THESE WOMEN WALKED WITH GOD

THE SAGA OF CITEAUX
THIRD EPOCH

THESE WOMEN
WALKED
WITH GOD

By

REV. M. RAYMOND, o.c.s.o.

THE BRUCE PUBLISHING COMPANY
MILWAUKEE

Rosary College Dewey Classification Number: 922.2

Library of Congress Catalog Card Number: 56–13337

© 1956 by The Bruce Publishing Company
MADE IN THE UNITED STATES OF AMERICA

To

MARY IMMACULATE

Queen of Citeaux

Mother of all Cistercians

AND TO

THE COMMUNITY OF MOUNT ST. MARY'S ABBEY

AT

WRENTHAM, MASSACHUSETTS

The Pioneer Trappistines of the U. S. A.

FOREWORD

These women walked with God — *why don't you?*

That is the burningly personal question put by this third volume in THE SAGA OF CITEAUX; and it is put bluntly. Fifteen women step from out the long dead past, stand before you, and say that in the situation you face today there is absolutely nothing new — except, perhaps, your own confusion.

They can say that without fear and with great force; for their day was as tumultuous as yours; their world, in as universal an upheaval. They saw all liberty and life threatened; they felt the continent of Europe sway; and knew their civilization was sick to its very soul. Yet they held on to intellectual clarity, never lost interior calm, and achieved perfect personal integration — for the sole purpose of showing you how to walk, no idle fancy

Do not think that a literary conceit. Take it in no mere figurative sense. Your time is altogether too precious, your life too short for any toying with trifles now. So when it is said that these fifteen women of Citeaux have been brought to life for the sole purpose of showing you how to walk, no idle fancy is being spun, but sternest and most important personal fact is being put before you. You need to learn the lesson these women have to teach; for you live for the same ultimate purpose they did, and in a milieu almost identical with theirs.

Your century has seen two world wars; theirs saw four. For the Fourth, Fifth, Sixth, and Seventh Crusades embroiled the manhood and the military might of those times just as completely as did the war in Europe from 1914 to 1918 and the recent global conflict. You have shuddered at the savagery shown in anti-Semitism in Germany under the Nazis; they shuddered at similar savagery shown not only in Germany but in England, France, and Portugal as well — and all against the

Jews. You look now on a Central and Western Europe cringing
in fear before a menace that rose far to the east and moved on
until the whole civilized world is threatened. Lutgarde, Hedwig,
the three Idas, and the rest of the women in this volume saw
the same; for the Mongol, Genghis Khan, was as powerful, as
ruthless, and, in his own way, as successful as any of your
modern dictators. With even greater speed than the Nazis or
Reds of your day, he and his Tartars swept whole nations and
countries before them; and they ruled the conquered peoples
with as high and harsh a hand as do those who have set up
the Iron and the Bamboo Curtains.

A-bombs never fell in the thirteenth century, but devastation
as complete as that of Hiroshima and Nagasaki was seen. Events
both world-shaking and world-shaping were as common then
as now; but nowhere will you read of anxiety, fear, or a sense
of frustration gripping the souls of men and women and ruining
their lives as you know them to be doing to countless of your
contemporaries. The secret? It is told in the title of this book:
they walked with God! That is the one lesson these women
have to teach; that is the one lesson it will profit you to learn —
for the year 410, which has fallen over Eastern and Central
Europe, may yet fall on you!

That was the year Alaric's West Goths sacked Rome. For the
first time in eight hundred years the city fell. A civilization
came to an end. In your day a civilization is dying. Your world
may yet become as dark as did the world after Rome fell; but
if you learn the lesson taught by these women of Citeaux you
need never walk in anything but brightest light.

Three contributing causes to the fall of Rome, little noted by
most historians, were lack of *humility,* lack of *simplicity,* and
lack of *obedience.* The same three causes are hard at work
today. That is why these fifteen women, who lived and died
seven hundred years ago, are as modern as this morning and
have a message more timely than anything you will find in

tomorrow's paper; for they lived under a Rule which can be summed up in the three words: humility, simplicity, and obedience. It was written by a man who had diagnosed the cause of Rome's fall and who saw, as few have seen, why his civilization was rubble. That man was Benedict of Nursia. His Rule rebuilt Europe and founded your Western civilization. His spirit can yet save your world. You will see that spirit "incarnated" in these women who walked with God; for, being Cistercians, they lived his Rule to the letter.

THE SAGA OF CITEAUX is a pragmatic work. Its purpose is to spread light where there is darkness, bring joy to those in sorrow, lift fallen hearts to highest hopes, give courage to the most disconsolate, and urge every man, woman, and child who reads it to look up, and laugh into the eyes of the God of love. In every volume humans who were human are to be found. But the thrill planned for every page is the portrayal of how divine these, and any other human, can become. The "First Epoch" showed a few men rebellious enough to be gallant to God; the "Second Epoch" introduced a family that overtook Christ; this, the third volume, though published fourth, shows what happens when you do overtake Him — you *walk with God!* The last of the series, published out of turn because of Gethsemani's centenary, tells the climax of life for any who would live rightly — you become burnt-out incense; for your life has been one long, loving adoration of the God who made you.

There is the answer to your day's perplexing questions; there the solution to your pressing, most personal problems: God, known and loved! God, walked with day and night! But to find that answer and employ that solution you will have to become humble, simple, and obedient. In a word you will have to become *reverent!* Then you will do what these women did.

It was a woman who first taught you how to walk. Her greatest concern was that you one day learn to walk alone. When you succeeded, she was proud and happy. She was wise in her teaching and entitled to her joy in your success; for physically you must walk alone. But these women of Citeaux teach the opposite lesson and know the opposite concern. They never want you to walk alone for so much as a single half step; for they know that your happiness in time as well as eternity, your joy on earth as well as in heaven, your life and all real love, both here and hereafter, depend entirely on your learning to walk always with God. It is a spiritual walking they teach; but you are a spiritual being and live life at its highest level when all your walking is in this spiritual realm.

Neither your century, nor the three before it, taught much about the spirit. You have learned more about matter, machines, and technocracy than you have about that which makes you human. But in time of crises truth is seen in naked clarity. That is why your day is waking up to human dignity and seeing that it lies in that which differentiates you from all other living beings — your spiritual soul. Your real thinkers are convinced at last that Communism is not only threatening your way of life — but that which makes you live, and life worth living — your very soul. Atheism is alerting your world to God. What a blessing! Hence the timeliness of the lesson these fifteen women have to teach.

They teach it quickly; for each "life" has been reduced to the closest compass possible. All are brief; some are even abrupt. But brevity was necessary so that the full gamut might be run and no man, woman, or child, no matter what his or her state in life, level in society, physical or mental condition, could say that there is not, herein, a model for them. Queens, with the wealth of entire realms in their hands, are seen alongside peasants who were paupers; healthy daughters from the well-to-do middle class are found leading the same love life as the sickest of the sick — a leper; women of highest intellectual acumen which has been further sharpened by the best the educational world of that day had to offer, are shown in the same community with those who cannot so much as learn the language of the country wherein they reside. Yet these extremes, so common in your own society, fuse into splendid unity as each woman does what every human being longs to do: *falls in love.*

You do not live until you love. You do not love until you give your heart away. You do not give your heart away until you have found GOD. Then you live and love because you walk with Him who is Life and Love, and you know the happiness for which you were made. But such love demands deep humility, utter simplicity, and an obedience that amounts to complete surrender of self.

Your learned men have given you much on the philosophy of women; more on the psychology of women; but how little, how very, very little, on the theology of women. But now that insecurity of life and instability of civilization is alerting you to reality and opening your eyes to truth, you know that whatever does not set up resonances that ring in eternity is nothing more than "sounding brass and tinkling cymbal." Therefore, what you want to know is the place God has for women in His ever wise, all-over plan for man. That is not difficult to discover. For the first book of the Bible tells how triumph over Satan and salvation for humankind comes not through the hands of the dominant male, but through the heel of a woman. The last book in the Bible describes that Woman clothed with the sun, the moon under her feet, and stars in her hair. Could God be more explicit? In His plan woman is at the base and the apex.

God made woman different from man, not inferior. She is the "weaker sex" only in that which makes man closer kin to the beast — his muscles; not in that which makes him really man — his morals. These women teach that which inspires to reverence and kindles to highest chivalry: the fact that into the more delicate body which God formed to share with Him in the mysterious patience and power of procreation, He

breathed a more sensitive soul, so that women, strong and passionate, might share with Him in the mysterious and mighty
work of man's redemption and salvation.

Across seven hundred years of time, then, comes the silence
of these women of the thirteenth century and proves to be a
shout to every man and woman of the twentieth, telling them
that the crying need of the day is *simplicity*. How you need
that hallmark of every true Cistercian: that single-mindedness
which alone can integrate character and unify life!

As you read their lives you will discover that with these
women it was not so much a matter of having a single principle
to live up to, as of having a single Person to live with. For
to them life was not something, as it is to so many of your
contemporaries, but Someone — the Holy One of God — *Jesus
Christ*. It was with Him they walked. It is with Him you must
walk if you would simplify life, enjoy sanity, and achieve
sanctity.

Alexis Carrel looked at your day and its decadence and said
the cause of it was your *loss of a sense of holiness*. A noted
Swiss writer studied that statement, asking himself just what
was this "sense of holiness" which your day has lost. He finally
answered that it is a sense of the presence of God — not the
God of the philosophers and the scholars, but the living, personal, and only God, the God of the believers, the God of the
Christians. It was with that God these women walked; for
they never lost that saving sense of holiness which they now can
help you recover. Actually it is a consciousness of that strong
gravitational pull, set deep in your being, which is ever drawing
you back to the God who made you, and uniting you with Him
who is the center of all being. It is a consciousness of His Christ
and your Christianity. It is a keen awareness of the fact which
so many look on as a luxury for the few, but which is actually
the duty of every human being: high holiness which is named

sanctity. You must be holy, or die without ever having lived — and die forever!

Friends of God take consolation from the fact that more and more people are asking if the widespread mental confusion of your day is not, in ultimate analysis, a moral problem. What an answer is given such people in our English word "holy." It comes from Anglo-Saxon word *halig* which means "sound," "whole," "healthy." It is obvious, then, that the health of the world depends on the world's holiness. Equally obvious is it that the holiness of the world depends entirely on the sanctity of the human individual — people like you. That is why you must meet these women of Citeaux.

The facts for the accounts of their lives have been taken almost exclusively from the Bollandists — that handful of Jesuits which Donald Attwater characterized as "one of the most learned groups of men in the world." What is found on their pages is genuine. But all that is to be found there is not to be found in this book. For, with ruthless hand, the charm, warmth, and rich color which characterize many of their legends has been sacrificed for cold clarity. One truth was to be bas-reliefed. It is found in every life, albeit with different background. It is the truth that you will never live until you have lost your life; you will never love until you have given your heart away; you will never walk aright unless you walk with God.

Grateful acknowledgment is made by the author for kind permission to quote from the following: *The Public Life of Christ* by Archbishop Goodier, published by P. J. Kenedy & Sons, 1933; "Saints" by Clare Booth Luce, in *Saints for Now*, copyright, 1952, Sheed and Ward, Inc.; *So Near Is God* by Fr. James M. Gillis, published by Charles Scribner's Sons, 1953.

CONTENTS

xv

THESE WOMEN WALKED WITH GOD

ST. LUTGARDE

The Woman Who

Loved

Without Measure:

Sine Modo

"Behold here what you are to love, and how you are to love"
Sister Portress' every gesture was eloquent with disapproval.
The large outside door, long noted for its solemn silence, was
closed with a decided click and the lock sent sharp echoes darting
from wall to wall of the dim vestibule. Keys, hitherto slipped
soundlessly behind ample apron, rattled now as Sister turned
sharply and headed for the tiny visitors' parlor on the left. As
she closed the dark door, she exclaimed in a disdainful whisper,
"Lutgarde, a novice!"

After straightening a chair that needed no straightening,
Sister Portress began to dust a table that was utterly free of
dust. A sentence that had sting to it accompanied each sweep
of the dustcloth. "What's coming over Mother Prioress? . . .
Taking the likes of that into the community! . . . Lutgarde!
. . . What will the townsfolk say? . . . What can she be thinking
of? . . . What will people think of this convent? . . . Lutgarde,
a novice! . . . Oh, what a scandal! . . ."

The Portress' fears were far from groundless. Already the
town was talking — and not everything said was complimentary

3

to St. Catherine's, the Benedictine convent and school which stood just outside the walls of St. Trond, a tiny Flemish town sedately set in what is now the province of Limbourg in northeast Belgium, but was then a part of the empire which was much more Hohenstaufen than Holy or Roman. For all of a month the name Lutgarde had been on almost every tongue, but this latest development had many in the town thinking and talking as Sister Portress was thinking and talking as she tidied a parlor that needed no tidying.

Sister had known Lutgarde for six years now. How well she remembered the day in 1194 when Lutgarde's parents brought her, a girl of twelve, from her native city of Tongres, some twelve miles to the west of St. Catherine's, and requested the nuns to prepare her for marriage. They were well-to-do people, her parents. The father was of the middle class, her mother, a member of the nobility. They were excited that day as they told the Prioress that everything but the date had been set for their daughter's marriage, even the amount of the dowry having been agreed upon.

How that entrance had set the nuns talking! They studied Lutgarde minutely. And it was not long before all agreed that she was an exceptionally fine catch for any man; for she had looks, ability, position, personality, and wealthy parents. But not many months had passed before all that changed; for her father plunged his all — even the promised dowry — on a business venture that went completely awry, and as one of the nuns put it when the groom-to-be heard that the principal had been lost, he lost interest.

But how had Lutgarde been affected? Sister Portress stroked some chair rungs vigorously as she recalled that before two weeks had passed, this high-spirited girl was carrying on as if she had never been betrothed. "That one," muttered Sister as she set a chair back in place, ". . . a novice? . . . Why, that girl is man-crazy!"

That was a false judgment on Sister's part, but no one could accuse her of rash judgment; for no one could count the number of times she had opened the door to young men in the past six years and shown them to this very parlor after they had made the one request: "Lutgarde, please." Sister paused as she thought of the young noble who had haunted that parlor these past two years. Then as she began energetically dusting again she thought of the soldier who had but a month earlier set the whole countryside buzzing by laying a bold ambuscade for the girl, determined to carry off by force one who would not go with him willingly. "And that one wants to become a nun!" Sister Portress wagged her head. "Why, all she ever thinks about . . . all she ever talks about is love — love — love."

This was true enough. But little did Sister know of what love Lutgarde was thinking at the moment, nor of what love she had been talking about ever since the soldier set the ambush which Lutgarde escaped by daring and deeds which showed her possessed not only of resourcefulness but surprising reserves of physical strength.

The Portress did not know these things; for she had not heard how just a month earlier, in the very parlor where she now worked, and by the very table she was dusting needlessly a second time, there had stood the Son of God while Lutgarde sat in one chair and her young noble leaned out to her from another which he had brought as close as he had dared. They were talking about love, then, too, when suddenly Lutgarde looked up and saw a pierced hand pointing to a Heart that held a wound, and heard the strange, stern command: *"Behold here what you are to love, and how you are to love."*

God has to ready His weapons

The Bollandists tell us — or rather it is Thomas of Cantimpré, Lutgarde's confessor and the man who wrote the life upon which every other word written about Lutgarde must depend — that the girl turned on her lover and used words which must have stung the young noble then as much as they astound us now. But Thomas of Cantimpré wins credence here; for this all happened in the year 1200, a full four centuries before Margaret Mary Alacoque was born, and seven hundred long years before the League of the Sacred Heart with its Apostleship of Prayer had made the picture of the Son of God pointing to the wound given Him after His death on Calvary's cross well known and loved. The apparition must have been as startling and strange to Lutgarde that day in 1200 as the apparition of the glorified Christ had been to the cowering Apostles in the Cenacle that first Easter night. Beside herself with fright and outside herself with wonder, Lutgarde rained words on her human lover that must have set him reeling.

God looked down on a very disordered world that first year of the thirteenth century. For Germany had in its Henry VI a man who had inherited from his father, Frederic Barbarossa, not only the same fierce nature; but the identical mad ambition to dominate the entire world. Henry turned the last years of the twelfth century into a veritable nightmare for Pope, princes, and people as he dreamed of uniting the West, subjugating the East, freeing the Holy Land, and thus taking his place beside such mighty world conquerors as Charlemagne and Constantine. To make that mad dream come true, he killed countless human beings in city after city, tortured and burned the inhabitants of hundreds of villages and towns, and left corpses strewn along numberless country roads. He had all Europe groaning under the threat of his tyranny.

Fierce as was this foe, there lay in the deep south of the continent one more subtle and more dangerous. For years the Moors in Spain had been a source of constant annoyance to Christendom, and with their military prowess, a real threat. But now, with the birth of an intellectual freedom never before known, they were far more dangerous; for in their Arabian misinterpretation of Aristotle they had something that could have undermined the entire structure of Christian truth by generating a spurious Rationalism.

Yet these threats in the political and intellectual spheres were as nothing compared to those in the moral realm. And since it is morals that make man, it must have been the sight of immoral men in France that moved God now to ready His weapons. For, as so often in history, zeal had begotten zealots and real fervor generated fanatics. Peter Waldo, the banker of Lyons, meant well when he began to live, and to exhort others to live, the poverty preached in the Gospels. But his followers, in their effort to simplify Christianity, all but suppressed it. They rejected the veneration of the saints, the doctrine on purgatory, Transubstantiation, the priesthood, and the hierarchy. These "Poor Men of Lyons" moved into Languedoc where they found an atmosphere heavy with heresy. For here thrived that hydra-headed thing which the infant Church knew as Gnosticism, which St. Paul had faced in Simon Magus, and which a few centuries later was called Manichaeism and found in Augustine of Tagaste a willing disciple but in Augustine of Hippo a fierce opponent. In the twelfth century it had appeared in northern Italy, where it was propagated by the mysterious Patarines. From Italy it moved into southern France, thanks to the Cathari, and was there named Albigensianism because of the quasi-headquarters established at Albi under the protection of Count Raymond of Toulouse.

Even today the peasants of Provence swear "by the double God," little knowing they are mouthing an error as old as man and a heresy as old as the Church. That oath is a legacy from Lutgarde's time when some men again explained the prevalence of evil by inventing a god, the author of matter and all that is evil, and placing him beside the one true God, whom they called the Author of spirit and all that is good. This erroneous over-simplification of the ever present problem of evil is one which, if carried to its logical consequences, would not only destroy the universal Church of Christ, but ultimately sweep away humanity itself; for logically it leads to the denial of the Incarnation, that supreme and all-holy union of spirit and matter effected when "the Word took flesh and dwelt among us"; and ultimately to the condemnation of marriage, the family, and every true and solid bond of human society.

In Languedoc the wind, sown when Lutgarde was a schoolgirl, was being reaped now as a whirlwind. God had to ready His weapons, for while "the perfect" of this sect, in their strictness of life were outdistancing even the truest of Christian ascetics, the lower classes were literally wallowing in sins of the flesh, which, they had been taught, were inevitable and due, not to themselves, but to this god who was the Principle of Evil.

Indeed God had to ready His weapons. History tells us that for Henry IV of Germany and the rest of the Hohenstaufens God had readied Innocent III. For that intellectual threat, dormant in Arabian Aristotelianism, there was Dominic Guzman, who would found an Order whence would come the *Philosophia Perennis* thanks to the intellectual fearlessness of Albert the Great and his "dumb ox" of a pupil, Thomas Aquinas. But for the hydra-headed thing that had overrun northern Italy and southern France, God needed more than the sword for the flesh which He would put into the capable hands of Simon de Montfort, more than the sword for the spirit which the Dominicans would wield so effectively by the eloquence of their words and the greater eloquence of their lives. What God needed, and what secular history does not tell about, were hearts that would serve as scabbards for the sword of His justice, which sin is ever unsheathing and placing in His all-just hands. What God needed was what the Apostles lacked that day they could not expel an impure spirit from a boy. God needed hearts whose systole and diastole would be prayer and penance; for the spirit down in Languedoc was most impure. He knew one such heart beat in the breast of this eighteen-year-old girl to whom He had His Son bare His own breast that she might there see what she was to love and how.

Of course Lutgarde was bewildered that day she banished the young noble from her side with a few sharp, strong words, but there was nothing that could banish from her memory the brilliance of that vision nor deaden the echoes of that majestic voice. She had seen Christ. She had heard Him speak. A wounded hand had pointed to a wounded Heart; and a strange, sad voice had issued a stern command. Alone with herself she tried to doubt, to dismiss it all as a dream, to deny that it had ever happened. But sharper than a shaft of sunlight stabbing into darkness, she would see the hand, the Heart, and their wounds; and clearer than voice across still waters would come that stern command. No, she could not question its reality. But what was she to do? How was she to love that wounded Heart — and love It as It had loved?

Sine modo — Without measure

It was this perplexity that caused her to gather a group of schoolmates and set out on horseback for her sister's house. There a sympathetic ear would listen, even if an enlightened mind could not direct.

While on this ride she looked up to find that she and her companions were suddenly entering a semicircle of horsemen who determinedly fanned out before them. When the leader of the group barked a nervous command, Lutgarde recognized the voice of the young soldier who had so often called at the convent school to protest his love and plead his cause. In a flash she divined his intent. Leaping from her mount she darted into the dense wood that was near the road. No horse could thread his way through those trees. So the frightened Lutgarde was soon beyond pursuit.

The townsfolk of St. Trond had a topic of lively conversation that night, and a subject for excited speculation the following few days. What were they to think of this girl, Lutgarde — and what were they to do about her? Where had she gone? Had she become lost in those woods? Should they try to find her, or should they leave that to the soldier who would so boldly steal her away?

Days passed. The town talked. So did Lutgarde. For just as stars began to cling to the high branches of the taller trees that night of the ambuscade, she had stumbled to the door of her sister's cottage and all but sobbed out a story that had the elder sister wondering whether Lutgarde was delirious or deranged. She heard how a lover's call at the convent school had ended in a vision of the Sacred Heart, then how a ride, begun with the innocent intention of visiting her, ended in an attempt at a violent abduction. The older sister's immediate counsel was rest. But sleep and food and the quiet of the cottage in the woods served only to sharpen Lutgarde's determination to find out exactly what Christ was commanding when He had said, "Behold here what you are to love, and how you are to love."

The older sister finally directed her to Father Bernard, chaplain of St. Catherine's. This wise priest listened in silence to the whole story Lutgarde had to tell, then quietly and kindly asked many questions, not only about the vision and the attempted abduction, but about her past life, her manner of praying, and her relations with God. He then asked the somewhat anxious Lutgarde to give him time for reflection and prayer. One day, then two, then three passed. Father Bernard prayed and reflected and prayed some more. For not only was the picture the girl had drawn of the Sacred Heart as new to him as it had been to Lutgarde, but the girl herself puzzled him. She readily admitted she knew she was pretty and was quite sure she had been vain about her looks; confessed that she loved nice clothes and was very much alive to the fact that she could wear them attractively; stated frankly that she had not only been flattered by the attention of young men, but took immense joy in being in their company; even how pleased and proud she had been to have had them calling on her at the convent school — and one of them even thinking of stealing her away. Father Bernard admired the honesty of the girl, but, probe as he would, he could find nothing in her person or her past life that would merit the extraordinary visit from Christ. He found her a normal girl in almost every way; a bit above normal in looks and personality, but possessed of all the strengths and weaknesses of any young woman as endowed as was she. Vivacious, she certainly was; but flirtatious, as some had whispered, no. His final summary was: a thoroughly good girl who tingled with life. When it came to giving his verdict about the vision and its command, he was without puzzlement. For only two words filled his entire horizon. They were *sine modo*.

Father Bernard of St. Catherine's had but to borrow from St. Bernard of Clairvaux, a man who had died less than a half a century earlier, but who already had been canonized. "Do you ask me what is to be the measure of your love for God?" this Cistercian abbot had written. "I answer that He is to be loved *sine modo* — without measure."

To anyone who has looked long at the corpse of God naked on a criminal's cross, no other answer is conceivable. His love for man was without measure. Man's love for Him must be the same.

To Lutgarde, after that vision in the parlor, this explanation was acceptable. What she next wanted to know from Father Bernard was the way in which she was to live and love *sine modo*. The answer to that question had not been as easy as the first. The priest told the girl very honestly that she could give measureless love to God by becoming wife and mother; that the same was possible even in the single state; but if she was looking for the surest and safest way, she would turn toward a convent.

That is why St. Catherine's Portress had been set dusting things that needed no dusting and muttering things she thought needed to be told.

But because the Portress was not the only one in St. Catherine's community who considered Lutgarde's entrance as extraordinary, her novitiate produced some rare spiritual phenomena. Though the nuns did not know it, the irresponsible schoolgirl had died the day of the apparition in the parlor; and while Lutgarde retained all the energy, vivacity, generosity, and lively unselfishness which had made her so vivid a personality while at school, she focused all these on a single object the moment she entered the convent: the Heart with the blood-red wound. That is why the latest novice did what every Benedictine novice is supposed to do: she sought God. But she did it in such a way that she started tongues wagging; and wagging tongues often deeply wound.

Lutgarde knew every nook and corner of the convent and the convent school's grounds, and her six years there had acquainted her intimately with the routine of the religious. She knew the times for the Office, the light manual labor, and the *lectio divina*. Often she had risen with the nuns and out of a schoolgirl's curiosity watched them while they were in choir during the vigils. The daily Mass was obligatory for the students as well as for the religious. And she had even spied on the more friendly members of the community while they worked, walked, read, or recreated. She had little to learn about the externals of the life. And that made her very different from the ordinary newcomer who has to spend so much time getting acquainted with the physical layout of the convent, and give so much attention to the schedule of the day. Yet this was not the thing that stamped Lutgarde the novice as different; it was the aura the girl carried about her person and the atmosphere which surrounded her every action.

Most novices are awkward even in their most graceful actions;

for they are actually hyperconscious of every member of their bodies: their eyes, heads, hands, hips, feet; the very arch of their neck gives them no inconsiderable concern. There is a pose for religious that has been canonized by art. It is seen in the statues and pictures of the saints — and in the postures of most young novices. Some time or other each attains that required angle of the head, fold of the hands, and lowering of the eyelids; but because attained with such self-conscious effort their very modesty is immodest; their recollectedness, a distraction; and all their gracefulness, without grace. There was little of this about Lutgarde, though all admitted she was very modest and seemingly ever recollected. Therein lies the explanation of what so puzzled her sister religious that it led to something of a persecution of Lutgarde.

The seniors of the community had seen other girls arrive and watched with interest, not always devoid of real amusement, their willing but awkward efforts to adjust to convent life so that they could serve God with what is called "religious decorum." The holy eagerness with which these newcomers go about each task is inspiring, but their overeagerness to look holy as well as to be holy causes the indulgent smile. It is this strained attention and manifest effort to conform to that "decorum" that is called "novice's fervor."

But Lutgarde's external composure was achieved with so much effortlessness, and her absorption in prayer was so evident, all knew hers was something different from ordinary "novice's fervor." Yet they did not know what to make of it. For only the Prioress knew what she had seen that day in the parlor, and what she had heard the day she asked Father Bernard to explain the command on what to love and how. That is why some of the seniors good-naturedly summed up Lutgarde in the adage "every new broom sweeps clean"; to which others replied, not so good-naturedly, "new brooms also wear out."

Of course these remarks ultimately reached Lutgarde's ears

— as they were meant to. When the new novice spoke of them to her Mistress and asked what they connoted, she was told much about the various phases of the spiritual life and the different depths to genuine spirituality. She heard a goodly amount concerning the enthusiasm of beginners, the energy that comes from the emotions, and the speed with which such things pass. She was told not to worry about the remarks, nor even about the temporary quality of a "novice's fervor." "It is a phase we all have to pass through," Lutgarde was told.

But Lutgarde did worry. She did not want her fervor to pass. For if it did, if she lost this burning desire to chant the Office well, to have her heart and mind centered on God as her lips formed the words the Holy Ghost had inspired the shepherd-king to put into his Psalms of praise; if she lost any of her love to assist at the Conventual Mass and offer herself every day with the Host; if she lost any of her fiery determination to do all things well, and to do them just to please God, how could she say she was loving as He had loved or that she was living *sine modo*?

When days are crowded as Lutgarde's with long Offices, the Mass, much reading, and a little light manual labor, they pass swiftly. A few months had passed before Lutgarde sought out Mother Prioress to ask if she should do as so many of the nuns had advised her to do: abate this eagerness of hers and be "more normal."

The good Prioress deemed it prudent to tell the girl much about the subtleties of the devil and to caution her against over-taxing her strength. Everything she said was true. Too often has this enemy of God deceived those who would be God's special friends and deluded them into so straining that they have snapped. God, who expects everyone to be strenuous, never wants anyone to strain. Then the Mother Prioress likened the fervor of novices to straw fires. "They flame high," she said, "but they die soon."

This well-intentioned effort to calm Lutgarde's fears served only to thoroughly frighten the novice. She would rather lose life itself than the love that had come to her from that vision of the "most beautiful of the sons of men" pointing with a wounded hand to a Heart that held a red-glowing wound. Now, after listening to the nuns, the Mistress of Novices, and the Prioress herself, Lutgarde grew afraid. In agony she asked herself again and again if she was going to prove another frail and fickle woman; one of those who, after a promising beginning, settle down to a mean but satisfied mediocrity. Her heart bled with the fear that these older nuns might be right, that hers was only a "novice's fervor." In tears she pleaded with Heaven that this might never be, even as her whole being shook with self-distrust.

In the midst of this torment there came to her one whose Immaculate Heart had been shaped to receive a sword; and from the lips of the Mother of God Lutgarde heard the soul-lifting words, "No, beloved daughter, what you fear will never come to pass. Instead, under my protection, your fervor will ever increase." Her fear dissolved in tears of gratitude.

A calmer and more confident Lutgarde heard the barbed remarks about her piety as an ever more fervent Lutgarde went about the duties of the novitiate. The year passed. Few knew that this young novice, whose first duty it was to seek God, had found Him. Yet all were convinced that she could be admitted to the profession of her vows. She had balance and stability about her, and a maturity that was marked; there were even whispers that this former charge of theirs, who so many had thought man-crazy, had been granted mystical graces. So in 1201 Lutgarde solemnly promised God to live poor, pure, and obedient to Him in the person of the Prioress of St. Catherine's Convent at St. Trond, where she would make every effort daily to "prefer nothing to the love of Christ." It was the Benedictine profession of five vows. It was the marriage ceremony wherein a Flemish girl of nineteen married the Eternal Son of God.

Lutgarde discovers the secret

But true love never runs smooth, even when that love is the love of creature for Creator and of God for His elected spouse. Lutgarde soon learned that even in a world made wondrous by a divine romance, all was not moonlight and roses. Little, if anything, can be kept utterly secret in a convent of nuns. So, somehow or other, word soon got around about the apparition of the Sacred Heart and the visit of the Woman with the Immaculate Heart. That word stirred strange feelings in the very human hearts of certain consecrated females. Some watched Lutgarde to see if they could learn from her something of the special ways of God; others watched to see if they could not detect much of the subtle wiles of Satan. For even in the most deeply religious soul there is a skeptic who never fully sleeps.

Since those who allowed this skeptic to become wide awake were more articulate than those who did not, life was not made too pleasant for the newly professed nun the first year after her novitiate. Yet this seeming human smallness was really part of the great God's ever effective strategy. For Lutgarde possessed a positive genius for making friends. It had shown itself while she was at school; it would manifest itself again in later life. But had it been allowed free scope these early years of her religious life, we may never have had a *Saint* Lutgarde. In an atmosphere clouded with suspicion and chilled by distrust, friendships could hardly grow. So Lutgarde came to know a deep human loneliness. But the human heart, especially the heart of a woman, must have love. So when the young nun's very goodness drove even good people from her, she was forced by the insistent need of her womanly nature to plunge yet more deeply into the life she had vowed to live. Thus she came to know an intimacy with

God that is granted to few. Gertrud von Le Fort has, perhaps, summed up this phase of Lutgarde's life perfectly in that poignant line: "I will go into deepest sorrow that I may find my God."

Since Lutgarde was a Benedictine, her lifework was to seek God. It was St. Bernard who wrote, "It is God alone who is never sought in vain, even when He is not found." That sentence, however, should be taken in conjunction with two other lines of his; one which asks the pointed question, "What doth it profit a man to follow Christ if he fails to overtake Him?" and the other which is an exclamation that can profoundly move every sincere soul: *Quam bonus Te quaerentibus, sed quid invenientibus?* — "How good Thou art to those who seek — What wilt Thou be to those who find?" Lutgarde sought. Lutgarde found. Lutgarde overtook Christ; for she learned what the "liturgical life" really is.

The Mass, Liturgy's crowning act, was the heart of her day. Around it clustered the canonical hours of the Divine Office, the Liturgy's most perfect prayer. And St. Catherine's, like all Benedictine convents, was meticulously careful about vestments, altars, and all objects of art. They had to be strictly liturgical. But Lutgarde, by an intuition which was a special grace, saw that one could sing liturgical chant daily, engage in liturgical prayer seven different hours of the day, be surrounded by liturgical art all her life, and morning after morning assist at Mass made liturgically perfect by liturgical altar and liturgical vestments, yet never for a single split second live in its deepest depths the liturgical life. For while life is made manifest by motion, the liturgical life is not the liturgical movement. The ability to follow the Mass in the Missal, sing plain chant, read an *Ordo*, and pray the Office; sensitiveness to the changing seasons of the ecclesiastical year and the habit of naming the weekdays as days of feast, fast, ferial, or vigil, can alert one to the existence of the liturgical life, but will never constitute liturgical living.

For the liturgical life is more than living *for* God. It is even more than living *with* God. Peter, James, John, and the rest of the Twelve He chose to be His Apostles lived with Him for three intimate years; yet at the Last Supper He had to ask, "Have I been so long a time with you, and you have not known me?" (Jn. 14:9.) Never will that question be asked of one who leads the liturgical life as Lutgarde led it back in the dawn of the thirteenth century; for by her intuition this young nun saw that, while the essence of the liturgical life might be living *for* Christ, *with* Christ, and *in* Christ — or as St. Augustine so pithily put it: *vivere in Verbo* — its quintessence is allowing Christ to live in you. And she would have the quintessence.

Exquisitely exact, as it is, as a description of the contemplative life, Augustine's *vivere in verbo* needs Paul's injunction, "Let this mind be in you which was also in Christ Jesus" (Phil. 2:5) as complement and elucidation. For there is a passive element to the liturgical life, if we may name it such, which for certain individuals is more important than the active. So true was this in Lutgarde's case, that in retrospect one can claim that her vows equivalently said, "Here are my hands, O Christ; with them, work. Here are my feet, Lord; with them walk where You will. Here are my lips, that from this earth You may yet sing to God the Father, praise and pray. Here, O Jesus, is my poor heart and every member of my human frame; with it, and in it, and through it, live, suffer, sacrifice, die . . . that God may be glorified and the souls of men know life." Christ accepted that offer — literally.

But let us neither read nor write this life as so many lives of saints have been read and written — backward. The posthumous glory that comes after canonization seldom shone from them as they hurried along to overtake Christ. To keep Lutgarde in focus we will see her as a girl of nineteen who has been bewildered by the fact that God has singled her out for a work she little knows the nature of as yet, but which she is trying to accomplish by being as fervent a young nun as she can be. She is striving to love God "with her whole heart, her whole soul, with all her strength, and all her mind," as He has commanded; striving to love Him *sine modo* as St. Bernard has specified. Yet, despite the fact that she has heard from the lips of Christ's own Mother that her fervor will not fade, she is still troubled. For true love is always humble and never without some fear. The fact is that Lutgarde has yet a lot to learn about living with God and allowing God to live in her. In these early days her very consciousness of the presence of God is far from perfect, and her manner of walking and talking with Christ can be improved. For instance, when a sister religious asks her for some little help, Lutgarde turns to her Spouse and says, "You wait here, Jesus. I'll be right back." In later life there will be no such leaving on her part, nor any need for Him to wait; for He will be within her, and she will find Him in everybody else. But at the moment she is only learning — and there is very much to learn.

The elements of the Benedictine life could hardly be fewer or more simple. The three essentials are the Divine Office, manual labor, and "Lectio Divina" — that meditative reading of the Sacred Scriptures and the early Fathers of the Church, which is really a form of mental prayer. But ineradicably set in the soul of each of us is a greediness for God which, if not recognized, will lead many a one in the cloistered contemplative life into a form of spiritual gluttony, and many a one leading the cenobitic life into error. Perhaps it was their knowledge of this that had some of the older nuns spying on Lutgarde when they learned she was rising during the hours appointed for rest and going to the chapel to pray. As has been said, no secret is absolutely safe in a convent. These elders most likely were ready to warn the newly professed of the cloistered world's capital sin if they found her overtaxing herself. Imagine their surprise — and embarrassment — when one night they saw Lutgarde filled, as it were, with light and radiating a brilliance which not only momentarily blinded their bodily eyes but simultaneously filled their souls with a sweetness they had never before known. One may safely hazard the guess that after such an experience, instead of finding spiritual gluttony in the soul of Lutgarde, they found spiritual jealousy rising in their own. But Lutgarde learned that she must be more discreet if she would keep the secrets of her love.

As time went on, she learned much more. Her most important discovery was that these extraordinary visitations were not the substance of sanctity at all; that genuine holiness is a matter of giving, not of receiving; that constant intimacy with God lies in an unfailing faith, not in these flashes of vision. She had heard Christ say to Thomas, "Blessed are they who have not seen, and yet have believed" (Jn. 20:9). As wonderful as were those moments of rapture when she saw Christ, much more wonderful she learned it was to walk with God hour after hour by keeping her soul alert to His indwelling and the ear of her heart ever attentive to His call of love. Devotedness to duty is not only the acid test of sanctity; it is the surest, sharpest criterion of the genuineness of any supernatural phenomenon. If after some extraordinary happening such as the radiance of that light that came from Lutgarde while she was at prayer, the person involved is found to be more humble, generous, charitable, unselfish, and zealous for the ordinary duties that make up the day for the ordinary religious, one can safely conclude that it was not the Spirit of Darkness who had come in the guise of an Angel of Light. And for the next four years Lutgarde gave all at St. Catherine's an example of devotedness to duty such as had not been seen there before. This, to the initiate, was far more convincing proof of her love for God and her intimacy with the other world than many of the things that were rumored about her then and are repeated now.

Thomas of Cantimpré would have us believe that in these earliest years of her religious life, Lutgarde was given gift after gift from on high, and received visitation after visitation from those close to the Throne of God. This could well have been; for God was readying His weapon for no ordinary task and would soon be asking this young nun for what only heroic generosity could give. Yet wide reading in medieval hagiography generates a healthy skepticism, which at rock bottom is genuine judiciousness. So when, through the Bollandists, one hears Thomas of Cantimpré tell that Lutgarde was endowed with the power to heal with a touch, a sign, or a prayer, and that the fame of this gift so crowded St. Catherine's with those seeking cures that the convent life was seriously disturbed, echoes of identical happenings in other convents are started, and one grows suspicious. When Thomas goes on to say that Lutgarde prayed God to take back this His gift lest she become a menace to the welfare of St. Catherine's Community and that God, when taking back His gift, asked the nun what she would have in its place, one grows skeptical; for he has heard this tale so often about others. Thomas claims that Lutgarde asked as replacement gift a clear understanding of the Psalms. That is intelligible enough; for Lutgarde had to sing these Psalms from dark to dark of every day and, after the Mass, have them constitute her chief means of praising God. Yet when Cantimpré goes on to say that, once this gift was given her, it was Lutgarde who found God's largess too disturbing; for the insights granted proved too powerful for her simple mind; so once again she begged God to play Indian giver and take back His gift; one again is slow to accept, for in medieval hagiography all this is narrated about many another nun. But there is one thing Cantimpré has chronicled about these years that wins unhesitating credence; and that is the story of the "exchange of hearts."

Lutgarde was one day talking to Jesus in that intimate manner which characterized her prayer when she heard the Christ ask, "What would you have Me give you, Lutgarde?"

The young nun made a reply which, recalling the apparition that had changed her life, is not so strange. She said, "Lord, I want Thy Heart."

"You want My Heart?" exclaimed the Christ. "It is I who want *yours*."

"Take it," replied the nun . . . and the "exchange" was effected.

Thomas wins credence here, for he gives what is perhaps the first record of something we have learned much of since. It was in His very first apparition to Margaret Mary that Christ took the Saint's heart, put it in His own, then returned to her a heart-shaped flame saying, "To serve as your heart I have shut in your side a little spark from the most living flame of my love. It will burn you unto the last moment . . . and from now on you shall be called the well-beloved of My Sacred Heart." Those may not have been the precise words Christ used at St. Catherine's at the dawn of the thirteenth century, but that is exactly what He did in this "exchange of hearts" — He put something into Lutgarde that "burned her unto the last moment."

Once this "exchange" had been made, St. Benedict's Rule took on a much more personal meaning for Lutgarde. It spoke with real intimacy to her. For at the close of his "Prologue" Benedict has sketched the whole purpose of life and its ultimate goal in two brief lines which say: "by sharing now in the sufferings of Christ, we may merit to share with Him His Kingdom in the life hereafter." These lines told the nun just what the liturgical life is — it is letting the Sacred Heart beat in her so that once again Christ might know the poverty of Bethlehem, the loneliness of Egypt, the humble hiddenness of Nazareth, those heart-breaking frustrations of the Public Life, but most of all that He might know again the pain of the Garden and of Golgotha. Lutgarde suddenly realized that He, the New Law's sole *Leiturgos* — its only High Priest and lone Victim — must live on; for, although the Redemption of man has been

achieved, the salvation of men is continually being won. That
is why she and others must give their hearts to God that His
might beat in them.

"Jesus, What Are You Doing to Me?"

Four years passed quickly. To Lutgarde it seemed but yesterday that an ambush had been laid for her by a soldier, and that
she had sat beside a young noble only to be startled by the
Christ of the wounded Heart. For all the four years, though,
she had seen little else; for ever singing in her veins were the
words, "Behold here what you are to love, and how you are to
love." And for all these years she had been striving to live and
love *sine modo*. How successful she was is attested by the fact
that, in 1205, although she was only twenty-three years of age
and a religious for less than five years, she was unanimously
elected prioress of St. Catherine's Community. Her sincerity had
won the tribute that is its due — complete trust. Lutgarde's
simplicity had disarmed the most skeptical; and while all were
not ready to accept her communications as divine, no one was
unready to admit that she had been sincerely seeking God and
striving with every ounce of her surprising energy to serve Him.
Because that service had been so markedly unselfish; because her
obedience had been prompt, unquestioning, and from the heart,
the nuns knew she was worthy to command, and they were
willing to obey.

It was a tribute. But if Lutgarde had protested to Christ about
His gift of healing, as her earliest biographer would have us
believe, and then later of His gift of understanding the Psalms,
now she had real reason to look up into the eyes of Christ and
ask, "Jesus, what are You doing to me?"

The First Superior in a Benedictine house is really the only
superior. He or she is omnipotent as far as the subjects are
concerned. Here is authority — all of it — in the one person.

Some of it may be delegated to what Benedict called "deans," but ultimately all of it belongs to the First Superior alone. As prioress, Lutgarde had dominion not only over the temporal goods of the convent, but even over the minds, hearts, and wills of each member of the community. She was not only responsible for every purchase made, but for every extra prayer or penance offered by the latest postulant or the oldest professed. Nothing could be done legitimately without her knowledge and consent, whether it be to bake some bread, make a skirt, buy thread, sell a manuscript, speak with an outsider, or even go to Holy Communion. There can be no question about the existence of authority in a Benedictine house, nor can there be any slightest doubt about the existence of order there since everything is ruled by obedience to this sole authority. In the very "Prologue" to his Rule Benedict states explicitly: "We are about to establish a School of the service of God"; then in his first chapter asserts that he is setting down a Rule for "the most steadfast class of monks, Cenobites" who serve God with the service of soldiers "under a Rule and an Abbot." Discipline can be all but felt in those words. Authority is supreme according to Benedict — a boon for subjects, but a burden for superiors, as Lutgarde was soon to learn.

She had seen the Sacred Heart of Jesus. She had had that life-molding experience called the "exchange of hearts." But to be prioress of the community at St. Catherine's and to rule it as St. Benedict wanted it ruled, she had only her native endowments of intelligence, energy, and initiative, coupled with what skills she had acquired in human relations — and her ever flaming faith. It was this last which aided her most in the trying task. Her responsibility made her keenly conscious of the necessity of following Benedict's Rule to the letter, if that were possible; for on the scales of God the worth of all her works would be balanced against the weight of this Rule. She became ever more Christ-conscious; for that is the essence of the Rule; and

it was this that brought her to her final vocation and to the one
work which an all-wise God had decreed before the dawn of
time would be her life's work. From the hints given by Thomas
of Cantimpré, the facts of history, and the marked femininity
that was Lutgarde's, one can follow the evolutions without great
difficulty.

Woman's intuition is a gift from God given her because she
is a woman and destined to become a lover. Love sharpens her
intuition, and her intuition sharpens her love. That is the way
it was with Lutgarde. She had fallen in love with Christ of the
wounded Heart; and from reports that reached her as prioress of
what was going on in the world, she knew He was suffering.
She suffered, too, and would share ever more with Him.

In France, Philip Augustus was acting very like a certain
Herod after John the Baptist had told him the truth about the
woman he had as "wife." Philip had repudiated his lawfully
wedded Ingeborg. When she appealed to Rome, he imprisoned
her in a convent, intercepted the legates Celestine III had sent
to investigate the matter and interned them at Clairvaux; then,
in open defiance of Christ's Vicar, married Agnes of Meran.
Pope Celestine died shortly after; but as soon as Innocent III
had received the tiara, he wrote to Philip saying, "The dignity of
being a king does not dispense you from your duties as a
Christian." When Philip turned a deaf ear to every exhortation,
Innocent laid all France under interdict. Across the water, in
England, John Lackland openly opposed the Pope and was
proving to the world not only that he was not the soldier his
brother Richard the Lionhearted had been, but that he was
not even an honest man. Here the Pope's representative would
be clothed in a cope of lead and left to die. Small wonder
England was placed under interdict and John finally excommunicated. Spain presented an even more shameful picture;
for there the Christian kings were outraging the sanctity of
marriage and, instead of uniting against the common foe — the

Moors, were fighting among themselves. As for the Empire, Germany and Italy writhed in torture as Philip of Suabia and Otto of Brunswick fought for the throne. The former would be assassinated and the latter excommunicated and deposed before Lutgarde had found her one life's work; but now, as she pictures the Church of Christ, her woman's intuition tells her what perhaps only the genius of Innocent III and the sanctity of Francis of Assisi and Dominic Guzman were telling them; namely, that great as was the need of the Church for the swords of the Crusaders, greater far was her need for those who would wield the sword of the spirit by prayer, penance, poverty, and preaching. Lutgarde found herself aching to comfort the Christ she knew to be in agony. But how?

That question puzzled her, and it puzzled the confessor to whom she put it; for there seemed to be no more that the nun could do. St. Catherine's had grown steadily in the spirit of love ever since she was elected prioress and was manifesting it by ever greater mortification. Yet none equaled, far less surpassed, the Superioress in giving God that tender tribute of love called self-denial. Her German biographer tells us she made a pact with her body never to grant it a single gratification, no matter how innocent. That seemingly extreme act was the result of her position as much as anything else; for she had to be a pattern to her flock. That is why she was the first in every exercise and the most mortified member of the community. Yet her whole soul, her whole being, now demanded that she give more. All her confessor could say was, "What more is there to give?"

When word came that Peter of Castelnau, who was serving as Papal Legate to the Albigensians, had been murdered, Lutgarde's womanly intuition told her what theology had failed to tell her learned confessor. She suddenly concluded that, if she was to love the Christ as He had loved her, she must have deeper solitude, follow a more rigorous way of life, and live in a milieu where she would know that intimacy with Christ which the sister of Martha had known. She was unable to give any other than a woman's reason: "she knew it to be so because she knew it to be so." But actually she was hearing in her soul the love call of the Sacred Heart to share with Him the role of Vicarious Victim. She was on the threshold of her life's work. But before she crossed it, her Benedictine confessor wisely insisted that she consult some learned and able director.

John de Liro, priest of the diocese of Liège, was noted for his holiness of life and deep learning. Lutgarde sought him out and told him everything that had been churning in her soul. He listened carefully, then asked for time to reflect. To be a victim, even a vicarious victim, he knew was the call of every Christian. Versed as he was in Mystical Theology, he saw how the "Do this in commemoration of Me" of the Last Supper, which was spoken directly to the Apostles and through them to every priest of the New Law, held overtones of meaning for every person baptized in the name of Jesus Christ. Still he hesitated. This doctrine, as old as Christianity, as true as Christ Himself, was little spoken of in the early thirteenth century. The picture Lutgarde had drawn with such vivid words of the Sacred Heart of Jesus, and her story of the "exchange of hearts," were as strangely new to John de Liro then as they would be to a Brahmin of India or a Bonze of Japan today. Perhaps more strange. Yet the candor of soul, the burning sincerity, the glow of love that radiated from St. Catherine's Prioress, told him he was dealing with no mere emotional woman or any false mystic. The more he prayed and reflected, the more he grew convinced that the conclusion Lutgarde had reached, thanks to her womanly intuition, was the correct one: she needed more seclusion than St. Catherine's could afford, she needed an environment that was different from that created by her office as prioress, she needed an atmosphere where her love for Christ could breathe more freely. The decision he reached surprised

Lutgarde. There was a sharpness of detail and a finality about it that frightened. His words were few: "You are to go to the Cistercian Convent at Aywières in Brabant," was all he said.

She could understand easily enough why he had specified the Cistercians; for their houses for men and women dotted Europe, and from them arose in steady column the white aromatic smoke of loving praise. For St. Bernard had not only made the twelfth century glorious with his sanctity and that of his brethren, but had assured the thirteenth and following centuries love-filled braziers wherein men and women could fling themselves as so much incense to be burned for the glory of God. Since women will never be outdone by men where God is concerned and self-sacrifice the manner of devotion, the Cistercian nuns came into being almost as soon as the men. In 1098, SS. Robert, Alberic, and Stephen had instituted a reform of the Benedictine life that was very literally a reformation — for they went back to the letter of the Rule, fearlessly expunging every accretion the centuries had brought to what Benedict had inaugurated at Subiaco. They were laughed at by the contemporary Black Benedictines, and seemingly with reason; for they knew a frightening sterility for over a decade of years. Then came Bernard of Fontaines with his thirty noblemen, and there followed a growth and diffusion of the Order that is still a marvel to men. At first it was decreed that the White Monks would have nothing to do with the spiritual direction of women religious. But a convent at Tart, near enough to Citeaux for contact, finally won from a reluctant group of abbots recognition and acceptance into the Order. They then had a growth and diffusion almost as marvelous as had the men.

This Order appealed to Lutgarde. For the Cistercian monk and nun were stamped with the unmistakable stamp of simplicity and austerity; their houses were citadels of silence where poverty, prayer, and penance ruled supreme. She knew that by becoming a Cistercian nun, she would be gaining that solitude she craved and would be enabled to pour herself out more generously. But she shrank from the house John de Liro had named; for in Brabant, French alone was spoken, and she knew nothing of this tongue. She did not raise a real objection, but she did mention the fact that there was a flourishing convent of Cistercian nuns at Herkenrode, where her native Flemish was spoken. But John de Liro said, "Aywières" — and that was all.

Lutgarde made no immediate move; for human prudence questioned the advisability of going to a convent where she would not understand superiors when they spoke, and they would not understand her when she spoke. Lutgarde listened to this human prudence for a time. Then one day a saintly friend who is known now as "St. Catherine the Wonderful" came to St. Catherine's Prioress and asked the direct and disturbing question, "Why do you delay to do what is commanded you by Divine Providence?" Up to that moment, owing to a blindness she could not explain, Lutgarde had not looked upon the advice of John de Liro as Divine Providence. She was ashamed of her lack of faith, and yet there kept tugging at her being human prudence bolstered now by a religious doubt: Was she not vowed to live and die at St. Catherine's? And was she not the lawfully elected prioress? How could she in justice leave this place? The climax came only when Christ Himself appeared and somewhat abruptly said, "Go to Aywières. Such is My will. If you go not, I shall abandon you." Lutgarde went.

Waste the world — and God wants

She went into the cloistered contemplative life as led by the Cistercians. This young woman, with all the sanctity and ability so far manifest, withdrew entirely from the world and, as far as it is humanly possible, buried herself while yet alive. It struck many as strange then. It will strike many as strange now. For it looks like wrapping that God-given talent in a napkin, and not "trading with it until the Master comes." It looks like sheer waste. And it will continue to appear such unless we look closely and see clearly that the cloistered contemplative life is living with the identical purpose that was God's when He took flesh of the Virgin "and dwelt amongst us" that He might give up the ghost on Calvary. Golgotha and contemplative cloisters speak the one same truth, but even the devout and well-meaning would persist in making that a half-truth.

The corpse of God, sagging from nails on Golgotha's tree, speaks with poignant eloquence; but men seem determined to hear only half that message. They hear it tell of God's infinite mercy and His unbelievable love for sinners; too often they fail to hear it speak with similar insistence on God's unwavering justice and His infinite hatred of sin. Christ's arms are spread like the scales of a balance, and should speak to all the twofold truth: not only that the sinner needed to be saved, but more especially that satisfaction had to be made for the sin; not only that there was call for a Redeemer, but before that there was demand for a Repairer; that Jesus — or Saviour — of men, is first the Christ — or Anointed — of God. Too often it is forgotten that religion — and especially religion's highest and holiest act, that of Calvary — is a matter of justice; we must pay back *to God* what is His due. Sin is not only suicidal; it is Deicidal. As St. Bernard has said, it is the destruction of God as far as the human will, in its waywardness, can destroy Him. Justice demands reparation for such an outrageous attempt on Infinite Majesty. That the Christ of God, who was the Repairer of that sacrilege, should also be the Jesus or Redeemer of men is due only to God's measureless mercy.

In contemplative cloisters the same reconciliation of what seems opposed goes on as men and women lay down their lives that God may have His glory and the souls of men be saved. There was sin in Paradise; there had to be a Calvary with a cross and a God upon it. There is sin in the world today; there have to be cloisters where Justice will receive its due as men and women repent and repay for those who sin and do no penance. God will not be mocked. His mercy cannot give the lie to His justice. If we sing that "His mercies are above all His works," it is true only because Jesus Christ is true. And if His unwavering justice is not to open the clouds in another Deluge that would wash away the sinful race of men, or fire such as Sodom and Gomorrha knew fall upon our cities, there must be contemplative cloisters where Christ in His members can climb again the cross and die as truly as He died on Calvary. Redemption is over; salvation goes on. Justice and mercy erect cloistering walls and place behind them souls such as Lutgarde's; souls filled with sympathy and love for men and women who sin, simply because they brim over with love for the God of justice and mercy who is outraged by that sinning. In a world as noisy as ours there must be islands as silent as was the island mound outside Jerusalem when God died as Victim for men and Vindicator of Divine Glory.

Simplicity Is a Virtue

At Aywières Lutgarde was under the same Rule as she had been at St. Trond; yet she found things quite different. Here poverty was more pronounced. It showed itself in the food and clothing of the nuns, in the house and all its furnishings. The simplicity insisted upon shocked her at first; for she found things, even the church and its very sanctuary, bare. Yet she soon saw the purpose of this striking difference. Ornamentation, even when added for the glory of God, can distract. But the most notable change for Lutgarde lay in the "Horarium." The Cistercians would admit of not the slightest compromise with the letter of the Rule; so Lutgarde spent far less time in church than she had at St. Catherine's and much more time in the fields. St. Benedict wanted his followers to be self-supporting and had specified farming as the natural means.

The day at Aywières was long and rigorous. Lutgarde rose between one and two o'clock in the morning, and for the next seventeen hours let Jesus live in her, using every faculty of her soul and body for the identical purpose He had required from Mary a human body and from His Father a human soul: that as man He might repair man's sin and praise Divinity. She in Him, and He in her, first chanted the Vigils of the Canonical Office; then, on most of the days of the year, sang Matins and Lauds for the Office of the Dead. Thus the first two and often three hours of the day went to the direct praise of God and to pleading for helpless souls. After these long Vigils Lutgarde sat in the cloister, which more often than not, was cold, and warmed her soul by reading of God as He is written of in Sacred Scripture. With the dawn, she was back in church singing the Sunrise Song called Prime, asking the Creator of the day, who had brought her to the beginning of this new one, to grace her in such a way that its every hour would be spent for Him alone. From the church she went to the chapter room where this Hour of the Office was completed, and where she heard some words of encouragement, instruction, or correction, spoken by the First Superior. Not long after this exercise the bell would summon her back to church for Tierce and the Conventual Mass, whence she would go to the fields and work until early afternoon. In the winter season (from October until Easter) she would take but one meal a day, and that between two and four in the afternoon. In the summer season she was allowed a dinner and a supper. But at no time did she have breakfast.

Lutgarde's hands grew calloused from the four to six hours each day she spent with hoe, fork, spade, or scythe as she dug, planted, cultivated, or harvested in the vegetable garden or farm attached to the convent. It was here that she made the joyous discovery not so much that work can become a prayer, but that God can be seen as truly in the single blade that has just burst the cerements of the seed for a resurrection unto a new life as He can be in the countless stars in the heavens or the magnificent universe He ever holds in place.

The simplicity of the Cistercian regime pleased Lutgarde, but it was its ruggedness that won her heart completely; for in such a milieu she felt she could live and love *sine modo*. A simpler life is hard to imagine; a more difficult life for a mere mortal is hard to conceive, for in it human nature is denied everything human nature normally craves. Yet this is the life that Lutgarde lived for forty years. And the point Thomas of Cantimpré failed to make, and those depending on him have failed to stress, is that it was this simplicity and ruggedness, this rising in the dark to sing unto dawn, this going out while still fasting into fields where a sun could be merciless or a wind cuttingly cruel, this working away in a silence she could fill only with prayer and a human loneliness she could people only with the spirits of the other world, this day in and day out denial to her womanly heart of all a woman's heart naturally craves, this life, which looks more like death, this steady striving to live not only for God alone, but even with God alone, was the thing that changed Lutgarde from a good holy nun into the mighty saint God could use as He willed.

What Thomas has highlighted in his biography are really the results of Lutgarde's sanctity, not its causes. The graces, gifts, visions, and other supernatural wonders could have been given her at St. Catherine's while she was in the black garb of the Benedictines. But before her soul could be deepened and its newer depths filled with God, it was God's will that she don the white of Citeaux and know the simplicity, austerity, silence, solitude, selflessness, and that utter separation from the world that was characteristic of every house that was Cistercian.

There were whole continents in Lutgarde's soul that lay

utterly unexplored. In this strange convent where an alien
tongue was spoken, Lutgarde would discover them. Up to now
she had rightly conceived her vocation to be a call to adoration.
As a Black Benedictine she had fulfilled it to the best of her
ability in those long Offices and other liturgical functions that
all but filled her day. Whatever was penitential in the life, and
whatever she had added had been for the purpose of self-
purgation. At Brabant, however, she gradually grew conscious
of the fact that there was an apostolate open to her of which
she had never dreamed and one in which she could love as
had the Man with the wounded Heart and at the same time be
loving Him *sine modo*. She could be a penitent for those who
do no penance; a victim for those the world, the flesh, or the
devil had victimized; and all her self-sacrifice could be offered
for those who make no sacrifice. She would adore; her life of
adoration would be more intense than ever. But now her very
adoration would be supplication for those who never act as
supplicants. Lutgarde came to realize that the second commandment *was* like unto the first as her love for God spilled
over into a glowing love for all His rational creatures.

But this wondrous lesson was not learned unaided. She was
not long in Brabant when one day she found herself looking
into the eyes of the Mother of God and found them to be the
pain-filled eyes of the *Mater Dolorosa*. "What ails thee, dearest
Mother?" cried the startled Lutgarde. "Why are you, who art
full of grace, so haggard and pale?"

The Sorrowful Mother's reply came slowly and solemnly.
"My Son," she said, "is again being crucified by heretics and
bad Christians. His anger hangs heavy over the world. Do
thou appease it by prayer and penance and a fast that will be
seven years long."

The skeptic in us accepts that vision as reported by Cantimpré
without a question. For the request our Lady made of Lutgarde
is identical with the one she has made at Fatima, Lourdes, La

Salette, and Pontmain, to name the outstanding appearances she has graced our world with this past century. Different words may have been heard in those places, but the purpose was ever the same: to stay the wrath of God; and the means to do it have never changed: prayer and penance.

As a Cistercian, Lutgarde did nothing but pray and do penance. Yet our Lady asks a little bit more and begs her to direct it all to the one end: the conversion of the Albigensians. Knowing what we do of the lustful excesses this heretical teaching encouraged, and mindful of the Gospel story about the inability of the Apostles to exorcise a certain unclean spirit, we see that our Mother is but echoing her Son. Prayer and penance will alone purge the world of the spirit which so took possession of man that it had God one time grieving that He had ever made man; of the spirit which produced a Deluge, brought fire on Sodom, and unquestionably has been a contributing factor to the plagues visited on modern man in the shape of world wars, economic depressions, and universal unrest.

To the question so often heard about the contemplative life: "Why this waste? What good do such people do their fellow mortals?" our Lady, it seems, would point to Lutgarde. For although Simon de Montfort mustered his swords and astounded the world with his bravery, although Dominic Guzman gathered his preachers and proved by the eloquence of their lives and of their words that there is but one God and He is good; complete victory over the heretics and their heresy did not come until a cloistered contemplative nun gave herself to God in a fast on dry bread and thin beer that lasted a full seven years.

One would think that a seventeen-hour day, in which seven or eight are spent chanting the Divine Office and assisting at the Holy Sacrifice of the Mass, contained prayer enough; and that the hard manual labor for from four to six hours, plus the silence, solitude, and sleep on hard boards, along with a fast which allows but one meal a day for three quarters of the year — and that taken toward sundown — held penance enough. But not so our Lady. She knew that human nature could give a little more. So Lutgarde fasted even from the black fast.

The astonishing part of it was that when, under orders from superiors, Lutgarde added other nourishment to her hard bread and thin beer, her whole system revolted, and she became a very sick nun. Yet, when adhering rigorously to her meager diet, she enjoyed perfect health.

There is one aspect to this penance that Cantimpré did not expose. Yet, for Lutgarde, it may well have been its most painful aspect — and most profitable. The human body soon gets used to any regime; so it was not long before the fast lost its bitterest sting. But the thing that burned Lutgarde's being with ever greater heat, and which shaped her soul to the form God desired, was the fast's concomitants. To be made to appear singular, no matter at whose command, in an enclosed contemplative community, is a source of endless embarrassment and a real humiliation. Lutgarde's dry bread and thin beer made her singular. But to this was added that which can sear the soul of a sincere religious — the distrust made patent by superiors, of the genuineness of spiritual favors. For Lutgarde's good — and the good of countless others through her — God now allowed that skeptic we know to be but lightly sleeping in all of us, to become fully awake in the persons who were most important to Lutgarde's life: her superiors and sister religious.

At Aywières, as there had been at St. Catherine's, and as there would be centuries later at Paray le Monial, certain religious, far from accepting the visions and visitations to Lutgarde as heavenly, thought her in the power of Satan. From time to time her Cistercian superiors acted as would the superiors of Margaret Mary. Yet Lutgarde anticipated by four full centuries what the Christ of the glowing wounds would tell the other

Beloved of His Sacred Heart: "Obey your superiors rather than Me." Lutgarde obeyed her superiors; and it was this obedience that led to her vindication. Sickness from sustaining food, and health from a diet that under ordinary circumstances would prove famishing, witnessed to the truth of what God wanted from Lutgarde. But they did not tell the anguish that her soul suffered from the doubt and distrust of superiors and equals. That is why one can say that it was not the fast but the fast's concomitants that molded Lutgarde to the shape God desired.

Intent as she was in giving herself to God in God's measure, Lutgarde was hardly conscious of time's flight. Her fast was over almost before she realized the mystical number of seven had been reached. It comforted her greatly to learn that Simon de Montfort had subdued practically all of Languedoc and that the heresy no longer enjoyed dominance. But even with God one good turn deserves another. So a new vision of Christ was granted Lutgarde and a new request for another seven years' fast was made.

She had seen Jesus under many aspects now. She knew His wounded Heart from the very beginning. She had kissed His open side one night back at St. Catherine's where He called her from a sickbed when she was endeavoring to break a fever by inducing a sweat, and bade her get up and pray for those who were sweating in the fevers of their sins. Lutgarde arose immediately, dressed rapidly, hurried along the cloister, only to be met at the door of the church by the Crucified, who allowed her to kiss the wound in His side. But on this latest occasion Lutgarde saw Christ's wounds as five rubied fires.

Leisure to love

"Beloved," said the martyred Christ, "behold My wounds. Hear what they cry to thee."

When Lutgarde, frightened by the reproof sounding in His voice, finally asked what it was that the wounds were crying, she heard what everyone with the Faith should hear whenever a Consecration bell rings: "They cry to thee to hold My Father's wrath, kindled against sinners, in check. They cry to thee to see that My blood be not shed in vain and My death a waste. They cry that you move My Father to mercy by your prayers, works, and weeping."

Most of the visions Lutgarde had during this time occurred while she was assisting at the Holy Sacrifice, and all had to do with His wounds. It would seem as if the Sacred Heart would teach her that in this world it is the Mass that matters — and very little else. Again and again, she saw Him as standing before God the Father, His wounds opened afresh and glowing with living blood. More than once He turned to her and said, "Do you see how I offer Myself to the Father? Do you see how I am ever and always crucified for My sinners? I want you to do the same. . . ." Small wonder that this nun deemed her one role in life was to let Christ live in her that sinners might not die; smaller wonder that the Mass, which is the heart of the Cistercian's day, became, as it were, Lutgarde's entire day. With each fresh "white Heart-break of a Host," she felt her own heart break anew; and she kept the command of Christ to win mercy for men by her womanly tears.

Lutgarde wept often these years; for the realization that the will of Him who is Infinite Love and Power could be frustrated by finite man; that God's blood could crimson a cross, yet be shed in vain; that Christ's Heart could be pierced, yet prove a wasted love, set her weeping first for God and His frustrated Christ, then for the stupidity of sin-sodden men. All day long she felt herself to be on a cross, her hands held to wide-flung arms by nails that had been fashioned and driven through them by her twin compassion for God and man.

One day when Lutgarde, conscious of the furious burning of

these nails, was sobbing in grief, Christ came to her side and said, "You may cease weeping for My sinners, Lutgarde. From now on, I want you to pray in more peace; for the fervor of your heart will plead with My Father as eloquently as did the tears from your eyes — and sinners will be saved."

Lutgarde's "Mass" went on in greater calm after that; but on it went, day after day, week after week, until years had passed.

The Cistercian regime had given her a leisure she would never have known at St. Catherine's. That is what the crowded day of seventeen hours appeared to her: a complete leisure in which she could love God the way she now knew the Man with the wounded Heart had loved her. Freed from all the attention-absorbing details of office, Lutgarde was able to reflect on all that God had done to her and in her since that day Jesus had said, "Behold here what you are to love and how you are to love." She saw the steps by which He had led her to the present simplification of life and living found in centering all things in the Mass. At first Christ had focused her attention on His wounded Heart. Being a woman she soon was throbbing in sympathy for His wounded humanity. The next step was immediate: her whole being was filled with compassion for Him. The culmination of Christ's Passion was the Cross. But the darkening of the hill of Calvary was the kindling of candle flame all over the world as Golgotha is renewed in the Mass. That is why time ceased for Lutgarde as she assisted daily at her Conventual Mass; for she was in the Cenacle as Christ said, "This is My Body, which shall be given up for you; this is My Blood which shall be shed for you"; she was on Golgotha listening to the *Consummatum est,* and watching wide-eyed as the lance drew blood and water from His stilled Heart.

She understood His last command, "Do this in commemoration of Me." To her that not only meant that she was to stand in choir each day as some priest bent over a wafer of wheat and breathed upon wine, but that she was to be priest herself and take up the day's joys and sorrows, its pains and pleasures, all its prayers and penances and make them into wheat and wine that she might help complete His Passion.

Life had changed from something into Someone for Lutgarde; and He was the one she would love *sine modo* by making her life a Mass; for that was what He had done with His death.

It is not strange, then, to find Lutgarde's late years filled with concern for priests. They were Christ. Without them the Mass could not go on. That they might acquire sufficient sanctity she would pray, she would suffer, she would offer all she had and was. When opportunity offered — and it offered itself more and more as her genius for making friends once again came into play — she humbly but urgently exhorted priests to be Christ. That is why such names as Jacques de Vitry, who would die a cardinal, Bishop of Frascati; Foulques de Marseille, the Cistercian monk who would be made bishop of Toulouse and wield such a mighty influence in the founding of the Dominican Order; Blessed Jordan, the man who would be the Dominicans' second general; and others of lesser rank but perhaps of no lesser sanctity fill her late years. It is impressive and quite significant that Thomas of Cantimpré describes this solicitude for holiness in priests with the words *supra modum*. Lutgarde was being consistent.

One more step, natural in its order because of her total absorption in the Mass, was her craving for Holy Communion. But St. Pius X, with his *Motu Proprio* on frequent Communion was almost seven hundred years away; and although the early Cistercians had been advised to receive the Blessed Sacrament once a week, the practice was not adopted in many convents of nuns. In some houses the religious approached the holy table only three or four times a year. Lutgarde would have died had she been denied this contact with her Lord for that length of time. Yet her craving caused criticism. And this is understandable when we realize that even to truly holy people, weekly

Communion, in those days, appeared highly presumptuous. Mother Agnes, abbess of Aywières, heard so many complaints and harsh criticism of Lutgarde's conduct that she felt obliged finally to command the good Sister to receive Holy Communion less frequently.

Obedience to this command tore Lutgarde's heart, until Christ came to her relief — which He did in a highly dramatic fashion. As four centuries later, when superiors would forbid Margaret Mary the practice of the "Holy Hour," God would manifest His will by an alarming visitation to the community, so now at Aywières came a sickness such as it had never known, which grew in intensity until the Abbess lifted the ban she had placed on Lutgarde's reception of the Blessed Sacrament. God wanted obedience in the subject, but also proper co-operation from superiors.

Yet, even this palpable manifestation of His good pleasure did not succeed in banishing all antipathy. Years later, when Lutgarde is a blind, infirm, and sick old nun, she will have to be assisted to the altar rail by angels, because none of her sisters will help her to Holy Communion.

The un-martyred martyr

In 1235, in answer to Lutgarde's constant pleading for a greater share in His Passion, so that she could make her life a more perfect "Mass," God took sight from her eyes. The day she could not see, the aging nun was very happy; for the affliction brought her back almost twenty years to the night when she was agonizing because she could not prove her love by the absolute *sine modo* of martyrdom. Little Agnes, the winsome Roman virgin, who had shown her love for God by the shedding of her blood, had filled Lutgarde's every horizon that day almost twenty years before. And at the day's end she found herself burning with a holy envy that she might emulate the loving and lovable Agnes. So ardent, so violent was this longing that it burst a vessel close to her heart, and through a wound that suddenly opened in her side there gushed out the bright red proof of her love. It was Christ Himself who stanched the flow that night and satisfied her longing with the words, "Agnes' reward shall be yours, Lutgarde; for your desire is accepted for the deed, and this shedding of your blood will be equal to martyrdom." Thomas of Cantimpré goes on to tell how two nuns testified that Lutgarde carried the scar of that wound all her days.

Now a new stigmatization appeared. Whenever now the blind old nun would look intently with the eyes of her soul on the agonizing Christ, drops of blood would form on her brow and fall as they had once fallen from Him in the Garden — and Christ knew Gethsemani's red sweat again in His chosen member, Lutgarde. Small wonder that the Blessed Henry Suso has said that "one of these victim souls is dearer and more valuable in the eyes of God than thousands of good souls who live at their ease." And we can understand his other remark to the effect that "though these souls are few in number, God allows the whole of Christendom to rest on them, so that if they did not exist, the world might perish."

But with all her intimacy with the Divine, with all her supernatural gifts, Lutgarde not only remained, but in later life became more and more warmly human. This, perhaps, is the surest proof of her genuine sanctity. For, to find one growing old gracefully; to see ever newer spiritual strengths come as physical weakness increases; to discover a robust youthfulness in the soul as the aged body gradually breaks down, and to meet a glowing humanness in the obviously holy, is to come face to face with one who has really met God and lived a lifetime in His company. Such was Lutgarde. For, if one had the time and patience to page through the Bollandists, studying every reference to this woman's human contacts, a delightful volume on human friendships as the result of warm intimacy with God could be written.

One of the most charming of the many stories that could be told of Lutgarde and her humanness is that involving Sibyl de Gages. This favorite of fortune, born and reared in one of the best families of Hainaut's nobility, had been first a canoness at Nivelles, but was called by God to the Cistercian life at Aywières. One of the first assignments given her was the care of the aged and sick in the infirmary. She did not like it. Both her natural background as a noble, and her religious background as a canoness, joined to make the assignment repugnant. When she found that her biggest task was to lead an old, blind nun called Lutgarde, who seemed to have some very queer ideas and be overfond of some strange devotions, Sibyl grew restive. She wondered if she had made a mistake in changing from Nivelles. Daily her impatience with, and antipathy toward, the blind old nun increased — and she showed it in no mistakable fashion. Lutgarde, with that superkeenness of the blind, could all but see the unfriendly expressions on Sibyl's features. With the wisdom that comes with age and grace, she simply smiled. Weeks passed, and with them Sibyl's discontent. When the duty of leading this blind and ever more helpless old nun to the chapel and back again to the infirmary, feeding her at mealtimes, and aiding her in and out of bed, filled Sibyl with a joy she could explain it only by saying, "Lutgarde is so lovably human!" The more important truth, of course, is that Lutgarde was so genuinely saintly.

A hurried reading of these Bollandists might give one a very wrong impression about Lutgarde's late years and the Cistercian solitude in Brabant; for Thomas of Cantimpré has filled his pages with the names of Lutgarde's friends. It is only after one studies the text carefully and notes that practically all the women named were sister religious at Aywières, and that the priests listed were either confessors to the nuns or mere passing guests,

that one feels no uneasiness about the strictness of the enclosure
at the Brabant convent and the depths of Lutgarde's solitude.

The dead live — the living die

But no law of enclosure binds the souls of the blessed or even
of those in purgatory. Hence we find Lutgarde in almost constant contact with her friends during her sunset years. John de
Liro, the priest who had sent her to Aywières, died while crossing
the Alps on his way back from Rome. Shortly after his death,
he appeared to Lutgarde garbed not only in the white of a
virgin soul, nor only in the martyr's red which his strenuous
labors had won for him, but in a blue that was explained as
signifying the reward that was his for his life of prayer and intimate union with God. Lutgarde saw in this her own future
raiment.

Many who had been friends on earth came back to thank her
for her prayers or to beg for them either for themselves or
others. Thus Blessed Mary of Oignes, who on her deathbed had
exclaimed, "There is no one on earth who has more power to
free souls from purgatory than Lutgarde," came one night long
after her death to arouse Lutgarde and plead with her to rise
and pray for the soul of a priest who had been a mutual friend
of theirs and who was now being judged. Father Baldwin, it
seems, had allowed temporal concerns to obscure his priestly
mission; and now God was weighing things in His faultless
scales. That invention of Infinite Mercy called purgatory yawned
wide with its merciless flames for this priest who had been somewhat worldly. Lutgarde prayed, and Father Baldwin entered
eternal rest much sooner than he would have without so kind
a friend in heaven as Mary of Oignes and so powerful a friend
on earth as Lutgarde.

The list is long of those who appeared either after a stay in
purgatory to thank her for their liberation, or before it to plead

with her to help them. It holds the names of many who graced earth's highest offices, such as that of pope, cardinal, bishop, abbot, priest, as well as those who walked earth's lowlier roads. Innocent III is there, as is Blessed Jordan of Saxony, Cardinal De Vitry, Abbot Simon of Foigny, Blessed Mary of Oignes, along with Lutgarde's own blood sister, perhaps the very one to whom she had fled the day of the ambuscade.

And the purpose of all this? — Perhaps God would have Lutgarde remind us that there is a temporal punishment due to sin — and a place for its payment; that prayer and penance can prove profitable to departed friends; that love can leap the grave; and such similar truths relating to that wondrous thing called the "Communion of Saints." Unquestionably Lutgarde shows that three worlds can be made one in the cloistered contemplative life, and that these solitaries, whom so many consider worthless beings, are among society's most profitable servants.

Mindful as she was of the other world of suffering and sufferers, she was never allowed to be unmindful of this world with its insufferable woes and incurable waywardness. Once again she stands forth as proof of the power of prayer and penance and the incalculable value of the cloistered contemplative life.

It is at times of crises that people get most impatient with "the waste of the cloister." When the world seems to be reeling, these good people would have monks and nuns leave their solitudes to help stabilize the staggering, stumbling world. There is a stinging challenge in such complaints — but no fuller or more convincing reply could be given than the one given by Lutgarde and the third long fast of seven years on bread, beer, and a few vegetables. For there was a crisis then — as fierce as the world or the Church has ever faced; for out of the East had come what was a real yellow peril.

Genghis Khan, with his merciless Mongols, had conquered all Asia from China to Persia. On tiny, shaggy horses as fleet as the wind, these hard, yellow warriors had killed between five and six million men as they swept on to their amazing conquests. When Genghis Khan died in 1237, he left to his sons an Empire larger than Alexander had ever dreamed of or Napoleon aspired to. Yet, they were not satisfied. They would make it vaster still. Finding Asia not wide enough, they swarmed into Russia, spilled over into Poland and even to Hungary. Western Europe grew pale with dread as the little yellow men rode on into Bohemia, which was then part of Germany. Definitely it was a time of cruel crisis. Yet Lutgarde was unmoved. . . .

Not so her confessor. Father Bernard came to her and begged with fiery insistence that she plead with God to spare Germany, France, and the Western World. This was in 1242, the third year of Lutgarde's last fast. She turned to her confessor and quitely said, "I am just beginning to call on the Lord. Fear not, these Tartars will never come into our country."

Father Bernard, taking her words as prophecy, departed relieved. But the picture that Thomas of Cantimpré draws is so filled with menace that one wonders how Father Bernard could have had such faith in the words of this aged nun. Thomas says, "The Tartars had destroyed Greater Hungary to the east and Lesser Hungary to the west; they had done the same to greater portions of Turkey, Greece, Bulgaria, and Russia; they had killed the powerful Duke of Poland, laid waste his lands, and put his people to the sword; now they threatened Germany and France."

Seemingly, these men were invincible. Yet Lutgarde had calmly said, "These Tartars will never come into our country." She was right; for the following year Oktai, Genghis Khan's son, who had led the army after his brother, Batu, died. Deprived of a leader, the little yellow men broke up into small bands and gradually drew back toward Asia. The Western World was saved. But by whom?

"I am just beginning to call on the Lord. . . ." What had Lutgarde been doing for three years? — She had been fasting and praying for what was a greater peril than that of the little yellow men with all their savagery. Frederick II, whom the Pope had crowned head of the Holy Roman Empire, was a far greater menace to Church and Europe than was Khan with all his Mongols. In 1239 Christ had appeared to Lutgarde to say that His Church was threatened by a very powerful enemy and that incalculable harm would be done souls if someone did not pray and do penance. The blind old nun immediately launched into the fast which would end only at her death in 1246. But on her deathbed, she would be able to say to Thomas of Cantimpré, "Fear not, dear friend; this man will be humbled by the prayers of the faithful and will soon depart from this life, leaving the Church in peace."

Frederick, though ward of one pope and crowned Emperor by another, waged relentless war on the Papacy. His was the mad ambition of his forebears: they would suppress the Papal power. Cynic, skeptic, and profligate, this Prince is reported to have said, "The world has been deceived by three great imposters: Jesus Christ, Moses, and Mohammed. Two of these died in honor; the third, Jesus Christ, was hanged on a tree. And they are fools who assert that God, the omnipotent Creator of this world, was born of a Virgin. Man ought to believe nothing but what he can understand and prove by reason." From such a blasphemer what disaster could not have come to the Church and the world?

Although excommunicated, he managed by wiles and deceits to retain his crown. A year after Lutgarde's death he set up an antipope. But two years later the Saint's prophecy was fulfilled when Frederick died. Before two decades had elapsed, the Hohenstaufen dynasty, which had been such a thorn in the side of the Church, came to an end.

It is her German biographer who says, "Without Lutgarde's prayers, tears, and fasts what an entirely different course would the history of many souls and even the Church herself have taken!" With reason we might add: "the world!" For the influence of this weak woman, hidden away in a solitude of Brabant, living in silence, and in her old age groping about in the darkness caused by being blind, gives light to thousands on thousands yet, as she makes them realize that only they can really change the world who walk with God.

As the spring of 1245 was slowly flowering into summer, Lutgarde's soul was lighted one day by the eyes of a smiling Christ. The vision brought her back to the earliest days of her intimacy with Jesus when she had first looked into those eyes. She now read love and approbation in those blinding depths, and learned she had read aright when the God-Man said, "Your labors are all but over, Lutgarde. I cannot bear that you be separated from Me much longer. But this last year I ask three things of you: first, give constant thanks for the graces you have received throughout life from Me; secondly, pour yourself out in ceaseless petition for the salvation of sinners; finally, burn with an ever increasing flame of desire to come to Me."

Those three points make not only a perfect preparation for death but are an exquisitely perfect plan for life. God loves the grateful, the generous, the loving soul; and thanksgiving, petition for others, and an ardent yearning for the face of God was not only the substance of Lutgarde's last year; it was the summation of her life. Small wonder God came for her.

It had all begun in a parlor where two young people were speaking of love. It all ended in a cloister far from her native town and where her native tongue was seldom heard. But by the time Lutgarde was ready for the unending vision of the eyes of Christ, she knew only one language, and she spoke it *sine modo;* it was the language of love: sacrifice.

On June 16, 1246, Christ came to her for the last time on earth. Forty-six years earlier He had said, "Behold here what you are to love and how you are to love." For forty-six years she had done it. Now all He could say was, "Give Me back My Heart,

Lutgarde, that with It I may love you for all eternity without measure."

The pagan may be wise as he counsels us to see to it that there is *"modus in rebus."* But from this cloistered contemplative the Christian can learn that the only way to live — the only way to love — is without measure.

Since we are all cowards at heart, says Belloc, courage is one of the virtues we admire most. Margaret Yeo applies the truth and asserts that because we are cowards, we shrink before sanctity. If the courage we have seen in Lutgarde to love "without measure" has not put the coward in us to flight, then perhaps these two Moorish women who met Christ's challenge to follow Him so courageously that one can say that, as far as in them lay, they gave "measure for measure," will not only win our admiration, but will shame the coward in us to death.

In less than forty-six days these two women won what Lutgarde spent forty-six years longing for — martyrdom of blood. The "of blood" is added, for it would seem safe to say that, just as there is a Baptism of Desire which is fruitful, so, too, there is a Martyrdom of Desire which will win the martyr's palm, especially when that desire is manifested as was Lutgarde's by a life which has merited from many the title of "white martyrdom."

There are many gaps in the story about to be told, and no amount of research will fill them. But the essentials are all there; and these, despite the gaps, are worth unfolding not only to kill the cowards in us, but to delight the child that never dies in man or woman. This may read like a chapter from the Arabian Nights with a Christian twist to it, but the story is true even though it is strange. It opens not in a Persian garden but in one not too unlike it . . . and shows what love can do!

BLESSED MARY and BLESSED GRACE

THE MOORS

Who Paid Christ

Measure for Measure

A fierce little houri!

It was noon in the little town of Carlete in Spain's Saracen-dominated province of Valencia. From the high balcony of the mosque's minaret there sounded the muezzin's call to prayer. At its first note Zaida and Zoraida, daughters of Almanzor, the town's ruler, took their mats in their shuttered women's quarters, turned toward Mecca, knelt, and prayed, *La ilaha ill' Allah!* "There is no God but the true God." For such is the faithful Moslem's prayer of praise which he must lift five times a day. As a general rule, Moslem women do not pray, but Zaida and Zoraida seldom followed the general rule; and this day, high in the summer of 1178, they kept their beautiful faces to the east longer than usual and borrowed phrase after phrase from the Koran, calling Allah the "Living One," the "God who sees," the "One who pardons," and begged him to watch with special care over their brother Amed, who but recently had headed north toward the city of Barcelona, in the country of the infidel.

Zoraida, the younger of the sisters, was the first to move. As she turned gracefully to put her mat back in its place, she com-

51

plained a bit sternly, "It is at times like this that I wish Amed had far less charm." Zaida's dark eyes lit with surprise and interrogation. Zoraida saw it and her own eyes flashed as she said, "Were he not so wise, so skilled in what they call diplomacy, he would not be heading north; nor would you and I be turning so suppliantly to the east. Were he more like Father, or even our elder brother, Almanzor, he would never be sent to negotiate with those Christian dogs."

From her crimson lips to the wisp of black silken hair that had fallen to her forehead, Zaida's slow smile spread. As she gently pushed the black curl back into place, she said, "And it is at times like this that I think you should have been a man. Amed is right. You are a houri — and a fierce houri at that. But now I have a puzzle. Why is it that we fear so when he is on what is really a peaceful mission?"

"There can be no peace with those infidel dogs," cut in the younger sister.

"I say it again, Zoraida: you should have been a man. Such fire. Such fierceness. But look, Amed has gone merely to negotiate the exchange of war prisoners. Our King Zaen thinks him the most capable diplomat in the realm. Why is it that when Amed rides out to battle, we do not fear as we are fearing now?"

"Allah fights with him."

"Doesn't Allah go north with him?"

"Of course. Of course," was the impatient reply from Zoraida, "but diplomacy can be more dangerous than actual war. I fear far more for Amed when he is in the council chamber than when he is on the battlefield. Those infidel dogs are treacherous. They bite the very hand that feeds them; and in their bite there is poison. I wish King Zaen would forget that Amed is so charming and so capable, and leave him here to help Father rule this town and Pintarrafes."

"He has Almanzor for that."

"Almanzor." Zoraida spoke the name slowly, and the shadow

of a frown moved across the olive forehead where dark curls clung. "Come, let's get out of this hot place. There is shade by the pool in the garden."

A few minutes later the two sisters were stepping across wide brown flags under the blazing Valencian sun. The girls were heading for the far end of the garden where blood-red poppies were mirrored in the waters of the pool they bordered. Some tall feathery palms and a few orange trees made an inviting shade beside the pool, and a rosebush, heavy with blooms, climbed a jagged wall. Zoraida led the way. She plucked one of the poppies as she passed the pool, strode into the shade, and threw herself into the thick, soft grass. Her wide red skirt flowered out as she struck the grass and Zaida said to her, "There are times, little sister, when you are more beautiful than any flower — and this is one of them."

Caressing the poppy, Zoraida said, "If I could feel as cool as this flower feels, I'd be content not to be as beautiful. But it was Almanzor I wanted to talk about. You say he helps Father rule Carlete and Pintarrafes; and you are right. But I've been wondering a lot about our elder brother of late. He will inherit all of Father's offices. But I'm afraid he has not inherited all of Father's character. Let me tell you, our Almanzor can be cruel. Father was never that."

"What makes you think such a thing?" Zoraida asked.

Zoraida plucked a few of the poppy's red petals, let them fall idly to the grass, then looked far out over the garden's wall to where the Montes Universales rose range after rugged range with Pina Roya, their highest peak, shimmering in noonday's sun. Slowly she brought her gaze back, picked up the blood-red petals she had dropped, and flicked them into the pool.

"I have seen something in Almanzor that tells me not only that he could be cruel, but brutally so," she said.

"Zoraida! What makes you say such a thing?"

"I don't know, but there is something in his eyes, and at times in his voice, something that I can almost feel as I watch his fingers at times, something that tells me if he were really aroused, he would have pity for no one, not even for you or me."

"Zoraida!"

"Oh, I know. You think me disloyal. But let me tell you, Almanzor could be ferocious. Father is getting on. Almanzor will soon be ruling two towns. Let us hope he reserves all his cruelty for the infidel — those Christian dogs."

"You hate Christians, don't you, Zoraida?"

"Don't *you?*" came the surprised reply.

Zaida bent over and played her hand through the pool's still waters. "What do we really know about them, you and I? And why should we hate anyone we really do not know?"

"They are infidels. That's enough. They are dogs. They are . . ."

"Human beings," cut in the elder sister. "And I'm secretly hoping Amed will have opportunity to study them up there, especially the women. . . ."

"He wouldn't look at one of them!"

"Oh, I don't mean that way. I want him to learn something of their freedom, their manner of life. Amed is quick to observe. Give him the slightest opportunity, and he'll learn all and tell us when he gets back."

"If he gets back with his life, I will have learned all I want to learn about Christians — men or women. I know all now. They are dogs. . . ."

"And you're a fierce little houri," countered Zaida with a laugh.

Zoraida laughed, too, got up from the grass, and moved deeper into the shade where a bench stood close to the roses. "Well, why wouldn't I be an houri?" she asked. "They are nymphs of Paradise, aren't they? And don't our men call Valencia a 'little bit of Paradise fallen to earth'? I was born here. I'm Valencian to the marrow of my bones. But seriously,

I wish Father would speak to our King about not sending Amed on these diplomatic journeys. They frighten me."

Voices in the night

At the very moment, Amed was entering the shade of a dense wood, some miles to the east and north of Lérida, the last Moorish town he would see on this long journey that had brought him across so many thin or dried up streams, over hot, dry plains, on into mountains that finally would bring him down into Catalonia. It had been blazing hot all the way. The sun was as merciless up here in the north as it had ever been in that *huerta* of which the Valencians were so fond and justly proud; so Amed was happy to lead his sweaty men and sweatier horses into the green shade of the woods. When he noted the angle of the shadows and realized that soon the muezzin's sunset call to prayer would be sounding in the land at his back, he was congratulating himself on having come so far north and off the beaten path that led to Barcelona; for these woods would serve as shelter from more than the sun. They were in Christian country now where it would be wise to ride warily. He sat loose in his saddle, let bridle rein go slack; and as his black Andalusian steed single-footed over last year's leaves, Amed looked leisurely from right to left. "If we could find some water, this would serve as a place to camp," he said to the man who rode almost at his shoulder. "This has been a long day."

"It's been a hot one," was his companion's only comment.

A few hours later Amed reined in his steed. His nearest companion did the same; but when his horse shook his head and stretched forth his neck, Amed smiled and said, "Let him go. Let him drink. We will camp here." They were at the side of a tiny stream that dropped from a little ledge and meandered among the trees.

That night as the moon shone into the little clearing where the band of Moors sat, Amed told his men that the next day, in Alfonso II, King of Aragon, they would be facing a descendant of that first Alfonso, who was called "The Fighter," the man, who, by taking Saragossa in 1118, had begun the decline of Moorish domination in Spain. When one of the men ventured, "I thought we were going to Barcelona," Amed laughed and said, "We are; but Barcelona and Aragon are under one king, and he has made the dual kingdoms one of the leading Mediterranean powers." Then he told a story that sounded almost fanciful as he traced Alfonso II's ancestry back through his mother, who was daughter of Agnes of Poitiers and Ramiro, the brother of Alfonso the Fighter. This Ramiro had been a monk in a French monastery when his older brother died after willing his Kingdom of Aragon to the Knights Hospitallers. The people of Aragon rejected this arrangement, and the Pope freed Ramiro from his vows so that he could accept the Spanish crown and carry on the dynasty. His brother, Alfonso, had ruled Aragon and Navarre; but his grandson, Alfonso, thanks to his father, Ramón, Count of Barcelona, had added that kingdom to Navarre and Aragon.

"This man is every bit as great a fighter as was his namesake, and all his prowess is directed against us. He has many valuable prisoners — many more than we have. And King Zaen expects me to win their release. Allah be with us tomorrow is all I say tonight."

With that, they broke up, each stretching out on the ground to sleep the sleep of weary men. No muezzin with his before-midnight call awoke them. But shortly after midnight Amed stirred in his sleep, settled back again, only to rise again suddenly and sit up wide awake. It was no call of the muezzin he heard; it was music; solemn, slow, with a strange yet soothing rhythm. It was distant and though at times it rose in volume, he could tell that the singers did not come any nearer. But who were they — these singers of music the like of which he had never heard? Amed was now tensely alert, for he had just asked himself what would a choir of men be doing at this hour of night in such a wood. As a Mohammedan he believed in the existence of angels, but never had he any personal experience with them. Was this to be his first? He tensed even more. He was not afraid, but he was fully excited. The singing went on and on. He would have liked to investigate; but the darkness, the denseness of the strange wood, and his own fears of spirits kept him in his place listening.

Only as the east silvered with the first light of dawn and the slight breeze of the new day stirred the tallest tops of the trees, did the singing cease. Amed marveled that he alone had been awakened by the night-long chant. Then and there he decided that he alone would investigate the source of the music. So, as the last star withered in the brightening sky and a few of his men stirred, Amed said, "I'll be back. Wait here for me," and set off in the direction whence the song had come.

It was not long before he came to a clearing in the forest whose center held a strange-shaped wooden house. Amed knew spirits had need of no such abode and he felt easier in mind. Carefully he reconnoitered. Then he saw two oddly robed figures move out to a tree and begin to fell it. Curiosity brought him closer and closer until at last he was within speaking distance. His opening question startled the workers with its suddenness, not with its subtlety or strangeness. It was simply a request to be told where he was and what direction he should take for Barcelona. But that was merely to open conversation. What Amed wanted to know was who these strange men were, what they were doing here deep in the wood, and what was the meaning of last night's almost endless song.

When Amed came back to his followers, he issued a peculiar command and gave a puzzling explanation of his own actions. They were to go back to Lérida, the last Moorish town they had touched, and wait for him. If any asked his whereabouts, the only answer to be given was that he was on a special mission of investigation. It had to do with Christians.

Now comes a lacuna in the story. Nothing more is said about the prisoners of war in any of the available documents. But Amed shows himself in all subsequent events to be of such a character that no one will be guilty of rash judgment if he or she concludes that he went to Barcelona and negotiated the exchange to the satisfaction of all.

Barcelona itself fades from the story entirely. We do not so much as feel a breeze from the Mediterranean, let alone look upon its lovely blue waters. And the catfooted Andalusian steeds with their doughty riders go out of the picture, too. All we see is that humble wooden monastery, whence came the night-long chant which led Amed to the discovery of the handful of Cistercian monks who had but recently come into Catalonia to found what was one day to be the "Royal Monastery" of Poblet, whose magnificent abbatial church stands even today to impress visitors and take them back through seven centuries of time to the day when Spain was more Mohammedan than Catholic, and remind them of Pedro II, "the Catholic," who made the dual kingdoms of Aragon and Catalonia a papal fief.

Amed was fascinated by what he found that morning after listening all night to what was actually a night Office for a feast of the Blessed Virgin sung with all possible solemnity. His inquisitive mind wanted to know more about these strange, silent men whose Abbot said they give up what Amed and other men call life because Christ had given up life for them. The atmosphere of peace captivated him, and his curiosity was at fever pitch because of what radiated from these men: contentment and even joy. How could it be?

He had dismissed his companions without telling what he had discovered; for he knew their one question would have been, "Are these men infidel dogs or followers of the Prophet?"

The answer to that question would have had one effect on his Moors, who were not only fierce fighters but fanatics where Christians were concerned. The reply he told them to give to any who would inquire as to his whereabouts was true: he *was* investigating some Christians; but little did he dream what the results of that investigation were to be.

When a week had passed and Amed felt almost forced — so strong was the attraction — to ask the Abbot if he might stay a while longer, he suddenly thought of home and his family. He well knew what his father and brother would say and do if they learned that he was not only dwelling with Christian monks, but actually enjoying his stay and even admiring their manner of life and many of their beliefs. He felt sure that Zaida would not only understand his feelings but even sympathize; for this elder sister of his had inherited all the winsome qualities of his dead mother. She was quiet, deep, loving, and very lovable. Amed thought of her as possessing everything a woman should possess and was both very proud of and very deeply fond of her. When his thoughts ran on to Zoraida, he chuckled. His pride in and love for her was different, but very real. Here was a being all fire and flame, he thought. But when he pictured himself telling her of his stay, he could see the flash of her dark eyes, and the color mount in her satin cheeks, and all but hear her tirade. How often he had told her that instead of being behind the shutters of the women's quarters, she belonged on a fleet-footed Arab steed and should be flying over the plains or climbing into the country's rugged hills. He smiled as he admitted that his admiration and love for this baby sister was seemingly more lively than what he had for Zaida.

But then his smile faded and his forehead furrowed as he pictured himself talking with Zaida about the things, the deep things, he had learned at Poblet. Yes, it would be with Zaida, never with Zoraida, that he would talk about such matters. His older sister would be interested in the fact that the Christians worshiped what they called the "one true God" even more fervently than any follower of the Prophet worshiped Allah. They prayed, and even sang their praise to Him longer and more often than any Moslem. Seven times a day, without any muezzin's call, these monks assembled and, instead of turning toward Mecca, lifted their minds and hearts to Heaven. She would be as fascinated as he had been to find them doing so many things that the Koran prescribed; they purified themselves, prayed, fasted, and gave alms as the Prophet demanded. More, they did not fast as so many Mohammedans, merely in the one month of Ramadan; these monks abstained from meat the entire year round, and denied themselves the usual meals of men every day. That would all interest her; and what he had found most inspiring would intrigue her — the way the monks prayed for the dead. Mohammed had enjoined all his followers to do the same, but it was seldom even in the mosques on Friday — the Moslem Sabbath — that even the imam pleaded with Allah on behalf of those who had died. Could it be that these Christians were more sincere in their beliefs than the Moors?

The longer he stayed with the monks, the clearer he saw the similarities and mighty differences between Islamism and Christianity. He began to suspect what critical scholars later affirmed; namely, that Mohammed's acquaintance with Christian dogma was very superficial. To Amed the story of the Annunciation, as given by St. Luke, was far more appealing than what he had heard and read about the same Angel Gabriel's call of Mohammed, which had constituted him the Prophet of Allah and the Apostle of Arabia. This tiny doubt was the seed of conversion. Of course the dogma of the Incarnation bristled with difficulties for this Moslem. But when the Abbot quietly pointed out that Amed was laboring under a lifelong prejudice and would have to clear his mind of all preconceived notions before he could ever judge aright, the Moor's dark face lit with a smile; and he said, "But it is all too good to be true: this tale about God becoming man that men might become like God."

The wise Abbot returned the smile. He did not argue. He simply said what he had said from the beginning, "God loves us and gave Himself up for us. What shall we do in return?" He admired the nobility of the Moor and felt sure that grace would work its marvel if this deep-thinking man were given time enough to reflect. So he often left him alone as he himself went away to pray. One day he ended their short talk by handing him a copy of the earliest, warmest, and perhaps the most authentic of all the lives of St. Bernard of Clairvaux, that written by William of St. Thierry, St. Bernard's intimate friend, saying, "I think you'll like this man."

Amed read that life with avidity. He was charmed by the many stories William had worked into his biography and was completely captivated by the character of St. Bernard. As he laid the manuscript aside after its first reading, Amed told himself that, if a man of Bernard's intellectual and moral stature could believe in One whom Mohammed named merely a prophet of Allah, he himself would be wise to ponder the tenets of the Christian Faith; so he begged leave to stay on another week.

The weeks lengthened into months, and yet King Zaen's diplomat made no move to leave the monastery of Poblet. It was not the arguments the Abbot and the Guestmaster presented with such calm; not the unanswerable proofs from history; not even the magnetic pull of the moral grandeur of Christ as seen in the Gospels that finally won him. What he found irresistible was the overpowering persuasion that came from the silent, humble, recollected, austere, yet joyous lives led by the men themselves. What he found on the yellow parchment under the names of Matthew, Mark, Luke, and John, which claimed to be the authentic picture of the Christ and an infallible portrayal of His doctrine, he saw in these monks as they rose night after night to sing to God, then lived out their long day in an atmosphere of prayer. At last he flung himself at the Abbot's feet and begged to be made a Christian. After months of instruction he was baptized and took the name of the man he admired most — Bernard.

Generosity makes man God-like

The story of Bernard, the Moorish noble who was received not only into the Catholic Church but into the Cistercian Order at Poblet, is one of the most delightful that appear in the Menology of the Order of Citeaux. But this volume of THE SAGA OF CITEAUX is exclusively given to women; so we may dwell only on those incidents in Bernard's life that affect our two main characters, his sisters Zaida and Zoraida. Yet it would be unkind, not only to him and our readers, but even to God, if we did not point to Bernard as proof that grace builds on nature.

His sisters saw his charm. King Zaen knew his worth. His father and brother almost envied him his many abilities. Yet were any one of them or each of them asked to name the secret of Amed's success, the outstanding trait of his character, and the deep source of all his charm, the answer would be: his generosity; for all knew him to be generous even in his thoughts. A century or so later Thomas Aquinas would name this trait magnanimity. The word literally means large soul; and therein lies a perfect description of those whose lofty minds never dwell on what is mean, whose hearts are large, never harboring anything as sickly or as shriveling as revenge, whose whole bountiful person is really prodigal. God fashions such men and women that we of lesser stature may not lose faith in human nature and may know some warmth in this cold and selfish world. Amed the Moor had been generous — Bernard the Christian would be more so.

The pleasing personality which had made him so successful a diplomat did not vanish when he donned the cowl, and a wise Abbot determined to use for the King of kings what had been used so often and so fruitfully for Valencia's King. In due time Bernard was made Cellarer of the monastery; and, if there is any office that needs a diplomat, that is it. He did not disappoint his Abbot. In fact it soon appeared that in this converted Moor the Abbot had for Cellarer one who was just what St. Benedict demanded: a man who was "wise, mature, and sober"; one who, when he could not give the brethren what they desired, would send them away happy because of his pleasant words. But there soon appeared a fly in the ointment. Some of the brethren, who had never yet been hurt by Bernard, feared now that he was too openhanded with the poor.

St. Benedict had commanded his followers to be generous, but this Bernard seemed more than that; he appeared prodigal. Some of the less magnanimous and more nervous finally went to the Abbot and accused the Cellarer of having ruined the monastery by the way he had emptied the granary and the cellar.

Bernard's reply to the charge was that of a diplomat. He did not say a word. He simply led the Abbot and the accusing brethren to the granary and cellar. The first was found running over with grain; the second, stocked high with wine and oil. The Abbot smiled. The Cellarer walked away. The brethren looked in awe and whispered something about miracles.

It was not the first, nor would it be the last time that the brethren would use such a word regarding Bernard's works. Among his duties as Cellarer was that of taking care of the sick. Here again his magnanimity showed itself. His very presence brought cheer — and as many thought — health. More than one of the more credulous told how they had been cured by the Cellarer's sign of the cross. Exaggeration perhaps, but tribute nevertheless to character.

But to move on to that part of Bernard's story that has to

do with his sisters: let us say that after some time he won from his Abbot the strange and most extraordinary permission to set off for Valencia and the town of Carlete. From what we know of Bernard's character, it is safe to say a double motive urged him on. His love for his family was great, but his love for Christ had become greater. He felt he could use his powers as a diplomat and get his father and brother to realize that all they had heard about Christians and Christianity was not true. He hoped he could be an apostle. With his sisters he knew he could go further than with his father or brother. The girls could be converted. But deeper even than these desires was the secret of his heart, his craving to give back to Christ what Christ had given up for him. Bernard the monk never forgot what Amed the Moor knew. So, once he had seen his family, he would move out among the Moslems and more than likely be greeted by them as were all Christians.

"Your brother is back"

Zaida and Zoraida had heard about the return of the men who had set out with Amed on that mission to Barcelona. For a time the account they gave of his failure to return with them satisfied all, even the King. But when more than a year had passed, doubts and questions arose. Yet the reputation Amed had won by years of loyalty to the King banished most of the doubts and served as answer for the questions. But, when the silence grew so prolonged, even Zaida grew fearful.

Her younger sister had early concluded that the Christian dogs had poisoned him. She told Zaida again and again that there had been treachery somewhere.

"But, Zoraida," replied the calmer sister more than once, "proof of such is always found. Something comes to light sooner or later. Since nothing at all has been heard of Amed, let us go on in hope."

"Fool!" was the word she received for that bit of encouragement. "You don't know those Christians." The year passed. At its close their father, Almanzor, died; and their elder brother of the same name took over the government of the two towns. Zoraida seemed to fade with the year. Her color went. Her spirits dropped. Zaida saw it and grew concerned.

Then in May, 1180, Valencia took on the vesture that had won for her the name of "bit of Paradise." The *huerta* was vivid green under a golden sun. Off on the high hills trees lifted proud heads to a sapphire sky. Zoraida responded to nature's awakening. She sparkled with gay life. Zaida thanked Allah and prayed that her sister would be like the seasons and go from blossom and bloom to full flower.

But then came word from Lérida. Zaida heard it first and found it filled with delight and danger. Their aunt in that city had seen Amed — but had found him a Christian. How was she to tell Zoraida? That fiery one so loved her brother that news of his being alive would set her whole being aflame. Yet her hate for Christians was so fierce that Zaida feared to tell her.

She was spared any decision; for hard upon the first news came a more exciting report: Amed was in Valencia. He had called on Almanzor. He was even now in conference with the elder brother.

Zoraida was in the garden when the word was given her. For a moment she stood as one stunned, then whirled and danced with wild delight, before setting off to find Zaida, calling to her in a high excited voice as she entered the house. But at the door of the women's quarters she stopped and stared, Almanzor stood there, and his face was as if set in stone. He spoke. His words were like steel.

"Your brother is back," he said. "A madman. A Christian. A monk. I did not kill him because he begged to see you. See him. Change him, or die he shall."

Almanzor turned and was gone. Zoraida found herself staring at a stranger. The strong black beard did not fully conceal the hollowness of the cheeks. The head was shaved save for a thin fringe around the crown. A shapeless robe, more gray than white, hung from the shoulders to the heels. It was caught at the center by a leathern girdle enclosing a dark scapular, which had a hood attached. Zoraida stared and might have screamed at finding this strangely garbed man at the door of her inviolable quarters had not the stranger smiled.

"Amed!" cried the girl.

But not until his two arms went out and the old familiar voice had said, "My fierce little houri, come here," did Zoraida fling herself into her brother's arms.

For the next two weeks Almanzor was not at home. Business in Pintarrafes was his excuse. But Zaida knew that was but a pretext. Her elder brother, like her father, could rule both towns from Carlete. This absence boded no good for Amed, who kept calling himself Bernard. But Almanzor was not the only one who had stormed at Amed. After the first excitement of his return had worn off, Zoraida flamed out at him day after day as he tried to tell her about Christianity and life at Poblet.

The diplomat in Bernard faced the most difficult task of all his experiences as it came to grips with the inbred hatred of Christianity which was now fired to a new fierceness by a sisterly love that was deep and could be dangerous.

"I could kill you myself," she cried one day after Bernard had quietly said he would never take off the monk's robe. No one, looking at her impassioned face that moment, could have doubted her word.

But love finally conquered. One day Zoraida, with her sister, listened as Bernard coursed down that avenue of truths called Christian dogma. Wise in human ways, the perfect diplomat never forgot for a moment that he was talking to a woman; so with the skill of a master he cleverly mingled with that invincible logic enough emotional appeal to win heart as well as head. He began with God the Creator and ended with God the Rewarder and the Reward, showing, in between, the fall of man, his need for a Redeemer, and the divine solution to that otherwise insoluble need. He told how Gabriel had called Mary "full of grace" and saw that both sisters were listening intently to this tale about the Maid of Nazareth. On he went making even the passionate Zoraida see it all through his eyes until finally he had his fiery little houri looking on the Madonna with love and on the Pietà with a woman's warm compassion. God had once again supernaturalized the natural as He used a sister's adoring love for a brother as a channel of grace and conversion.

Down by the pool in the garden, Bernard baptized them. Zaida asked to be named "Mary" after God's own Mother. Zoraida showed readiness to protest. She, too, wanted to bear the name of the Immaculate One. But when Bernard smiled and said, "You shall bear her name, my houri, but we shall pronounce it 'Grace' — for that fits you perfectly, both naturally and supernaturally," she agreed with her usual enthusiasm.

But now real difficulty faced them. They knew Almanzor was having the house watched. He had already sent two servants to see if all was well. Bernard and the two sisters knew what such solicitude meant.

"He's inflexible," said Bernard with a smile.

"He's brutal," flashed the newly baptized Grace. "I have always said he could be cruel. Now we shall see it. But, Bernard, did you not say Christ wanted witnesses? What was the name you gave those whose blood became seed?"

"Martyrs?"

"That's it. That's what we shall be — and in our father's own house."

"You've changed your name, but not your nature, little houri," put in her elder sister. "You may be called Grace, but you are still fierce. But think a little. Almanzor does not yet know that we have joined Bernard. He does not know we are Mary and Grace. Why could we not slip out of this house and away from Valencia itself. Why could we not escape into Christian territory?"

"Seat of Wisdom!" cried Bernard. "Indeed you have been well named Zaida — I mean Mary. Listen . . ."

He then told how he had converted their aunt up in Catalonia before coming home and outlined a plan for them that sounded most feasible. The two sisters were to lock Bernard in their father's house, go to Almanzor, tell him of their inability to bring Amed back to Moslemism (saying nothing, of course, about his having converted them!) then suggesting that the family honor would be best upheld, not by killing Amed, but by banishing him forever from the realm. If they were successful in this, Bernard would accept the sentence, but hide in a nearby wood where Mary and Grace would join him as soon as possible, then the three would make their way to Catalonia and their aunt's house. From there Bernard would return to Poblet and the monastic life. He smiled as he concluded all arrangements by saying, "I'm passing up martyrdom for you two; I hope I'm not passing up heaven."

It worked. For though Almanzor fumed, stormed up and down, called on Allah, cursed, swore, threatened to brush the two sisters aside and strangle his brother with his own two hands, Zaida restrained him with the repeated, "Think of Father! Think of the family name." It restrained him somewhat, but Almanzor did not come to a full pause until Zoraida flashed out with, "Fool! What good is a dead dog? A live madman may one day come to his senses, but can a dead one?"

Bernard was banished. He left his father's house under Almanzor's guard but not under his gaze. The elder brother swore he would not so much as look at the renegade.

But the very next day the same Almanzor was out in the

woods — and his one desire was to lay his bloodshot eyes on that same brother; for early that morning word had been brought to him that, under cover of the night, Zaida and Zoraida had left the home taking enough with them for a long journey.

In a flash Almanzor saw it all. He had been tricked. His younger brother was still the clever diplomat. He had played on the sympathy of his sisters and not only won freedom for himself but even had them ready to accompany him to some other abode. But Almanzor would show this Christian dog what resources the ruler of Carlete and Pintarrafes had. The head of the guard which had escorted Amed out of town was called and questioned. Within a few hours a cordon of horsemen had been thrown around the only wood that could serve as shelter for the banished one. Then a slow systematic beating of those woods was begun. It went on without results that night and into the next day. But late in the afternoon as some of the searchers, led by Almanzor himself, drove their horses to a stream for a drink, they suddenly came upon the monk as he was carefully making his way back with water for his sisters in their concealment.

Almanzor rose in his stirrups to drive his spear through his brother's body but caught himself just before the thrust. "Where are your sisters?" he cried, as the rest of the band encircled the monk. Almanzor should have known better. Amed would never cringe before danger nor be stampeded into fright. All the elder brother got for reply was a slow smile. It infuriated him. "Where are Zaida and Zoraida?" he all but screamed.

"Dead," said Bernard quietly.

When he saw gleams of fright, unbelief, and suspicion flash one after another in his brother's eyes, he added, "I buried them in Christ Jesus last week down by the pool in the garden."

Again Almanzor rose in his stirrups, and again the spear was poised for the thrust. But just as quickly as he had risen, he sank back in his saddle, wheeled his horse while calling out the savage command, "Bring him in alive," and started back for Carlete. For just as he was about to hurl his spear, the import of his brother's words pierced his infuriated mind. Amed was not saying that he had killed his sisters, but that he had christened them. A cold fury came over him. He would find those two and undo the work he should never have allowed Amed to do. He might need his younger brother for this task. That is why he commanded that he be brought in alive. Before leaving the woods he gave orders that one group should not return until it had found the girls.

Two days later Almanzor was sitting in judgment. Before him was the ever flaming Zoraida, who insisted that everyone call her "Grace" and who refused to answer a single question until her bidding was done. Almanzor expected fire and much of it from his younger sister; but when Zaida showed a steadier, more controlled, and, hence, fiercer flame, the Ruler of Carlete and Pintarrafes knew he was beaten.

Bernard was placed with his back to the wall of his father's house. His two sisters were forced to sit at a table facing Bernard with Almanzor sitting between them. Then a soldier was commanded to nail Bernard to that wall by driving a long spike through his head. Almanzor gripped his two sisters by their wrists: "Open your eyes and see how an infidel dies. Watch this follower of the Crucified."

It was a needless command; for Mary and Grace would not have missed the sight for all the gold in the world. Bernard had told them what martyrdom meant; and cruel as was the spectacle, they saw its glory and both prayed and encouraged Bernard as the hammer blows fell.

Rage, blind, brutal rage, seized Almanzor when Grace turned to him and said, "Thank you, kind Brother, for sending Bernard to heaven. Won't you be as kind to us?"

His answer was to order his sisters beheaded.

There is no pity in a Moor when Christians are in question. So swords did Almanzor's bidding even though the necks they sought were those of two beautiful women.

They vest in red

The story sounds fanciful, almost fantastic. Never would it be accepted as other than touching legend were it not for two realities no one may blink. In Catalonia today there is — or at least there was before the Spanish Revolution of 1936–1939 — a tomb to which countless pilgrims come annually to pray with confidence to a Saint they claimed was more than generous, to a Saint they said was magnanimous. They called him St. Bernard of Alzira. If you asked about his life, they would only say he had been a Moor by the name of Amed who became a Cistercian at the monastery of Poblet. The other reality is founded on firmer rock, one which no revolution will ever overturn. It rests on the fire-spawned granite which is the foundation stone of the infallible Catholic Church. It manifests itself in the fact that on June 1 of every year, throughout the entire Cistercian Order, monks and nuns bend over in prayer as they chant the Divine Office in honor of Bernard, Mary, and Grace, the Moors who gave "measure for measure" to the Christ. The prayer of that Office is for love — the love which enabled them to bear time's trials in a way that merited eternity for them. For hundreds on hundreds of years that has been the pleasure of the Order of Citeaux, but it was only in 1701 that the Church declared these three Moors "Blessed."

Mary and Grace won what Lutgarde hoped for. When Cistercian priests vest for Mass on June 1, red — the red of martyrs — is the color they don. And love is the burden of their prayer of petition. They want a love that will pay measure for measure.

Asceline was in the convent before she had reached the age of the use of reason; but the use she made of it after reaching that age not only kept her from ever aging, but showed her to be most reasonable. That reasonableness won for her the title of "Blessed" — and life holds no greater success. It won for the Cistercian Order another title to greatness.

Lutgarde, as we have seen, came to the Cistercians from the Black Benedictines. Mary and Grace live in Cistercian liturgy, not because they were Cistercian nuns as some enthusiasts have claimed, but simply because it was their Cistercian brother who was God's instrument for leading them to martyrdom. Now we approach a relative of the greatest of great Cistercians, St. Bernard of Clairvaux; and we find that she was at first an Augustinian.

All of which proves not only that there were many roads that led to Citeaux in the centuries that are gone, but that even today there are various ways that lead to God. Asceline had one of her own. It could be yours.

BLESSED ASCELINE

The Girl

Who Always Walked

With God

Education and environment shape souls

Russia has demonstrated for the world that environment and education can mold souls and crystallize character. But the environment is bad, and the education is nothing but indoctrination. So the souls are shapeless and the characters horrible distortions. Yet this mid-twentieth-century madness can serve to set in relief a marvel of the Middle Ages. The Iron Curtain, though immaterial, is certainly an enclosure. So for didactic purposes let us call it a "cloister." And that soul-destroying system of indoctrination, which is the only training of the mind and will allowed behind that Curtain, can, for the same purpose, be called an "education." Our modern psychologists and students of character have asserted the sculpturing powers of education and environment. But it waited for the Reds to take those assertions and translate them into frightening facts.

With their Iron Curtain they shut out the Western World and created an environment of their own. With their system of indoctrination they crammed their people into their classrooms and created an educational system that again was their own. Today we see the results. Russia will go down in history as the first nation that took the very souls out of its people by managing environment and monopolizing education. It presents the opposite side of the picture to the one drawn in the late twelfth century when a true cloister shut out the worldly world and gave a soul a real education about this and the "other world."

It lies in a Word: God-consciousness

Asceline was cloistered with Christ almost from infancy; and for the next seventy years received nothing but a Christian education.

The sources whence the matter for this short life has been drawn take us as close to the fountainhead as it is possible for humans living in the twentieth century to get. The main sources are the *Cistercian Menology* and *Lilia Cistercii,* both written by Chrysostom Henríquez. Though they were published in 1630 and 1633, respectively, they actually go back to the end of the twelfth century; for the *Menology* is little more than a digest of a life written in 1198 by Blessed Goswin, who had been Asceline's confessor; and the account in the *Lilia Cistercii* was compiled exclusively from documents secured from the convent at Boulancourt, where Asceline spent most of her life. Besides these we have the story written by Father Des Guerrois in his book, *La Sainteté Chrétienne,* a book that comes from the Boulancourt archives. Then there is that scholarly record drawn up by Pierre Le Nain in his *Histoire de l'Ordre de Cîteaux.* Finally we have that careful and critical work of l'Abbé Jobin, *St. Bernard et Sa Famille.*

The sources are plentiful and safe. Yet little that is found in those "lives" will be found in this. For while they are replete with wonders wrought by the saintly one, this is concerned only with the wonder of her sanctity. They tell of marvels she worked after arriving at holiness; this will tell how she arrived there. For unlike the Bollandists, who aim at giving faithful rescripts of all they find to be authentic, we give simply the fruits of their fidelity. Our purpose is professedly pragmatic; for while none of us may ever enjoy the gift of tears, the gift of prophecy, the ability to read hearts and heal bodies; while none of us may ever enjoy the visions and revelations Asceline enjoyed after arriving at sanctity, no one of us need ever be without the joy of that which brought her to sainthood. It lies in a motto; it lies in a word.

Frederick William Faber has said that one motto *lived* is enough to make a saint. Asceline proves him correct. For from all that Jobin, Le Nain, Des Guerrois, and Henríquez (and each depended ultimately on Goswin) say about Asceline, we take but one outstanding fact; and we take it from the lips of the Beata herself. Speaking to her confessor one day late in life, she very honestly declared, "I know nothing good of myself except this: *I have always had God present in my mind.*"

There is the secret of Asceline's success in life — God-consciousness, or that constant living in the presence of God. There, too, is our lesson for living. For no simpler, surer, safer way to the heights of holiness could be devised or advised. "The Spirit breatheth where He wills," of course; but we, too, can breathe in and with the Spirit if we but will! Asceline shows us how.

She was born about 1120 at La Ferté-sur-Aube, not far from Clairvaux. Some have called her the niece of Clairvaux's great Abbot, St. Bernard. But that can hardly be; for of that family only Guy and Humbeline married. The latter, we know, never bore a child; and history tells that of the former's two children one girl married Bartholomew of Sambernon and the other we shall meet in the course of this narrative as the Prioress of Poulangy. So Asceline cannot be related to Clairvaux's great Abbot as closely as some would have her be.

Yet, when we call her cousin, we are still in difficulty; for there is question about the degree. Some would call her first cousin, naming her the daughter of either Holdoin or Haynon, two brothers of Bernard's saintly father, Tescelin. But perhaps Jobin comes closest when he names her the granddaughter of one of these men. So, while the distance may be greater, the relationship is more true. Bernard and Asceline were of the same blood.

But that detail need detain us little; for here we are proving no thesis on heredity, physical or spiritual. We simply say that Asceline proves the truth of the Gospel adage: "as you sow, so shall you reap." Or, to be more explicit, she proves how true it is to say:

> *"Sow a thought, and reap an act;*
> *Sow an act, and reap a habit;*
> *Sow a habit, and reap a character;*
> *Sow a character, and reap a destiny."*

The thought she sowed was God. The destiny she reaped was Godliness.

We cannot discover the names of Asceline's parents. But there is unanimity and uniformity among authors in saying that her father died when she was an infant, and that her mother, on the advice of St. Bernard, betook herself and her daughter to the convent of Augustinian Canonesses at Boulan-court. There our story really begins.

That Asceline entered the cloister almost before she was weaned need not surprise us; for Chapter 59 of St. Benedict's Rule details the procedure to be followed when children, even infants, are offered to God by their wise parents. It is a beautiful and deeply significant ceremony the Saint prescribes; for he ordains that the parents, in the presence of witnesses and by a public act, make a formal petition to the abbot about receiving their child. Then during the holy Sacrifice of the Mass, they are to make the oblation, which Lanfranc tells us was a host and a chalice which held some wine, symbols of the body and blood, the life of the child. If it were possible, the child would hold both host and chalice in its hands at the Offertory of the Mass; but, if he or she was too young, then this oblation, along with a document testifying to the dedication of the child, were wrapped with the child's hand in the very cloth of the altar, to signify that the child was given entirely to God.

Some persons, of course, will be horrified at the very thought of such an act, indignantly asking what right parents had thus to sacrifice the life of their child. But is it not strange (and indicative!) that these same persons are not moved when they read of kings and queens espousing their newly born children to other children who have yet to crawl out of their cribs? After all, a marriage to the Son of God seems a pretty fair match for any parents to make for their child.

It is just possible that Asceline's good mother did not make any such petition, oblation, or dedication. It could have been that she merely took the child to the convent as a matter of convenience, and kept her there to be educated. Reading the *Dialogues* of St. Gregory the Great, especially his account of St. Benedict's life, we learn that it was just such a procedure that led to the founding of those monastic schools which, after the fall of Rome, not only formed Europe, but even fashioned, to an enormous extent, the culture and civilization that is ours in the West today.

At any rate the historical fact, to be admired or lamented, is there: Asceline, while still a child, hardly more than an infant it would seem, "entered the convent." Before anyone says she thereby lost life, let him look a bit more closely at some facts about her.

Souls take on beauty

Grace supposes nature every bit as much as skyscraping spires suppose supporting walls and deep foundations. Like any girl, then, Asceline wanted play and playmates. What the play was is open to conjecture. It is safe to suppose that, if any of the doting nuns fashioned a doll for the child, it was given some pious name. But about her playmates there is no need to conjecture; for every extant biography gives an incident which demonstrates clearly that Asceline was alerted early to the constant companionship of one whose perpetual presence too many of us totally ignore — her guardian angel. The incident merits repetition.

While still very young, Asceline, like every normal youngster, was tempted. Today it may be jam or the cooky jar — or even the dials on a TV; then it was cheese. It may have been only a tidbit; but to Asceline, then, it looked as luscious as did the fruit on that tree of the knowledge of good and evil to Eve in Paradise before the gates were closed. Like her first parent then, and like many a child since, Asceline reached for it. But unlike so many, she felt a tug at the sleeve of her — shall we call it, "habit"? Yes, it was her Angel. At least that is who the child "cloistered" from infancy took it to be.

Many today are ready to say it was nothing more than natural caution or at most the voice of conscience. But for all that, the testimony given by the grown woman need not be entirely cast aside. It at least shows that a mind can be alerted and a conscience formed by environment. When the environment is good and holy, the chances for the mind and conscience being bad are slim indeed. But that is not enough. That tug at the sleeve was not imaginary. We who live in this materialistic twentieth century need pause long enough to realize that the spiritual world is far from being a world of unreality. Thompson was stating fact, not spinning idle fancy when he sang:

> *"O world invisible, we view thee;*
> *O world intangible, we touch thee;*
> *O world unknowable, we know thee;*
> *Inapprehensible, we clutch thee."*

Asceline lived in the times of the Meistersingers, the Minne-singers, the Trouveres, and the Troubadours. Tieck, the great collector of the poetry of her times, tells how "Believers sang of Faith; Lovers of Love; Knights of knightly actions and battles; and loving, believing knights were their chief audience. The Spring, Beauty, Gaiety were objects that could never tire. . . ."

What did Asceline hear? The question is not irrelevant; for Andrew Fletcher touched a rare depth of psychology and soci-ology when he said, "Let me write the songs of a country, and I care not who writes her laws." The answer to the question, "What do people sing?" can reveal more than the temper of the times and the character of the people; it can uncover the very soul of civilization. So from the social, psychological and even the spiritual angle our question has point, especially when environment and education are the foci of our investigation.

The girl was in a convent. It is unlikely then that those tinkling trifles of the Troubadours about the flowers of spring or about fanciful love rang in her memory or came softly from her singing lips as she went about the house and grounds in her young, lighthearted way. What she was hearing day after day, and what was having its inevitable effect on her mind and heart, were the cadences of those marvelous Latin hymns, many of which are appreciated today not only as the greatest of hymns but as the greatest of poems. She may not have heard the marvelous *Dies Irae,* but she most certainly sang *Jesu, dulcis memoria.* She lived too soon to have been acquainted with the *Pange Lingua* of Thomas Aquinas, but she knew in-timately that song of the same name by Venantius Fortunatus along with his ever unforgettable *Vexilla Regis.* And if we do not realize that the atmosphere created by such music has effect on the soul, let us ask modern psychologists if the tom-tom beat of the jazz and the sensuous rhythm of the jungle music that pours incessantly from our radios day and night has any effect on the "psyche" of our young.

Asceline heard plain chant. Suffice it to say that Rockstro, who wrote the article on this kind of music for the *Encyclopaedia Britannica,* declared that "no more wonderful succession of single notes had ever been strung into melodies . . . than some of the Plain Chants of the Middle Ages." And Doctor Walsh echoes soundest criticism when he writes: "no more sublimely musical expression of all the depths there are in sadness has ever found its way into music than what is so simply expressed in the *Lamentations* as they are sung during the office called *Tenebrae* in Holy Week. Even more beautiful in its joyousness is the marvelous melody of the *Exultet,* which is sung on Holy Saturday. This latter is said to be the sublimest expression of joyful sound that has ever come from the human heart and mind."

Now just as clothes will bleach if left long in the blaze of the sun, so human souls take on beauty when exposed continuously to what is beautiful. Asceline not only heard music that was beautiful; she studied it.

That brings us to an incident in which innocence and naïveté mingle with sly, insidious subtlety. When Asceline was twelve years old, she was out in the open one day helping the nuns make candles, and her beauty so arrested one young man that he wanted to have closer association with her. He posed and passed as a professor of music and calligraphy; and as such he could come close to her by holding her hand while teaching her how to form letters, and by adjusting her bodily position as she sat to pluck the strings of a harp. Not many lessons had passed before the teacher was talking to the young girl about more than music and writing. When he finally asked her, "Don't you like me just a little?" he got a strange reply. Asceline, in all innocence, instigated a folly that could have been not only sinful but sacrilegiously so when rather naïvely she said, "I would like you much more if you were clothed in the habit of a religious."

Before many weeks elapsed, the music teacher appeared at the convent garbed in the habit of an Augustinian canon. Actually he had entered the monastery for men which stood close by Boulancourt, stupidly supposing that Asceline would be more open to his amorous advances now that he had donned the garb of a religious. At first the innocent girl was quite delighted, thinking that she had been instrumental in winning a soul from the worldly world and a man for God. But in very short order she became aware of her mistake. It was not long before Boulancourt was minus a music teacher and the neighboring Augustinian canonry missing its latest postulant.

But the experience bit into a soul as sensitive as Asceline's. It actually ended her adolescence. She aged under the fright of it. She feared that she had led the foolish youth astray. That, most likely, is why we find her and her mother living outside the walls of Boulancourt's convent for the next two years, under the direction of a holy old hermit. It was during this period that the girl tried to destroy her beauty lest it cause any other young man to be similarly absurd. She rubbed ashes and lye into her cheeks.

How deeply that lye ate into her skin none of her biographers tell, but that the whole experience, from the episode with the music teacher to the years under the hermit, ate into her soul is evident from the fact that she developed a God-consciousness that became so keen that she ever walked in the presence of her Creator and Lord.

Fortunately for Asceline, this God-consciousness had been given her almost from infancy; for both her mother and the nuns talked to her often about God. When still very young, she was told, as so many have been told, that it was God who had given her everything good and surrounded her with everything beautiful; that it was God who had made her and who loved her. It was the same truth that all wise mothers tell their young; but what is too often mere passing thought with many became habit with Asceline.

As the girl grew, her mind broadened and her soul deepened; and in the process, what had been mere singsong repetition of words gradually not only took on meaning but became both vital and vivid. This truth about God took on personal association, and the young girl's thoughts of her Maker became colored with affection. Slowly but very surely Asceline was acquiring the habit that would bring her to high sanctity; the habit of living in the presence of Him without whom there is and could be no life at all.

This affectionate remembrance of God, when frequent, does two very salutary things for a soul: it deepens its love for God and refines its knowledge of Him. Even the pagan Plato was aware of this fact and taught it explicitly in his "divine exemplarism." St. Augustine, so avid a reader and a close follower of this philosopher, perfected the teaching and, as it were, baptized it. Thus it was that Asceline was but following the advice of her spiritual father when she gradually acquired the habit her mother labored to instill: that seeing God in all persons, things, and happenings; that rising from the creature to the Creator; that awareness of God's all-pervading providence.

We marvel at the imperturbability of the saints. The heavens may fall, earth be shattered; but they seem unmoved. Here is the secret: they know what Asceline slowly learned, that every event of history, be it the history of an individual, a family, a nation, or the world, takes place under the gaze of God and with His, at least permissive, will. They know that what men might call cosmic chaos is part of God's all-wise plan, something that the Divine Mind has foreseen and the Divine Will decreed, at least permissively, to bring glory to the Trinity, complete Christ's Passion, aid man on to perfection, and thus lead the drama of Redemption to its fitting close.

This same God-consciousness is also at the base of all true humility; for as one gradually becomes aware that all the being, beauty, truth, and goodness in the world are but dim reflections of Him who is Truth, Goodness, Beauty, and Being, one grows ever more alert to the all of God and the nobility of man! That is true humility: the recognition of human worth in the light of Divinity.

Let any growing girl keep on telling herself, as Asceline was taught to do, that she is not only under the gaze of God and in the hands of God, but that her soul is a veritable breath of God, and she will need no lessons in *Noblesse oblige*. Asceline, because of this training, long before she became a Cistercian, had grasped one of the deepest and most fundamental truths of Cistercian theology and asceticism — man's nobility as an image of God. A single truth was shaping a character and carving out a destiny. Taking her own word about herself; namely, "I know nothing good about myself except this: I always have God present to my mind," you can trace the development. Her thought of God had given birth to the habit of ever living in His presence; this habit became ingrained in her character; that character led her on to her destiny, which was to have a heart ever throbbing with love and gratitude to God, spilling over in affectionate mercy and tenderness for men, and radiating inward peace and interior joy.

There is a ladder that leads to God

But saints are paradoxical characters. They have to be. Utterly imperturbable because aware of God's governance, they are ever in a ferment because so alive to man's almost continual frustration of that Divine Plan. Radiating warm joy because filled with the realization of God's love for them, they are ever grieving because of the rejection of this love by others. Because they are so conscious of God they are extremely sensitive to the sins of the world and the world's sinfulness. That is the explanation of the otherwise surprising fact that the ever gay Asceline often wept.

Along about 1150 the Augustinian nuns of Boulancourt decided to adopt the usages of Citeaux, and, if possible, become affiliated with the Cistercian Order. It was then that Asceline and her mother went to Poulangy, a convent that was already observing the Cistercian customs, and there lived under Adeline, the daughter of St. Bernard's brother, Guy.

The precise motive for and the exact meaning of this move is shrouded with obscurity. It would seem safe, however, to suppose that Asceline and her mother went there to observe and assimilate; for very shortly both mother and daughter would be back at Boulancourt, where Asceline would be prioress and be leading all under her along the path to holiness according to the customs of Citeaux.

It was at Poulangy that Asceline showed herself a fierce ascetic and one endowed with an extraordinary gift of tears. She was just thirty years of age — at the height of her virginal womanhood. She donned a rough hair shirt and would not take it off night or day; she scourged her flesh several times during each day; and at dawn each day was seen to weep so copiously that her tears were said to fill a small hollow in the stone floor of the church every morning. Exaggeration? Not when one loves. Not when one has a sense of sin. Not when one lives in the presence of the infinite God who is ever outraged by puny man. Not when one knows intimately the long, long story of man's ingratitude to God, and if that one is keenly alive to the fact that her own human nature can and yet may turn traitor to God.

Yet there is another explanation for the tears of the saints. How could they, who are so acutely conscious of the goodness of God refrain from weeping from sheer joy?

Asceline spent four years at Poulangy under Adeline. And while she was greatly consoled, strengthened, and edified by such contact with a close relative of St. Bernard, and though she profited from the spiritual direction Clairvaux's Abbot had given

Adeline and which she shared with Asceline, the greater comfort and consolation came from intimate acquaintance with St. Benedict's Rule. For no one who has so much as read that Rule can have failed to recognize the basic importance of Chapter Seven. This is the chapter in which the Patriarch of the West shows all the ladder that will lead to God — a ladder whose top rests on the bosom of God as surely as did that which Jacob saw.

If ever rules for practicing the presence of God were written, Benedict has written them in this "First Degree of Humility." *Deum semper praesentem* rings through that long paragraph of his like some strong musical refrain and must have made melody in Asceline's heart. Benedict terms it "fear," but it is that reverential fear which is only another name for great-souled love. Asceline could have assured the Legislator that she had lived ever mindful of the fact that she was being watched by God and it was thanks to the consciousness of this gaze, which she knew to be the gaze of a Lover, that made life so wonderful for her.

St. Bernard died in 1153. Asceline is supposed to have seen his soul enter heaven in the form of a dove. Shortly thereafter she and her mother returned to Boulancourt, and for the first time in our narrative we are absolutely sure of Asceline's status. We have seen her as a child being tutored in music by a man who was so taken by her beauty that he braved the religious life in order to win her attention. It is possible, but hardly probable, that she was a nun at the time. Later we saw her living under the expert tutelage of an old hermit. That is peculiar, but not an utterly unprecedented procedure for a professed religious. Finally we saw her at Poulangy. That she was living a spiritual life, and one much deeper than many a professed nun, has been clear from the beginning; but what has not been clear, has been her precise standing. But now at Boulancourt all obscurity vanishes; we not only see her as a nun, but as a Cistercian nun who has imbibed and even assimilated the basic Cistercian characteristics of simplicity, humility and generous, unquestioning obedience — and all out of love.

Her one practice of the presence of God shaped her soul to the only genuinely Cistercian form. St. Benedict has compressed the whole science of spirituality in what he calls the first degree of humility; and anyone who learns it as Asceline did by living it will become all that Asceline was — an artist in the most difficult of all arts, that of living life to the fullness of one's capacity.

Asceline's God-consciousness made her humble; for no one can live in the presence of God half an hour without realizing the startling and stimulating paradox of all human existence. To be conscious of Infinity and of self is to become alive to seemingly contradictory truths: the human individual who is incarnate weakness is seen to be important to Omnipotence; Omniscience is found depending on dull human minds; the eternally immutable God is recognized as exerting a constant loving care for His continually changing creature called man, who is made to His image and likeness and who can contribute much to the completion of His Christ's Passion. Humility can be called Janus-like inasmuch as it sees two opposites: God and man, and composes them in the one mind through the wonder of love.

She sees the Devil

By the time Asceline had returned to Boulancourt her lifetime practice had lifted her to the height Benedict promised to those who would climb the twelve rungs of his ladder. The fear of the first degree becomes fearlessness on the height of the twelfth because the consciousness of God's presence becomes the consciousness of God's providence; and the consciousness of His providence generates a love that casts out all fears . . . the one remaining fear is only another aspect of love; for it is a fear of sin or offense to the God who loves us. Of course both the fear of the first and the fearlessness of the last rung are matters of faith — but a faith that is so vital, vivid, vibrant that it is just short of vision. Such belief, far from being blind, is actually all-seeing.

Faith, the Gospel says, moves mountains. Asceline knew it would put out fires. One day, not long after her return from Poulangy, Boulancourt faced real disaster as a fire broke out and with what looked like a determination to gut every building rushed across the convent's expansive church and began eating away at the main building. When every effort to check its rush proved futile, Asceline took a crucifix from the wall and walked toward the flames, speaking to the God under whose gaze she had ever lived, and in whose hands was the strength of omnipotence. One slow step after another, each filled with earnest prayer, the nun advanced slowly and steadily; just as slowly, but just as steadily the flames went back. Soon Asceline was in the church. Smoke blinded her. Burning embers fell all about her. But on she went, slowly, steadily, prayerfully. By the time she reached the end of the building no tiny tongue of flame could be seen.

Miracle? Most assuredly not an ordinary happening. Asceline knew that He who walked on waters, commanded wind and wave, was master of every element, and Him they would obey. That is why she advanced so steadily toward what could have devoured her. The fame of the thing went far beyond France's borders, and the Archbishop of Cologne was so moved by the report of the holiness of the wonder-worker that he sent to Boulancourt a woman who was possessed and from whom the devils could not be driven by holiest exorcisms. Asceline's whole being was stirred by the mere proximity of the possessed one. Pity for the poor human and loathing for the spirits possessing her gripped Asceline. She turned to God with all the faith that had the leper crying, "Lord, if Thou wilt, Thou canst make me clean"; with the faith that had Bartimeus shout, "Lord, that I may see"; with the faith that is commemorated in every Mass by that *"Domine, non sum dignus";* with the faith that exclaimed, "Say but the word." And, as always, such faith moved the Heart of God. The woman was freed.

This brush with Satan led on to another encounter with him; for the Archbishop of Cologne was so happy about Asceline's success with the possessed one that he begged her superiors to allow her to come to his archdiocese. The request is understandable enough. What St. Thomas has said of goodness is especially true of the goodness we call sanctity: *diffusivum sui* — "it pours itself out"; "it radiates." But the granting of that request is not so easily understandable. Cistercian nuns are cloistered contemplatives. Yet Asceline went to Germany. Just what she did in the land is not told; but on the way back she stopped at the Cistercian Abbey of Vaux, in the diocese of Toul. Her reputation, of course, had preceded her. So a good holy monk, who had given himself to the Cistercian manner of life generously for years on years, asked and obtained permission to speak with the saintly nun and ask her advice on a matter that was disturbing his peace of soul and robbing his life of all tranquillity.

He told Asceline that he was thinking of leaving the Cistercian Order. Naturally she asked why. The monk gave the only defensible explanation: he would seek higher perfection, and felt sure he could find it elsewhere. Then he began to enumerate the reasons for this high and hopeful expectation. They appeared genuinely legitimate, and the man seemed aflame with true desire and alive with plans that seemed most feasible for the prosecution of his designs for higher perfection. But Asceline was not listening as sharply as she was looking. Her attention was focused on a devil who stood whispering into the ear of the monk the specious reasoning that came so eloquently from his lips.

Asceline told him whence his ideas came. The monk was humble enough — which means sane and manly enough — to recognize that what he had taken for inspiration was nothing but subtle temptation. He stayed at the Abbey of Vaux. Asceline came home to Boulancourt.

For the next decade her sanctity showed itself in the charming simplicity of her manner of life and the radiating joy that came from her as she made the Mass, Office, manual labor, and *Lectio Divina* her tribute of gratitude to God for allowing her to live so continuously in His presence.

The listing of her visions, prophecies, ecstasies, and miracles is not called for here; for these things were done in her and by her because she was a saint and very close to God, but they did not make her sanctity. No. It was taking that truth that "in Him we live and move and have our being," and not only making it live, but making it her life.

About 1175 she was elected prioress of Boulancourt. For the next twenty years it was her delight to show all her Sisters, especially the new arrivals, how easy it is to live with God, to walk with Him constantly, and thus become what He created them to be — saints. Her life cannot be told more exactly nor more briefly than in the words: she was a girl who always walked with God.

In 1195, on the Friday within the octave of Pentecost, she died. And as one would expect, she made the last act of her life a piece with all her living. She died joyously, proclaiming to all that this thing called death was but the beginning of real living; for it was bringing her face to face with Him with whom she had ever lived, but whom she saw as St. Paul tells us "dimly and in a dark manner."

Until the French Revolution, Pentecost Tuesday every year

saw a procession form at the *Monastère des Dames* at Boulan-court and march out to a chapel in the woods where Mass would be said in honor of "St. Asceline," at whose tomb in the convent church miracles were still being wrought. The liberating revolutionists ended all that. Today a few relics remain in the village church of Vassy (Haute-Marne). But the lesson she taught of living in the presence of God still goes on, and will make saints until the end of all revolutions and all time.

Asceline has just shown how one who walks with God sees through men, scares devils away, puts out fires, and lives in joy. But Asceline was never blinded as was Lutgarde, nor bludgeoned as was Bernard, nor struck with the sword as were Mary and Grace. One wonders if the same radiant joy would have come from her if she had lost her looks, or her sight, or her health, or her friends. Would she have walked so light-heartedly with God if He struck her?

That question can be answered: it has been answered. For there was a woman who, like Asceline, ever walked with God and whom God struck; struck her as the ancient Jews would tell you by the very word they used to describe her disease. Tsara'at means leprosy; but its literal translation is a "blow struck by God" or a "divine scourge." Aleyde de Scharbeek, a Cistercian nun of the Convent of La Cambre, near Brussels in Belgium, was struck by God — tsara'at — He made her white with that dread white fire, that devouring flame which the ancients took to be a divine vengeance. It made Aleyde white as snow, white as a Host. That is why she filled her world with radiance, the white radiance of joy.

BLESSED ALEYDE

The Woman

Struck by God

and Made

White as Snow

Struck by God

"And we thought Him as it were a leper, and as one struck by God."

Thus does Isaias describe the Christ seven hundred years and more before there was a manger at Bethlehem, a carpenter shop at Nazareth, or a cross on Calvary. In that short sentence the Prophet has crowded two tremendous histories: that of a sickness and that of sin. Looking ahead to what was a horror he had to look back to what was hideous so that he might share in some way his vision with those who did not see. Peering down through long, long centuries as yet unborn, his eyes rest on an unsightly figure atop a skull-shaped hill outside a holy city. To tell what he sees he has to look back through the centuries that are dead and select from them what will unfailingly strike terror into the soul and use it to describe what shocks his eyes. He sees the Christ of God as Victim for the sins of man; he turns the gaze of his contemporaries on what has always been held as the most hideous of sin's consequences — a sickness, the mere mention of which caused shudders.

Inspired as he was by God, Isaias had told perfect truth, and told it perfectly. Almost eight centuries later St. Paul would say that Christ "became sin for us." Isaias says the same thing more strikingly when he says Christ was that sickness which was considered by all Jews as the punishment a just God inflicted only on the most heinous of sinners. *Tsara'at* was the word he used. It was the word he had to use; for what he saw was not so much God-incarnate, as incarnated sin; and that he could liken only to the most dreaded, detested, and deadly disease of his day — leprosy.

To read the early books of the Bible is to learn much about this frightful malady. According to the Law of Moses the leper was an outcast from society. He had to dwell far from inhabited places; go bareheaded so that he could be recognized at a distance; and should he, by chance, meet anyone, he had to cover his mouth with the folds of his garment and warn them off with the loud cry, "Unclean! Unclean!" The one afflicted was in the state of perpetual legal impurity, and to touch him was to bring on the same defilement as came from touching a corpse. Legally, the leper was a living dead man.

In the years before Christ, leprosy is said to have been one of the most desolating plagues of Egypt — its original country — as well as of Palestine, Syria, and the other Bible lands. The Jews made no attempt to cure it; for, according to them, it was an affliction from God; and only He who sent it could take it away. In the time of Christ it was still quite prevalent and, as always, was most fertile ground for despair.

From reading long in the Old Testament and in modern literature about the matter, it seems safe to say that the most common type starts at the skin, slowly penetrates to the inner parts of the body, affecting the flesh, muscles, tendons, nervous system, and even the bones, which it seems to gnaw away, as it were, and partly destroy. The extremities of the human frame suffer first — the nose, ears, lips, toes, fingers are either eaten away or fall off. Then the disease attacks the rest of the body, covering it with purulent, fetid sores. The flesh literally rots away; the bones are stripped and the joints loosened. The poor leper has to watch with living eyes while his body decomposes as it would in a grave — and his only hope of relief is death after a lingering agony in which the atrocious physical suffering may be surpassed by excruciating moral tortures.

That paragraph was not written to indulge in any morbid realism, but simply to orient us fully so that we can understand Isaias, understand this sickness, understand Christ, understand sin, and above all understand this saintly virgin who was, even as Christ, struck by God, and, more than Christ, not only *appeared* as a leper, but actually *had* leprosy.

But one further truth must be grasped. The Jews were right. They had a word for it; and their word was exact. Every leper is *tsara'at* — struck by God; and struck because of sin.

That truth needs stressing. Pain as pain is never a blessing. Sickness as sickness is always a curse. Death as death is never beautiful. For none of these appeared in the original plan of God. Sickness, suffering, sorrow, and death, in themselves, are man-made. They came from sin — only from sin; and, as such, can never save nor sanctify. But since Christ became "as one struck by God"; since Christ, in the words of Isaias "became like a leper"; since Christ, in Paul's startling language "became sin," every twinge of pain, every sickness, suffering, or sorrow can *in Christ* and by a Christian become beautiful, blessed, and beatifying. They did in the life of Aleyde.

In the Gospels we read of two episodes in which lepers figured prominently. And the contrast between their behavior and that of the little Belgian nun is so sharp that it merits slow study. Matthew, Mark, and Luke tell the story of the single leper who cried, "Lord, if Thou wilt, Thou canst make me clean." Matthew is sparing with his words. He simply states, "And Jesus stretching forth His hand, touched him, saying, 'I will. Be thou made clean.' And forthwith his leprosy was cleansed." Mark adds to that sketchy account by giving us a second scene in which he shows the cleansed leper broadcasting the goodness of God and the power of Christ, thus bringing multitudes to His side to hear His glad tidings. Yet even his account can be called meager. Luke has little more than Matthew. So perhaps it will be wise to let Archbishop Goodier retell the tale:

"As He [Jesus] passed down the lane a leper spied Him from the hut in which he spent his weary days. He had heard of Jesus, as by this time all Galilee had heard of Him. From a distance he saw Him; inevitably he asked himself if his own day of release would ever come, as apparently it had come to so many. The wondering led to hope, the hope to courage; the opportunity was before him; so he resolved to try. As Jesus came near, he limped from his place of hiding; in the middle of the road he fell down, first upon his knees, then upon his face; prostrate he showed the Stranger how deeply he already believed. Then he spoke; but it was not by way of petition. He did not ask to be cured; his faith went deeper than that; years of endurance, besides, had given him that quiet patience which is prepared for any doom. He did not ask; he did but say what he believed, and waited. 'Lord,' he said, 'if Thou wilt, Thou canst make me clean.'

"The response was immediate. Jesus understood; He always understood. . . . He looked down on the poor creature stretched out on the ground at His feet, who would not so much as raise his head. . . . He knew the sufferer's longing, yet also recognized his beautiful restraint. Here was one who had learned the one lesson of life, and was willing to abide by it: acceptance of the will of God; and He was touched to the heart because of him. He bent down to him where he lay; His hands reached out and touched him, a quite gratuitous condescension, and therefore all the more significantly mentioned by each of the three Evangelists who tell the story; for who without need would put his hand upon a leper? Then the words were promptly uttered, as if the Speaker were no longer able to keep them back . . . 'I will. Be thou made clean.' . . .

"Was ever so much contained in so few words? A perfect prayer, perfect because of its utter simplicity, and therefore receiving a perfect answer. A perfect petition, though the leper asked for nothing; he knew that Jesus knew, and was content to leave it there; such bribery Jesus could not resist. At once the change. Scarcely had the words been uttered than the leper felt his healing. The dead extremities took life, the muscles of his body softened down, supple once more, to their proper place and function; the joints responded to the brain, no longer stiff and hampered; the fresh blood rushed through the veins, tingling with the glow of health. And Jesus stood over him, smiling with interested eyes, glad for the healed man's gladness, made a yet more assured friend because of the upturned face, flushed with unutterable gratitude and love."

That story, told that way, will help us understand this story told another way. For the whole point of Blessed Aleyde's life lies in the fact that she was a leper different from any of the lepers we meet in the life of Christ; and for each of us who was born in sin, and who will have to suffer before he dies, she, as they, is highly significant.

The lone leper of the first year of Christ's public life surely furnishes every human soul with a cry it can make its own; for each of us was born unclean, and live with a tendency toward uncleanness. "Lord, if Thou wilt . . ."

Yet the lone leper in the last year of Christ's public life, the only one of the ten who came back to thank Him, may be more loved and appreciated by us who live in dark and ever darkening days. For he was a Samaritan; and when Jesus said to him, "Go; thy faith hath saved thee," the barrier between the Chosen

People and the Gentile world was being lowered, it was already beginning to fall. But the whole story has place here and can be told best, perhaps, by the same talented Archbishop.

St. Luke gives but eight brief verses beginning: "And as He entered into a certain town, there met Him ten men that were lepers, who stood afar off and lifted up their voice saying: 'Jesus, Master, have mercy on us! . . .'" The Archbishop describes the locality of that "certain town" and enables us to see why ten lepers should have gathered just outside it. He then reconstructs the scene in this manner:

"Into this town, on the third or fourth day of His journey, Jesus was entering as the sun was beginning to set; He had at last reached Galilee, and the twelve were glad. As He came up the road, He was easily recognized; it was the Wonderworker come back again; it was the Man who 'went about doing good.' The lepers knew all the stories concerning Him; for a long time they had hoped He might come their way; if He only would, how much might not be expected from Him!

"So thought ten poor lepers who for many a day had hung about outside the town. Common misfortune had drawn them together, to whatever side of the border they had originally belonged. They shared their sorrows and they shared their consolations; outcast by the rest of men, they were all-in-all to one another. At a distance from the crowd that gathered on the road these men saw Jesus coming forward. It was He at last; what might they not expect? They would wait until He came by them and they would ask Him. But what was this? They had hoped He would come on; instead He turned aside to go into the town. They must lose no time; they must bring themselves to His notice; yet with the crowd all about Him, and themselves condemned to stand apart, how could they hope to get near? Still they must not lose hope. On their crutches and maimed limbs they hobbled as near as they dared; encouraging each other, they eagerly raised their voices; at last, when they

were near enough to be heard, together with one accord they
cried: 'Jesus, Master, have mercy on us.'

"At the sound of their voices Jesus stood still. He looked across
in their direction. He did not go towards them; He was almost
unmoved; He saw them where they stood appealing, and it was
enough. Raising His voice, He called to them, 'Go, show your-
selves to the priests,' and watched them turn away.

"For indeed they lost no time in going. They had heard the
word; they had seen in His face the well-known look of assurance
and command which compelled men of good will to obey.
Though they were not healed, they knew that in doing His
bidding they would be rewarded. Round the edge of the little
town they hurried along to where the synagogue stood, with
the houses of the priests near by. And behold as they went, the
change came. Their limbs became whole and supple; it was easy
to walk, nay to run; they threw away their crutches and sticks;
they bounded along into the presence of the men whose
business it was to testify to their cure. This was soon done. . . .

"They were happy men that evening; in their joy they ran
into the village to celebrate their good fortune with their friends;
not for the first time in the life of Jesus was the Man who had
done this for them forgotten. There was one exception. Among
the ten was a Samaritan. . . . Him, too, the priests had certified.
. . . But after that, unlike the others, there were no friends for
him in the Galilean town with whom he could go and rejoice.
Nor after all did he need them. As he stood outside the dwelling
of the priests and realized what had been done to him, his
thoughts went back to the Man who had said the word which
had meant so much, and his heart was grateful; it was almost
sad with gratitude. Without more ado he hurried back; he could
now return more quickly than he came; whatever it cost he must
find the Man again and thank Him for what had been done.
Even as he went along, he could not contain himself; the place
resounded with his cries of thanksgiving.

"Jesus, it seems, had not left the spot where the lepers had accosted Him. . . . Perhaps He was waiting the issue of the miracle He had worked. He had the people around Him; there was much He could do for them. He spoke to them and waited. Then into the midst of the throng, regardless of all about him, shouting his joy as he came, rushed headlong the poor Samaritan. The crowd made way for him, curious, excited, yet shrinking a little. This man cared nothing for them all; in a moment he was down at the feet of the Master, pouring out his gratitude in words he did not reckon.

"Jesus let the good man have his way. Gratitude had not been too common an experience in His life, and He would allow Himself this consolation. Still it was a consolation with bitterness attached. He had healed ten; only one had thought of thanking Him; and that one was not of the house of Israel. He could not but feel it; and He would say so; perhaps what He said would bear fruit. 'And Jesus answering said: Were not ten made clean? And where are the nine? There is no one found to return and give glory to God but this stranger?'

"Still the man must have a yet greater reward; in generosity Jesus will never be outdone. He had been healed; his cure should be confirmed; he should be placed along side of others, pagans and sinners, whose faith in Him had transcended the faith of the people whom He called His own. 'And He said to him: Arise, go thy way; for thy faith hath made thee whole.'"

The right to call God "Father"

As the Samaritan leper, now made whole, goes his way, we jump the centuries and the seas and come to one who spiritually was a descendant of the Samaritan, since she was a Gentile, and physically his inheritor, since she was a leper. We find her, not as we found him, outside a town, but really outside her world! Aleyde had been placed in the Convent of La Cambre, near

Brussels, when she was a child of seven. The community and the community life was the only society she had ever known. The convent was her world. But now in late 1246, her physical world is bounded by the four narrow walls of the tiny cell which had been built for her years and years ago when she became "struck by God." Loving sympathy had chosen a spot near the convent church, so that the young nun, who had been stricken by this fearful malady, might be able to hear the Offices as they were sung in the choir. In no time it was seen to have been a great mercy to have placed the cell so close to where a tiny red flame told of a Presence in a pure white Host; for as Aleyde's physical world shrunk, there came to her spiritual universe an expanding that astounded all who learned of it. The center of that ever expanding universe was the White Christ in the tiny white Host.

Aleyde's story is a brief one, yet so filled is it with lessons for our day that it will well repay slow study.

She came to the convent as a child and walked into the hearts of all in the community. To her young eyes everything and everyone appeared wonderful. By letting all know just how wonderful they appeared, she enabled more than one aging nun to recapture the marvel and mystery of convent life and kept some of the younger sisters from losing their grasp on that same mystery and marvel.

Youth is always attractive. All is promise and prospect. The older and more experienced we are, the greater the pull of the child on our affections and interest. But from no one, perhaps, will energetic, unspoiled youth win warmer love or truer and tenderer care than from women who have had the Christ Child as their only Object of affection. It is not that the maternal instinct of such women has been stifled but rather that it has been purified of that possessiveness that can somewhat mar the magnificence of love. Nuns love children because they love Christ and find in the sparkle of children's eyes gleams from the Light of the World. So Aleyde would have been loved no matter how meagerly she had been endowed, but when it was found that God had blessed her with an exceptionally quick and keen intelligence, and a curiosity that seemed focused almost exclusively on God and the things of God, plus a surprising evenness of temper, she became more than what we commonly call "an attractive child," she became a universal favorite and the object of special concern.

When she asked to be taught "all about the Rule" some were amused by what appeared a strange whim for one so young. But there were others who thought it might be more than wise to humor that whim and so Aleyde was schooled in St. Benedict's "School of Divine Service" from the very beginning of her intellectual life. That is how it happened that when she was old enough to join the community as a postulant she had a firm grasp on the realities of the Rule.

One is forcibly reminded of the stories told about the young Aquinas who, while still a child, tugged at the robes of old monks and asked the one question: "Who is God?" Something very similar was Aleyde's recurring question, and the Rule made answer to her: "God is Love." But the interesting and the enlightening fact lies in how this answer was made to Aleyde.

Aleyde came to the community as a child of seven. Before she was seventeen she was head over heels in love with Jesus Christ. How did it happen? She had not seen this "most beautiful of the Sons of men." The Voice that thrilled all on the Mount of the Beatitudes, on the shore of Galilee's blue lake, and in the wilderness, had never broken on her ears. Yet He was her all! She had eyes and ears and heart for no one else in the world. She gladly gave her life with all its possibilities to Him and to Him alone. She did it by an act of the will. She did it by a vow. And that tells us exactly what real love is — it is a union of wills!

Of course it is true that instinct, bodily sensations, natural emotions, and affection play their part in love. But no one of them should ever be mistaken for it. Love is far greater than the sum of all these. It lies in the will — and the will is a faculty of the soul, which is an entity essentially different and really distinct from the body it animates and the senses to which it gives life.

While still a child, running about asking this nun and that to "tell her all about the Rule" Aleyde was causing some to say: "The Kingdom of Heaven is like to this," for she was as winsome as that youngster must have been whom Jesus stood in the midst of His Apostles in order to teach them the way to heaven. Yet she was far from being in love. It was only after some wise nun took her to one side and taught her St. Benedict's first degree of humility that the process was set in motion. That degree has been labeled "The Fear of God" — and the label is true. Yet it can be very misleading. Unless one is taught that this is a filial fear, the kind of fear that is the beginning of wisdom, the kind of wisdom that is the beginning of love, and the kind of love that is the beginning of heaven on earth, he or she has not been taught St. Benedict's first degree of humility.

Actually, this degree is one that develops the habit of living always in the presence of God. But even that truth will be misunderstood unless one realizes that when one lives in the presence of God he or she is living in the presence of Him who is our Father. That is the word that changes our whole outlook and attitude. That is the word which speaks of Providence and all that is connoted in that title: foresight, protection, plans for our future, personal care and guidance, a love-filled watching, waiting, and working. A father is one who not only begets life, but who devotes the energies of his lifetime for the sake of the child he has brought into being. Small wonder that St. Leo the Great cried: "The right to call God 'Father,' is the greatest of all gifts." This was the marvel that was taught Aleyde as soon as she had come to the age of the use of reason; for the thrilling truth in Benedict's first degree of humility lies not in the fact that God watches us at all times, but that He watches over us! He is our Father.

There is a fear connected with this degree, a very real fear. But it is the fear a loving son has lest he ever disappoint his mother; the fear a loving daughter has lest she ever cause her father to frown. It is a reverential fear, which is only another name for filial love. The practice of the presence of God turns out to be a constant loving effort to please Him who is our Father when it is taught as it was taught to Aleyde at La Cambre in the early thirteenth century.

Of course the nun had to tell the child how she was to please the Father, so naturally, she took her examples from the life she herself was leading and the only one the child was to know. She was told that nuns go to choir, read in the cloister, hoe in the garden, sew in the sewing room, paint and copy manuscripts in the scriptorium, and even take their meals and go to bed just to please God. They are sure He is pleased because their Rule is His will; and whenever His will is done He is loved and He is pleased.

The teaching was as simple as all that but that it had taken root and was growing straight and strong was evidenced when the girl kept on pleading to be allowed to join in the community exercises so that she, too, might make God happy. Little by little she was allowed such participation and what was begun as an indulgence turned out to have been an education; for when she was ready for the postulate she very sweetly said: "Jesus took three companions with Him to Tabor. They were the ones who saw Him shine like the sun. I mean to take the same road. My three companions will be manual labor, prayer, and contemplative reading; and I, like the Apostles, will know how 'good it is to be here'; for just like them, no matter from what I look up, I shall see 'only Jesus.' "

Call it naïve, as some of the nuns undoubtedly called it then, but such naïveté shaped a soul to sanctity. For this seemingly simple remark was really a resolve. It was the outgrowth of that practice of the presence of God which had her ever conscious of the watchful and loving eyes of her Father. The child had come to know the Father's only Son and how He had said two very important things as far as she was concerned. He had said: "I am the way . . ." and "I do always the things that please Him."

"I do always the things that please Him" echoed and re-echoed in Aleyde's soul. She remembered well her first lessons in the convent and saw that the old nun who had told her how to live in the presence of God and why anyone should go to choir, work in the garden or scriptorium, read in the cloister, had really been saying exactly what Jesus had said. When she learned more of the Rule she found that it was all centered on Christ, so she made most of her readings from those *Lives* of Christ that were written by Matthew, Mark, Luke, and John. From them she learned not only that humility is best expressed by obedience, but that love is shown by taking the chalice the Father gives and drinking it to the final drop, no matter what He has placed in that cup.

What is Love?

This was the lesson that gave her life that strange calm when the cruelest affliction came. But long before she was struck with the "white fire" of leprosy she had shown God and others what real love is and how it is distinguished from its mere semblances. As novice and young professed of the community, Aleyde showed that she was ever walking with her three companions and that no matter from what she looked up she saw what Peter, James, and John had seen on Tabor. Yet she would not claim that she was showing all the love that she felt she should show to Him who is Love. She knew there were deeper depths to this "passionless passion" which had seized her. Her complaint, if complaint she had, was that it was all "too easy."

Choir with its demand on attention and effort was all "too easy" for she enjoyed singing and found real happiness in taking David's psalms and making them her own tribute of praise to the greatness and the goodness of God. It was love, she told herself, but not love's purest and best gift as yet. This young girl, by some instinct or intuition, knew that her emotions and affections were not only engaged, but even on fire when she was discharging the *Opus Dei* — and she was happy that this was so; yet she told herself that God was giving her more than she was giving Him in these hours of the Divine Office. The same was true about her manual labor those early years. Her energy and enthusiasm communicated themselves to the others who worked with her and brought more than a smile of appreciation from older nuns; they won words of commendation from wise superiors. Yet Aleyde again told herself that this was not love at its highest; that once again God was giving her more than she was giving Him; for she enjoyed outdoor work and was really recreated by these hours of manual labor. As for the *lectio divina* that was done with relish for she well knew that if when she prayed she talked to God, then when she read, it was God talking to her. It was all "too easy." It was not yet love at its best.

The girl was right; for her instinct for God was at work when she read, her bodily energies found outlet in her labors, and her emotions and affections were inflamed by her choral duties. They were all parts of love, but no one of them was the real love she was to show years later when the same devotedness to detail, the same marked attention to the minutiae of the chant, the same diligence at manual labor and assiduity at reading were manifested, but little of consolation she used to know in her emotions, affections, and bodily senses. Aleyde was physically ill long before any in the community suspected it, and the unity of the composite is never more strikingly seen than in the way the soul's life is affected by the health of the body. Mental prayer is not easy when one's head is splitting with a sinus or a migraine headache. Neither is plain song nor manual labor when the whole body feels sore. But love is shown when the will sends one to choir with all the alacrity that had been evident when one was in perfect health; when the will has one assisting at the Holy Sacrifice with alert faculties despite the demands of pain; when the will spurs one on at manual labor and has the individual disregarding the drag of the tired muscles. Love resides in the will and is shown more in deeds than in words. Aleyde, growing increasingly ill, showed real love when she did her duty with all her will despite the fact that senses, emotions, affections, and even her instincts rebelled.

This little nun teaches a lesson that not only every religious should learn, but one that will prove priceless for everyone who is married and wants to know the deep joys of perfect married life. It lies in the fact that she gave and gave and gave. The least and most selfish of us is capable of an isolated act of heroism, but it is the heroism of a lifetime that marks the lover. So while we are not to discount the momentary generosity and unselfishness that marks a single act of loyalty or is shown in a solitary manifestation of trust and confidence, yet we are to remember that it is the settled and continued fidelity, the abiding habit of unquestioning confidence and that constant and continual giving of self that is love. The other things are only its shadow and semblance. Aleyde grew to this depth through twenty years of living in the presence of God and striving always to do the things that please Him.

Still she was far from those seldom plumbed fathoms where God and a loving soul carry on the Incarnation and the Redemption in a unity of wills that is simply ineffable. She touched them only when God had so touched her that a physician finally named her *tsara'at* — a leper.

White fire and a woman's will

The cold light of fear leaped in many an eye in the convent at La Cambre the day the news spread in the community. We little know the strength of our instinct for self-preservation until real danger is brought close to us. But once again we see how wondrously God has made us. Everything in the physical entity will draw back from the danger. Our senses shrink away from it; our emotions and affections are stirred to such an extent that we break out into a cold sweat; our impulse is to run away. But the will is master. It commands those emotions; it controls that impulse; it holds the brave to the spot and has them face the danger fully.

But that we are not all equally brave nor of equal strength of will was shown this day at La Cambre. All felt in their hearts a real sympathy for Aleyde; but only the few could bring themselves to show that sympathy openly by associating with the stricken one with the same freedom as before the doctor's verdict. Most shrank back from contact and some even shunned the atmosphere Aleyde breathed. We cannot blame them; for in those days leprosy was considered highly contagious and known to be unquestionably fatal.

Aleyde was keyed up by the announcement that she was a leper, and hence was keener in her perception than usual. She saw the fear in the eyes of all, she noted the shrinking away of even the bravest and the efforts of others to avoid her very presence. She was somewhat bewildered by it all but tried to be as kind and generous in her thoughts as she could be.

But she was human enough to feel hurt by the actions of the frightened ones and the attitude of the truly timid.

That night when alone in her cell she faced the fact fully. She asked and answered herself about the hideous thing called "white fire." She told herself frankly that she was "struck by God"; that she was a leper . . . and she felt fear grip her whole being. She felt it to the marrow of her bones. Yet she knew she had a deeper depth than blood or bone. She fought to hold herself there. She tried to form the word "Fiat," with little success. She was saying it in the depths of her soul, again, again, and again. But this fright seemed to freeze the word on her lips. Her habit of turning to and talking to the Father helped somewhat. She knew He was there; that He was watching her; that He was watching over her. She knew that this thing was nothing to be afraid of; that it was a blessing; that it had to be such since it came from His hand. Yet there was a louder voice clamoring for her full attention. It was the strongly resonant voice of instinct — a voice which tells us that we were never meant to die; an instinct that has us clinging to life with all our strength.

Aleyde wept this first night. Her Latin biographer describes her experience in words that are best translated as "she almost died of fright."

That should not shock us. It should open our eyes to the lessons this nun is teaching us. She is a "Blessed." From the tender age of seven she lived close to God. Now before she is forty-seven she is told that she has a disease which is not only incurable, but one that has been called, not too figuratively, "a living death." She knew enough about leprosy to know that her body would slowly corrode. She wept. How perfectly human! How like Him who was both human and divine! Christ, who so bravely said: "I have a baptism wherewith I am to be baptised, and how am I straitened until it be accomplished"; Christ, who "set His face steadfastly toward Jerusalem" and the death that awaited Him there; Christ, who rose from what was to be His last supper with song on His lips, but who was soon telling His most intimate disciples that His soul was sorrowful even unto death, and not long after that was sweating blood at the mere prospect of His Passion. Such was the impact of the vision of what lay ahead on the God-Man. Aleyde was but His follower — and a lone, little woman at that. The marvel is not that she wept, but that she did not borrow the words of Christ and turn to Him she so often had called "Father" and say: "If it be possible, let this chalice pass." She did nothing of the sort. She wept — and after hours of weeping, when emotion had just about exhausted itself and her sensation of horror burned itself out, her intellect and will assumed the ascendancy. Long before the bell for Matins — and it rang shortly after midnight — this little nun was praying: "Thank You, Father. I will use this thing for the glory of Thy Son."

Now the remarkable thing about that prayer is this: Aleyde knew about the Gospel lepers as few religious, and as practically no lay folk, know; for as a Cistercian she had made her *lectio divina* the Cistercian way. That means she not only read the Gospels, she meditated them as she read, and even contemplated their scenes. She saw the lone leper of the first year of Christ's public ministry and the ten of the last year with all the clarity Archbishop Goodier manifests in his descriptions. What is more, she had an even deeper, keener insight into their psychological reactions, not only because she was a woman with sharp intuitions, and a cloistered nun with a contemplative cast of soul, but because she now was *tsara'at* — struck by God, and could tell what that means as only lepers can.

Then again we must not forget that she knew the Christ as none of these lepers had ever known Him. To them He was the Wonder-Worker from Galilee; the Master; at most they may have hazarded the hope that He was the Messiah. But Aleyde knew Him not only as the Crucified Son of God but as the Glorified Son of Man; not only as the Good Shepherd and Divine Physician, but as the God-Man who loved her, and as the Man-God whom she loved. Her bodily eyes had not rested on His physical features as had the eyes of the lepers of Palestine, yet she could draw the line of His nose and reproduce every tender expression of His sensitive, strong lips; for she was a contemplative, and the eyes of her soul had rested on the face of Christ year after year. Her postulant's resolve, to see Him from no matter what she looked up, had been lived to the hilt. She knew Jesus Christ as only the contemplative saints can know Him.

With how much more faith, then, could she have said: "Lord, if Thou wilt, Thou canst make me clean." With how much more confidence could she have cried: "Jesus, Master, have mercy on me." She did neither. She simply said: "Thank You, Father. I will use this thing for the glory of Thy Son." No apology was made for her tears. She knew that He who had sweat blood understood perfectly.

Aleyde rose from her pallet physically weary but spiritually renewed. She went to choir as usual, but before she left church that morning she knew that nothing in her life was to be as usual again. She was asked to stand a little apart from the others as the Office was chanted. She gave a brave little smile as answer to that request and obeyed. But she felt the isolation. Still this was nothing compared to what happened during Mass.

In the mid-thirteenth century Cistercians were still receiving Holy Communion under both Species. When the priest came to Aleyde that first morning and offered her the Host, then immediately withdrew without offering her the Chalice, the hurt in her heart was so keen that she returned from the altar with scalding tears — bitterer far than any she had shed the night before, coursing down her cheeks. She thought she had been denied the Precious Blood and had received only a Sacred

Corpse. Jesus had become so dear to this nun that His Blood was most rightly called "Precious" by her; for to a great extent, it was her lifeblood. Thanksgiving that morning was tears.

Had she expressed the thoughts that flashed through her stunned mind or voiced the desire of her heart she would have said something like: "Dear God, let my health be shattered; let my body corrode; let them deny me my place in choir and forbid me to assist at Mass with the rest of the community; let them deny me my place in the common dormitory and my place at meals; let them build the tiny cell some have been talking about and place me in it as one to be shunned — all this I can stand. But, dear God, let them not deny me Jesus. Let them not take away my Lord from me." Aleyde was weeping as bitterly this morning as ever had Magdalene at the Empty Tomb — and her complaint was the same: "They have taken away my Lord. . . ."

The Chaplain dried those tears by his theology; but it took time and patience and much repetition. Finally Aleyde realized that Jesus is present whole and entire under each of the Species, and another adjustment was made.

Many adjustments had to be made by the community as well as by the little sufferer. At first, when the outward signs of her disease were few, she was allowed a corner of her own in church, in the refectory, dormitory, and even in the cloister. This segregation was the part of prudence and Aleyde accepted it even as charity, yet each request to stay apart brought home with greater force the fact that she would have to live her life alone — after almost forty years of the close cenobitic life as lived in a Cistercian convent. But Aleyde kept her eyes adjusted for the sight of Him whom Peter, James, and John saw shining whiter than snow. She was still able to smile even though the answering smile would come from a distance. But soon the "white fire" burned more fiercely and made itself apparent on her hands, her feet, and even on her face. Then she was told that they were going to build a tiny cell for her, near the church, but outside the regular convent building. There she could read, eat, sleep, work, and even discharge her choral duty. Once again Aleyde saw the necessity for the move and the charity in those who planned the building. But she saw that in effect she would be a solitary shut up in a tiny cell. A spasm of fright, very reminiscent of the first night with the truth, shook her. But it was only a spasm; for almost immediately her intellect and will asserted themselves and the little leper was praying quietly to One who was within her more closely than the sickness was in her body. She was saying: "You are nearer far than anything else can be. I will not be afraid."

The cell was built. The little nun was led to it. She entered with a smile on her somewhat distorted face and she kept her promise: she was not afraid. And the Christ who could not resist the faith of the leper who prostrated himself saying: "Lord, if Thou wilt . . ." nor the plea of those who cried "Master, mercy . . ." was so touched by this trust of the tiny Belgian nun that He appeared to her, smiled, and said: "Aleyde, you will never want. I shall be your Cellarer." When we realize that the cellarer, according to St. Benedict's Rule, is he who provides everything the brethren may need, we can see why the little leper knew she had received something better than a cure.

How we of the twentieth century, which is so filled with misery, need to look long at this leper and learn all that she teaches. How we need to learn that we can trust God even when He strikes us. Yes, especially when He strikes us! For then He is giving us opportunity to show that we love. How we need to learn that we need never fear those who can destroy the body, be they human despots or merely disease. How we need to watch this woman and realize that so long as we live on this earth the one and only thing that need ever cause us fear is the fact that we can displease Him who is our Father and our God, by sin.

But do not think that a life of love is a life without pain. We know that we love with our wills. We also know we are creatures with senses and sensitivities, with human emotions that can be as strong as a storm wind and as devastating as a tornado. So we need not be surprised to find seeming contradictions in the life of one whose life is all love. Did not St. Paul, under the inspiration of the Holy Ghost, tell us that he found a "law in his members that was contrary to the law of his mind"? He was really telling us that in the lives of each of us there will be two loves. And on that fact St. Augustine wrote one of his greatest works — *The City of God.*

That prelude is necessary to prepare you for the statement that our little leper suffered intensely when she was first placed in this tiny cell, close to the church, but outside the convent. The Cistercian cenobitic life is a silent life, but it is also a highly social life. Aleyde had lived for forty years in closer intimacy with her fellow religious than do brothers and sisters in the same family. In the convent at La Cambre she had spent all her waking hours side by side with her sisters. Never was she alone either in choir, at work, or in the cloister. And when day was done she retired to a large open dormitory where the entire community slept. Of privacy she knew only that of her soul. Of aloneness she knew nothing save that which came in moments of spiritual dryness. So her early days in this tiny cell taught her the stringency in St. Benedict's penal code. He would "excommunicate" a monk for some more grievous fault. He would cut him off from the community — make him take his meals alone, have him remain at the door of the church while the rest of the community praised God by the Divine Office. She saw now that apart from the profound spiritual significance of being separated from "the Body of Christ" which is the community, there was also the stinging social punishment of not being allowed to associate with the brethren. She reacted humanly to this solitary confinement.

But even this human reaction can be divinized; the natural can always be elevated to the level of the supernatural by that mind and will and memory which tell us of Him who so loved mankind that He would redeem it from its captivity and so loved God that He would make satisfaction for mankind's sins. Aleyde took not only the affliction of the body, which no one will deny was agony itself, but also the afflictions of the spirit, which the initiate know as greater agonies, and offered them all in union with Christ to the glory of the Father and for the good of men. She knew that she had been given a special part in the work God the Son took upon Himself when He became man — a work that will end only with the end of time, and the results of which will last so long as God is God. Her will with God's grace was the secret of her successful living with something that could have generated despair.

A Companion for the outcast

As the leprosy made progress the little nun became more and more helpless. Her hands and feet gradually became useless. Then it was that God showed how near He was to this sufferer; for a brave superior accepted the offer of a braver nun to live with the leper. Aleyde's earliest words to this attendant were: "Because you have come to serve Christ in me and me in Christ you will never contract this dread disease; and what is more, Christ will come for you before He comes for me, and you will never know the pains of purgatory. He will take you straight to heaven."

Naturally these words filled the Sister with consolation, but she wondered if she should accept them as true. She knew Aleyde was holy. She had seen the way she had accepted her sickness. She had watched her for years and could not but conclude that the little leper was near and even very dear to God. But were these words charity or prophecy? She did not know. She wanted to believe that they were prophecy, but she hardly dared; for she knew the awful purity of God and the immaculateness demanded before any soul can enter His eternal presence. But as the weeks slipped into months and she saw this leper touch a few others similarly afflicted and saw them depart as whole as ever was the Samaritan leper who came back to thank Christ for making him clean, she began to hope that Aleyde had prophesied in her regard.

Nor was it very long before she was awakened at night to hear Voices answering the almost toneless voice the sick nun was raising in prayer.

They spent Lent together and the attendant had reason to marvel when she noted that though Aleyde's body was really a mass of corruption, the tiny cell would be filled with the sweetest aroma whenever the little leper prayed — and it seemed she was ever at prayer. In Holy Week, as Aleyde lived again the marvels from the triumphant entry into Jerusalem through the Last Supper with its high priestly prayer of the Christ, its institution of the Holy Eucharist and the first ordination of priests of the New Law, on to the death on Calvary, the attendant became aware of the fact that she was living in an atmosphere that was suffused with a light that was not of earth.

Aleyde had insisted that she be awakened at midnight so that she might assist at the Resurrection. The heroic attendant agreed and, after arousing her, helped her to a prie-dieu. Through the open windows of the church and into the tiny cell came the happy chant of the Easter Alleluias. The Office moved on and the lessons were being sung when the attendant noticed the little leper shift her position on the prie-dieu. This was exceptional, for Aleyde's knees were so sick and sore that any movement was excruciating. Suddenly the chant of the responsory *Surrexit Dominus de sepulchro* . . . was begun. Aleyde's eyes, sunk deep in dark sockets, and looking like pools of fire, seemed to open wider and wider. The attendant followed their gaze and saw the sky above them open like some great curtain, while light, as from the face of some fiery furnace, poured down upon the convent, setting every building brilliantly aglow. The Sister attendant cried out in fright. Aleyde made a quiet gesture with what remained of her right hand which told the nun not to be scared. Then the tiny cell drank in, as it were, the torrent of celestial light, and the truth that the mystery the responsory told about was being re-enacted became plain to the Sister attendant. Christ, the Risen and Glorified had come to visit the soul of one who was as white as snow not only physically, but also spiritually.

As Easter Week moved on Aleyde's state became more and more agonizing. Once when the pain squeezed a cry from her the attendant was moved to such pity that she spoke of the words Aleyde had used the first day they dwelt together. "Sister," she said, "I have often heard you lament the length of your exile. I know your longing for heaven. I also know something of the agonies you endure. Tell me, please, that what you said to me the first day I came to you, is not true. Tell me that you will not live after me; that you will not suffer much more."

Aleyde looked her gratitude for such genuine sympathy but made no reply. It was only later in the day that she turned to the Sister and said: "Sister dear, what I told you that first day is true. You will die before me, and you will go straight to God. You must then help me even more than you do now; for Jesus has told me that the sufferings of these past years are as nothing compared to what I will yet suffer."

"Oh!" cried the attendant. "How can that be! How could God ask so much! Oh, Sister!"

Aleyde's sunken eyes lit with that smile which could not brighten any other feature but her eyes, so far had the leprosy progressed.

"And you can smile at such a prospect!" exclaimed the attendant.

"It is a happiness," replied the leper. "It is a great happiness to help God. Jesus has told me that there are certain souls that cannot be saved — cannot be saved, mind you — unless I suffer. That is why I am glad to remain here after you have gone. That is why I am happy that this body of mine can serve the Christ. But never forget what I said. You must help me from heaven. I do not like pain!"

Balancing God's Books

"I do not like pain." How that line speaks to us all! Think of how our century has brimmed and spilled over with pain. Think of how Nazism, Fascism, and Communism have made our days and nights misery. Think of what World War II did to our young men, to the souls of mothers, and the hearts of young wives. Think of the loneliness it made for millions of women and millions more of children who will never know their fathers. But think, too, of the real tragedy of our times which lies not in the deluge of pain which swamps our world, but in the woeful waste we mortals make of that which can be turned into a blessing and made meritorious. Think of what the wives and mothers, the aging fathers and the growing orphans could have done for Christ had they been as mindful of their roles in the Redemption as was this Belgian nun who was a leper!

Think again of what Aleyde is telling us who have become so cancer-conscious. Cancer is as common today as leprosy was in our Lord's time — and it appears just as incurable. How many of us can profit from the light in Aleyde's eyes — and the words that came from her swollen lips about saving souls by suffering. Cancer can prove a blessing for more than the one who has to bear it. It can be as salvific as was Calvary's Cross. All we have to do is what Aleyde did: unite ourselves and our suffering bodies with that Body which was nailed to Calvary's wood.

By the spring of 1249 Aleyde was little more than a skeleton. Leprosy had done its slow work and was now torturing her in the very marrow of her bones. She told her attendant that alternately she was experiencing the agonies of purgatory and hell. The explanation is simple enough. It lies in the fact that God is just. If Aleyde was to save certain souls that would never be saved except through her, she had to balance God's books. She had to expiate, to pay the price, to experience the punishments due to sin.

On June 11, the feast of St. Barnabas, she was given Extreme Unction. But the priest had not burned the cotton and the sticks he had used for the anointing, before the little leper looked up and announced to all about her that she knew from God that she had another full year to suffer.

Shortly after that, her prediction about her attendant was fulfilled. Christ took this heroic soul to Himself. Then the nuns of La Cambre showed their evaluation of Aleyde when even the most timid volunteered to take the late attendant's place. The leper needed special help now, for in 1249 she lost the sight of her right eye. She told her Superioress that God wanted that sacrifice for William of Holland who had just been elected King of the Romans. Aleyde offered it that William might defend the Church of Christ with bravery and even with chivalry.

The year 1250 had hardly been born when our little leper lost the sight of her left eye. Again it was for a King that she offered it. This time it was for Louis of France who for all subsequent time is to be known as "King St. Louis of France." Aleyde prayed that he might wage war well for the sepulcher of Christ. History tells us that this was the year Louis was taken captive, but who can say that it was not Aleyde's blindness that opened the King's eyes to heights of sanctity?

Winter melted into spring. May came with its snows of blossoms and its light winds laden with perfume from bursting buds. Aleyde corroded in her tiny cell. June brought its flowers and blue skies. Aleyde was burning with unseen white fire. Her joints were all loose now, and some of her bones were exposed. She admitted that she had never known such suffering, yet now, as never before, her pitiably hoarse voice sang only one song: *Magnificat anima mea Dominum!*

June 12 dawned. It was a full year since she had said that Christ had visited her with a message that she had a year more to suffer. Few seemed to have remembered. But Aleyde joyfully announced the fact to her attendant: "This day I shall die." The Chaplain and the Superioress were summoned. Before the community could gather near the tiny cell, the soul, which had been burned white by the white fire in her body, was with the Christ with whom she had been walking all these years as a leper.

Small wonder that the countryside rang with cries of "The saint is dead." Smaller wonder that the Cistercian Order glories in her as model for all who would walk with Him who walked to Golgotha. And no wonder at all that Christ's Holy, Roman, Catholic Church beatified her *per modum favoris* in 1702, then again by formal process in 1907.

The leper who would not ask to be cleansed — the little nun who was struck by God — has given the world another feast to celebrate on June 12 — and all mankind a lesson on what to do with pain. She has shown that the worst of diseases can be the greatest of blessings.

Orationi frequenter incumbere — "*To apply oneself frequently to prayer.*" Such is St. Benedict's fifty-seventh "Instrument of the Spiritual Art," as he calls it.

Such was the life of St. Francha.

Here was a woman who talked incessantly — as is perhaps slanderously said of many another woman; but unlike so many others, Francha talked to God.

Here was a woman who, because of her virile spirit of "no compromise," fed the fires of a family feud until it flared into a civil war. Though she lived secluded in a cloister, she set Guelphs and Ghibellines in such a furor, and stirred the princes of Church and State to such a bitterness and brawling, that no one less than His Holiness, Pope Innocent III, had to step in and lay the whole town under papal interdict. She left Italian society at the age of seven; yet for the rest of her life of forty-four years stirred that society to its very depths; then forty-four years after her death stirred it even more deeply and commanded more attention than when she lived.

Francha, daughter of the Count of Vidalta, entered the convent at seven, professed at fourteen, was elected abbess when twenty-three, sponsored the strict observance before she was thirty-three, founded a new convent before she was forty-three, and was dead at forty-four. Yet her life teaches but two large lessons for our living:

1. Sanctity is built on the principle of "no compromise";
2. To live that principle one must apply oneself frequently to prayer.

ST. FRANCHA

Abbess of Plectoli:

The Silent Woman

Who

Talked With God Incessantly

Buon Giorno

In 1175 (1173 according to some) Count Vidalta was rejoicing over the birth of his first, and as far as we know, his only child, Francha.

Vidalta had his foes, plenty of them, right there in the gay city of Piacenza; for he was leader of the Guelphs, the party which insisted on the supremacy of the Pope over the Emperor; and there were numerous Ghibellines in Piacenza. Count della Porta was the recognized leader of these secularists. But on the day Francha was born, her noble father would have thrown his arm around the neck of Della Porta and insisted that he drink to the health of the newly born and to the happiness of her parents. Since genuine joy is infectious, there can be no doubt but that the Ghibelline would have yielded and drunk.

If that had happened, there can be little doubt about Vidalta regaling his rival with the dream his wife is said to have had before the birth (as is so often told in the lives of saints of the Middle Ages); a dream in which she saw a little dog running back and forth with a burning brand in its mouth. Then he would have added with pride and an air of great secrecy that a holy hermit had interpreted the dream as meaning that the newly born was destined to do great things for God and His Church.

That reference to the Church would probably have ended the momentary friendliness, not only because these Italians were volatile, but because the feud between the Guelphs and Ghibellines was truly volcanic.

There is no record that the newly born started any fresh rumblings in that volcanic thing; but it is certain that she stirred that which was so volatile. *"Buon Giorno"* was ringing out all the day long.

Seven short years later the Count and Countess were standing at the door of the convent of San Ciro, but no *"Buon Giorno"* was ringing out. Their lips were smiling, but their hearts were somewhat heavy. They had just placed the sunshine of their lives under the care of the Benedictine nuns, and now faced back to an empty house. The noble couple were truly lonely for months after the deed; yet drew consolation from the fact that their child was safe and under the care of those who would have her grow straight in soul and tall in virtue.

They tried to convince themselves that Francha was only boarding at the convent for the purpose of education. But they had seen their baby emerge into childhood and, while proud of her precocity, were at times really amazed at her piety. Both felt quite sure that, given the environment of the convent, her natural bent would be followed. They had led her to San Ciro as a boarder to be educated; but in their heart of hearts they believed she would stay as a religious to be sanctified.

They were not wrong. Six years after they had brought her to the door of the convent, she was prostrate on the floor of the chapter room; and when Abbess Britia asked, "What do you seek?" Francha mumbled into the dust the prescribed formula, "The mercy of God and of the Order." She was asking admission into the Benedictine community as a novice. One year later she pronounced her formal, final, and perpetual vows. And from that day until the April day thirty years later, she lived a life of no compromise with the Rule, according to which she had vowed to live.

Her early biographers, of course, canonize her before she asked to become a novice. As a mere child of eight, they have her cultivating with rare success those basic yet crowning monastic virtues: humility and obedience; have her actually avid for rigid fasts and really enjoying long night vigils. Such a state of affairs is not absolutely impossible, all will admit. But all who are wise will likewise admit that such a state of affairs is not highly probable. Still there is a legend extant which makes it appear that she must have been instant in prayer. For the two deep channels of grace are prayer and the Sacraments. But in Francha's time to a child of eight or ten the only Sacraments available were Baptism, Confirmation, and Penance. Yet Francha must have had grace in abundance; for at her investiture an aunt of hers saw an angel, not the Abbess, clothing the child, and in place of the ordinary veil which covered only the head and shoulders, the angel was putting a veil over Francha that reached down to the child's toes — a sign that her dedication to God was complete and His response just as complete; a sign that she was robed in grace.

If she had not been assiduous in prayer before profession, she had to be after it; especially if she were to live up to her resolve to allow of no compromise. For atmosphere affects even the hardest steel — and the atmosphere of San Ciro Convent, while not lax, could hardly be called strict.

Day after day Francha had reason to pray, "Make me brave, dear God, and make me strong."

It really requires the strength of the omnipotent Holy Ghost to faithfully walk the straight line of the Rule when all others seem to be cutting corners and getting away with it.

Shakespeare has said, "Conscience doth make cowards of us all." It can also be said that conscience can make heroes of us all. It did of Francha; for the only approbation she sought — and the only approbation she got these early years — was from her conscience. The majority of her sisters in religion smiled at her strictness of observance and considered her a victim of profession fervor. Actually this fidelity was a product of the Holy Ghost's great gift of fortitude, which was given to her in abundance because of her almost constant plea, "Dear God, make me strong enough to be true, and true enough to be strong. Make me faithful."

Bend your back

Before Francha was seventeen, Abbess Britia thought her the proper person to be put in charge of the infirmary. Her physical age seems obstacle enough to such an appointment; but, when we note that St. Benedict has specified that this charge is to be given only to one who is "God-fearing, diligent, and careful," and that Abbess Britia was known as a wise woman, we can but conclude that Francha's soul had grown far beyond the years of her body. The explanation of this phenomenal growth lies in the use of that fifty-seventh "Instrument of the Spiritual Art" that St. Benedict gives in his Rule: *orationi frequenter incumbere*.

It will not be unprofitable to call up the picture painted by that verb *incumbere*. It shows you a man's back bent as he strains at pulling a long oar. Since St. Benedict added *frequenter* to that verb, you can understand why one says he means to be *instant* at prayer. Francha was.

The sick furnished the young Infirmarian with a double

spur for her habit of prayer; first St. Benedict insists that they be served as "Christ Himself" — and when one is face to face with Christ Himself, be it only in His member, the prayer of silent, loving adoration is inescapable; but since they were only His members, the human often obscured the divine; and Francha was forced to pray earnestly for patience, kindness, evenness of temper. She did. And her prayers were answered to such an extent that it was her sweetness, not her skill, that endeared her to every sufferer. Now let it be recognized that every sick person is, to some extent, petulant; every sick nun, if she be old, especially so. Francha had mostly old, sick nuns to serve.

Abbess Britia herself was confined to the infirmary in 1194 and 1195. In 1196 she was in her grave. Then the nuns of San Ciro did an astounding thing. They elected the young Infirmarian, who was at most twenty-three, their Abbess. That is not only tribute to Francha's virtue and real worth, but testimony of the deep desire the San Ciro nuns had for high sanctity. For Francha had always stood out as strict. Undoubtedly the community at San Ciro had been following the customs of the day in their interpretation of St. Benedict's Rule. Hence it could not justly be called lax, lukewarm, or mediocre. It was only when their observance was placed beside the text of the Rule and contrasted with the attempt Francha was making to live the text, that the discrepancy could be noted. By electing Francha the nuns said in effect they wanted to be strict, straight, and holy.

Perhaps no one in Lombardy was more pleased with the election than Ardicius, Bishop of Piacenza. He knew Francha; knew all about her spirit of "no compromise" and her life of continual prayer. He imposed the Abbatial Blessing and installed her with a happy heart; for he felt that she would not only do good to the convent of nuns, but to the entire diocese of Piacenza. Shortly after the ceremony he died, consoled by the thought that he had in his diocese a powerhouse of prayer that was ruled by a saintly soul.

His successor was none other than Gramarius della Porta. The wags of the town waxed eloquent with quips about the Guelph who was head of San Ciro and the Ghibelline who was head of the diocese. And there the matter would have ended, with everyone enjoying the wit of the wags and relishing their clever puns about politics and those in positions of power, had not the rivalry between the two factions become concentrated within the convent itself when Gramarius' sister, who was a nun there, began to feel an antipathy for her prayerful and strictly observing Abbess.

Since there was trouble even in Paradise, no one should be surprised to find daughters of Eve, even in religious garb, who are quite capable of ruffling the calmest waters. The first few years after her election Francha had reason to wonder if she were not in Eden; for the community responded to her every advance with something close to real eagerness. The tone of San Ciro lifted, and it soon became the envy and admiration of the religious world of northern Italy. But soon Satan had some of the nuns looking at the "forbidden fruit."

Exegetes have labored to tell us just what was on that "tree of knowledge of good and evil," that tree which was "in the midst of Paradise." They have not been too clear nor too convincing. But about the nature of the fruit that occasioned the trouble at San Ciro there can be no doubt. All hagiographers agree it was the grape — not the fruit itself, but its juice. The cook at San Ciro in the days of Abbess Britia used to take certain vegetables from the water in which she had boiled them and steep them in wine just before serving them. A trifling thing in itself. But what was the apple, if it was an apple, that Eve bit into, when considered in itself? Yet, look at the centuries of sorrow it produced. So with the wine.

There were no newspapers, radios, or TV's in Perugia in

these early years of this, the "Greatest of Centuries"; so people had time to think for themselves; time to share their thought in discussion; time even for gossip, both idle and not so idle. That is how it came about that in 1208 "the whole town was talking" about the cooking at San Ciro, and speculating as to whether the Guelphs or the Ghibellines would have their way. Francha frowned on the practice as an unnecessary indulgence, something that smacked of the worldly world and even of sensuality. The Bishop's sister, who may not have cared any more for the wine in the vegetables than she did for cheese on her spaghetti, used the incident to malign the Abbess and advance an ambition which she had kept secret for years, but now openly divulged. She would be abbess in Francha's place.

From our vantage point of the twentieth century it all appears trifling, this steeping vegetables in wine; but the historical fact is that the dispute did not stay within the walls of the convent. Words passed between the Della Porta's and the Vidalta's. The families had always been rivals: socially, politically, economically. Now they became such ecclesiastically. The feud spread from the immediate households of the Counts to all the relatives. Soon the entire city had separated into sides, and a veritable civil war was on. As has been said, the Italians are volatile! Of course the vegetables and the wine had long been forgotten before the Counts Della Porta and Vidalta had ceased rattling their stilettos. Not long after the blades had been unsheathed, even the families, as families, had sunk from the surface of everyone's consciousness as the long-drawn-out feud between Guelphs and Ghibellines, that impasse between Church and State, held everyone's attention and inflamed everyone's passions.

Gramarius had been a Cistercian monk at the Lombardian monastery of Columba before being elected Bishop of Piacenza. But in the heat of the affair he remembered only that he was a Della Porta and a Ghibelline. He let all parties know exactly what it was that he remembered and stirred such opposition that he and his clergy had to fly to Cremona if they would save their lives. It was then that Pope Innocent III stepped in and laid the entire city under interdict. Who can now doubt that a cow started Chicago's great fire, or that a pebble can cause an avalanche?

Rather than have anything like this occur, Francha would willingly have sacrificed her life. As it was, she showed herself ready to sacrifice her office. Her principles she would not sacrifice, no, nor even admit of compromise. But she could resign from her office and live with God in a place where wine would not set the entire countryside in ferment. She told God so in prayer. Prayer was her life. How often in prayer she offered herself as sacrifice to God. Now in prayer, from the Mother of God, she received assurance that soon she would be granted assistance and know some relief. Francha stayed on as abbess, praying incessantly for her persecutor, for the nuns at San Ciro, for the Della Porta's and the Vidalta's, for the Guelphs and Ghibellines, for the city and diocese of Piacenza, and for the whole Catholic Church. But it was a soul-shaking experience.

"It is better to build anew"

Then in 1210 there came to her a girl by the name of Carentia, daughter of Viscount Uberto, head of one of Piacenza's first families. This young lady had been exceedingly well educated. She was a Master of Arts, graced with a liberal education in Belles Lettres, and thoroughly schooled in philosophy and even in theology. Interest in the gossip of the town may have occasioned Carentia's first visit to the convent, but it was interest in God that kept her returning to this Abbess who was now harassed from within and without her domain. The Bishop's sister had not only convinced her brother that Francha was the wrong person to head San Ciro, but had even persuaded many of her sisters in religion that Francha was not to be followed in her spirit of "no compromise." Yet when Carentia sat in the parlor with this truly persecuted nun, all she heard was the praise of God and talk about the art of prayer.

In no time Francha discovered in this talented daughter of Uberto a kindred spirit, and soon she was confiding to her the desire of her heart: to rule a convent in which St. Benedict would feel as much at home as he had been at Monte Cassino, so exactly would his Rule be observed. Carentia discussed the matter with her, bringing into play all that philosophy and theology had given her. Soon she was aglow with the realization that, far from being a mere formalist who wanted the letter of the Rule for the letter's sake, Francha was more nearly a fundamentalist who wanted the words of her vows to be taken in their literal sense for the sake of God's glory. The exchange of ideas was mutually profitable, and soon Carentia found herself burning with a desire to glorify God as Francha had outlined, and Francha found herself aglow with gratitude to God for having sent her such an intelligent, sympathetic, enthusiastic, and energetic soul — the relief that Mother Mary had promised and one who would not only be of assistance but who would become a real sister as she shared Francha's heart more and more.

All through the year 1211 these consoling visits continued. So did the opposition from within and the condemnation from without. But one day Carentia burst in on Francha with a big idea. She told the harassed Abbess that the answer to all their desires lay in the Cistercian form of life, and that there was a convent of Cistercian nuns at Rappallo, a charming little town on the coast, east of Genoa. There she would go, learn all the customs, absorb the spirit, then return, enter San Ciro, and help Francha reform the convent.

Francha listened breathlessly; for, though she would not tell this ardent, enthusiastic young friend, Rappallo and its Cistercian convent had been her dream for years on years. Silently she thanked God for putting the idea in Carentia's head, and thus making her own dream come true, at least by proxy. Then a strange thing occurred: even as these two women talked about Citeaux, into their presence walked two Cistercian monks. They were looking for a night's lodging as they, at the command of the Pope, carried on a crusade against the Albigensians in northern Italy.

The monks got their lodging, and the nuns got encouragement; for it was no time before they were pouring out their ideas and plans. The two Cistercians could not be but intrigued by the similarity of Francha's position at San Ciro with that of St. Robert at Molesme over a century earlier. They entered into the plot and furthered Carentia's plan as far as they could by giving her letters of recommendation to the Abbess of Rappallo. The next day, just before they left, they reminded Francha that the failure of Robert's attempts to regularize Molesme led to the founding of Citeaux; hence, if she should experience a like frustration at San Ciro, it might be an indication that real success for her lay in following St. Robert's lead. They left with that bit of sage advice. Carentia also left. . . .

Late in 1213 Viscount Uberto received a request from Rappallo that he send an escort thither; for his daughter would return to Piacenza, and the daughters of the nobility merited company. Great was the rejoicing in the Viscount's circle of friends when word got around that his brilliant daughter would soon be home. Many a young nobleman became interested, and some of the bolder spirits even spoke to the Viscountess about marriage. Carentia, even at a distance, was creating a real stir among the Viscount's friends. But it was nothing compared to the stir she created when she announced after she arrived that she not only was already engaged but even fully married — for she had vowed herself to Jesus Christ to be virgin-bride of the Lamb of God.

It should not have been a surprise — not after her intimacy
with Francha and her year at Rapallo. But it was. At least to
all the young marriageable nobles. The Viscount himself was
not taken aback until Carentia told him her plan to introduce
Cistercian customs at San Ciro. Then he shook his head. He
knew human nature. He knew Italian women. He knew the
Guelphs and the Ghibellines. So one day he took Carentia aside
and said, "Carentia dear, your old father may be a fool in many
ways. He does not know all the philosophy and theology you
have studied. But he does know something about human nature.
So I want you to listen to him." The girl nodded. The Viscount
went on, "I have a plan that will help you with your plan.
Every cent that I was going to give as your dowry will go
into it. You want the Cistercian way of life. You can have it.
But, if you will listen to your old father, the only way for you
to have it is to take the money I offer, build a new convent,
and begin from the beginning there with your Cistercian customs. Remodeled houses always show something of the original
outline. It is better to build anew."

That sent Carentia flying to Abbess Francha. They talked
it over. Then Francha prayed it over and over. She first attempted a few reforms within the convent. They did not take.
She prayed some more. Then in 1214 she petitioned the new
Bishop Foulques of Piacenza for permission to leave San Ciro
for the purpose of founding a new convent. The reason offered
was the same as that given by Robert of Molesme in 1098:
"that she might better observe the Rule she had vowed to live."

Gramarius had died in exile at Cremona in 1210 while the
papal interdict still hung over Piacenza. Foulques succeeded
him. Whether he was a Guelph or a Ghibelline does not
appear. At any rate he granted Francha's request.

Piacenza's society buzzed with excited talk when it became
known that Francha was to leave San Ciro. But when it was
learned that Carentia was not only going with her, but had

won a half-dozen daughters of the nobility, from both Guelph and Ghibelline camps, who declared themselves ready to follow Francha and anxious to become Cistercian nuns, Piacenza's society was stirred to its depths. When the parents of the new aspirants once accepted the situation, they began to vie with one another in their offerings of land, vineyards, houses, and cattle. Francha was bewildered. She finally accepted a secluded place, thirty miles from the city, called Montelana.

The place was secluded enough to satisfy Benedictine prescriptions, and the house was habitable enough for those who would live the Cistercian way; but the soil was stubborn. The Abbot of Columba, who had been appointed Father Immediate of the enterprise, saw the difficulty and promptly advised a move. A noble lady of Piacenza had given him some property just three miles from the city. It would not be as secluded as Montelana, but the soil might prove more fruitful. Francha yielded, and her second attempt was made at what was called San Gabriele di Vallera. The soil was much better. This place could have supported a Cistercian community with comparative ease; but not far away was a convent called Ponti Tribbia, which had but recently been affiliated to the Order of Citeaux; so the General Chapter advised against a permanent foundation at Di Vallera.

Francha would have been nonplused by this action of Divine Providence had she not always believed both that God knows best, and that He has His own time for things. She prayed quietly. The solution, however, came much less quietly. Carentia broke in on her one day excitedly crying that her brother had just willed her a property at Plectoli, a good ten miles from Ponti Tribbia. Thus it was that the first Cistercian convent near Piacenza came to bear the strange name of *Santa Maria de Tertio Passu* — Holy Mary of the Third Attempt. On March 23, 1217, Bishop Ughullo di Cassadocca laid the cornerstone of the Church — and Francha's trial of almost twenty years was

over. She had her convent, her fervent community, and time
for prayer.

A strange vigil

Yet daytime did not suffice. Each evening she would ask
the Sacristan for the keys to the church. It seemed a normal
request, since the Abbess kept practically all the keys of the
house in her possession. But it was not long before Carentia
grew suspicious.

As Prioress she was responsible for the Abbess' health. Francha
had always suffered from stomach trouble. Carentia once succeeded in getting her to consider the advisability of taking
some medicine — a simple thing compounded from local herbs
— for her complaint. Francha was not enthusiastic. She was
not fully co-operative. With some hesitation she approached
the table on which the dish lay with the roots already cooked.
"I'd much rather suffer for Christ's sake and leave myself entirely in the hands of the Divine Physician," she said.

"It was the Divine Physician who gave medicinal properties
to these roots," was Carentia's quick reply. "I'm sure He wants
you to use them."

"I'm not so sure," said the now smiling Abbess, "but let us
see what happens." She took a knife and began to cut the
roots preparatory to eating them. As soon as her knife had
pierced the root, blood oozed out of it. Francha quietly placed
the knife on the table, folded her hands, and softly said, "I
believe I know now what the Divine Physician prescribes."
When she noted the frown on Carentia's brow, the Abbess
smiled more broadly and said, "Physical remedies are useless,
Carentia, when God sends a sickness for the health of the soul.
My pains are for my purification."

"But you suffer so!" objected the Prioress.

Francha turned and, as she moved out of the room, remarked,
"Far better to suffer in this life than in the next."

That ended Carentia's attempts at getting her Abbess to take medicines, but it did not end her obligation to watch over Francha's health. When she noted that she was becoming more and more hollow-eyed, she decided to investigate the rumor the Sacristan had set afloat by remarking idly that "most likely Reverend Mother uses my keys when the rest of us are asleep." Carentia remained awake one night and watched. Sure enough! Not a full hour after all had retired, Mother Abbess arose noiselessly and left the dormitory. Carentia listened. She heard keys turning in the lock of the church's great door; heard the door click as it closed after admitting the Abbess; then silence.

The next day Carentia used her authority as Prioress and told the Sacristan that she would take care of all the keys to the church and sacristy for the next few weeks. But one night she was awakened by the sound of the church's doors opening and closing. She felt in her pockets. The keys were there. She looked over to the Abbess' pallet. Reverend Mother was not there. Carentia sighed, turned on her side, and tried to sleep. What use was there in trying to care for a person who could work magic or miracles? The same happened night after night.

When the chaplain, a monk from Columba, came to hear the confessions of the nuns and give them a spiritual conference, the Prioress took him aside, told him of her experiences, and asked what she was to do about caring for the Abbess' health. The good priest laughed at her story and accused her of dreaming. Carentia invited him to stay and see for himself. After consulting his abbot, the monk accepted the invitation. During Compline one night, unknown to everyone save Carentia, he hid himself in the church. From his hiding place he watched Francha sprinkle each nun with holy water as they left the church in single file and headed for the dormitory. He saw the Abbess herself depart after a short visit to the Blessed Sacrament. He watched the great door close and heard the lock's click. He waited a few moments, then went over and tried the doors.

There was no doubt about it — they were locked. Then in the darkness he waited.

The monk chatted with our Lord in the Blessed Sacrament while he waited; and after laughing at himself, told our Lord that he was nothing but a muddleheaded monk to have ever entered such a pact with the Prioress; and as the slow-footed hour plodded on, he asked our Lord to forgive him for such stupidity and accept the tedium of the night in reparation. Then he heard the huge church doors opening. He had heard no keys being inserted in the lock, he had heard no turning of the keys. He looked; and there, as the doors swung back, he saw the Abbess, her hands still in the folds of her long sleeves, walking into the church.

When those mighty doors swung back after her entrance and closed quietly, the tiny fringe of hair on the monk's head must have been stiff and straight, and his palpitating heart in his throat.

The rest of the story is best told by a painting which hung in the Piacenza church dedicated to St. Francha, and which may still be there, unless it did not survive the last war. It shows Francha kneeling before an altar with her arms stretched out in the form of a cross. A human skull is resting on the table of the altar just in front of her eyes, while to the right a huge breviary is seen very precariously perched on the altar's edge with a thong tying it to the outstretched and upraised arm of the nun. The purpose of the device is evident. Like Moses on the mountaintop, Francha would grow weary at prayer; and when her arms would drop the least bit, so would the huge breviary. Its fall would be enough to awaken any drowsing Abbess. Cowering in a corner is the monk.

Oil in your lamp — your lamp burning

Francha could never get enough of prayer. The explanation

lies not only in the love of her greatly loving heart, but in the very nature of the prayer that she most used. She was not petitioning the Lord all day and all night. That, according to St. Thomas, is prayer in its strictest sense. But there, by strict, he means narrow. But God knows and we know that we have to petition. Christ Himself, when asked by avid Apostles to teach them how to pray, gave them and us a prayer that is filled with petition — and also with praise. When one knows God, one loves Him. When one loves Him, one has to praise Him. That is the secret of Francha's incessant prayer and praying. And that is the very soul of the Cistercian life. A contemplative soul is best described as one that lies ever prostrate before God, adoring Him with love, and loving Him with adoration.

But the convent at Plectoli was hardly fully organized and running smoothly when the Benedictine nuns at San Ciro were making history repeat itself as they imitated the Benedictine monks of Molesme a century earlier. The monks had demanded the return of St. Robert from Citeaux. The nuns now demanded the return of Francha from Plectoli. Their plea was based on the same grounds as that of the monks. But there the repetition of history halted; for this time the Pope did not sustain the demands of the Black Benedictines. Instead he graciously lifted the interdict from Piacenza and left Francha to her incessant praying.

That was in 1216. Then God granted her a peace she had not known since 1187, when she first adopted her guiding principle of "no compromise."

At this time she hardly considered herself well into middle age. But actually she was in her sunset years; for God had decreed that she should be in eternity before she had completed forty-five years in time.

During Paschaltide of 1218 she urged Carentia to summon Father John, Abbot of Columba and Father Immediate of

Plectoli; for she felt that this sickness, which had now prostrated her, was different from the one which so often had shaken her and stirred the Prioress' pity. The Abbot came, heard her general confession, anointed her in the presence of the community, then listened to an exhortation he could never hope to surpass, so solidly spiritual was it, and so soundly practical. He could but marvel at the intellectual grasp this nun had on St. Benedict's Rule and the virile directness which characterized her address.

"Continue to walk in the fear of God," was her first exhortation — and Dom John knew he was listening to one for whom that fear was nothing but love. Her next plea proved it. "Be ever grateful to God for the grace of your vocation." Then came the plea which revealed the drive of her life: "Aim always at ever higher perfection in the observance of the Rule and the Statutes of Citeaux. Admit of no compromise with either." All marveled at the spirit she put into her next few sentences. "Be convinced that zeal for prayer is food and strength for the soul, a protection against dangers of all kinds, and a bulwark in time of temptation." How well she could speak such truths, after living them for all of thirty years. Then came her typical Cistercian climax: "Cultivate true fraternal charity, humility and obedience. These virtues will open the Gates of Heaven, for they will be oil in your lamps that will burn brightly when you, as wise virgins, are awakened by the coming of the Bridegroom."

Her own lamp was ablaze with light when Christ came for her on April 25, 1218.

She was buried before the altar at which she had prayed so continuously day and night — the altar dedicated to the warrior archangel, St. Michael, who, himself, admitted "no compromise."

And there she stayed until 1266. Then, though, no breviary fell from the altar to awaken her, she, as it were, arose. For on the feast of St. Bernard that year, when the nuns assembled for Matins, they found their church filled with a perfume no incense had ever given off. As the Office proceeded, the sweet odor became so pronounced as to be almost stifling. The excited nuns sent a messenger speeding to Abbot William Quattrochi at Columba to tell him about the sweet odor which seemed to be coming from Francha's tomb. When the hard-breathing messenger burst into the Abbot's room, Dom William made a gesture that silenced him and said, "I know why you have come. Abbess Francha has already been here to tell me it is the will of God that her remains be more highly honored."

Dom William with two of his monks set off for Plectoli. At the door of the church they were met by the sweet odor and a group of wide-eyed nuns. The Abbot vested in alb, cincture, and stole and directed the two monks to set about exhuming the body.

Here the Abbess interrupted to tell that Carentia had insisted that Francha's remains be sealed in a leaden coffin and buried extra deep lest the nuns of San Ciro hire someone to steal them away. But even as she spoke, one of the monks struck metal not a foot below the floor of the church. Abbot William looked at the Abess. She merely raised eyes and hands to heaven and muttered, "A miracle!"

Dom William grew cautious. He told his monks to cease digging. He ordered the nuns to rope off the area where the grave was. Then he sent word to the Bishop of Piacenza that there was call for a special meeting of the diocese's wisest heads.

On August 28, an ecclesiastical gathering brilliant with miters, pectoral crosses, and rings, replete with rochets, simple surplices, and ordinary cowls bunched itself before St. Michael's altar to see a leaden coffin raised and opened. In it they found a rather well-preserved body floating in a sweet-smelling oil. More phials than the widow of Sarephta ever dreamed of were filled, and subsequently many more miracles than there were phials were claimed for this oil. The marvel had the effect Francha desired: it won for her a shrine — and the cult which finally brought her formal beatification in 1273.

In 1559 Abbess Lucia of Plectoli had a church built in Piacenza and dedicated to the honor of St. Francha, the woman who would admit no compromise and hence lived and died as every true Cistercian monk and nun should live and die — always talking to God.

Chivalry is a word we usually, if not universally, associate with men. It is a medieval term, and French in its origin; for the chivalrous knight was always a chevalier — a Christian warrior mounted on a horse. Valor and virtue are connoted by the term, because the code of honor of the medieval knight required that he protect women, children, and the aged by deeds of high courage and hard arms.

When we speak of the Crusades and the Crusaders, the same thing happens: we think of men, strong men and chivalrous knights, and course down from Godfrey de Bouillon and Raymond of Toulouse to King St. Louis of France and Don John of Austria.

But now, after seeing Lutgarde in Belgium, Mary and Grace in Spain, Asceline in France, Aleyde at La Cambre, and Francha at Plectoli, you may pause and wonder if chivalry and the spirit of the Crusades is limited to the male of the species. To allay all doubts we will go down into the newly established kingdom of Portugal, learn something of the lives of three Princesses of that realm, and contrast their conduct with that of the male members of the same royal household.

Chivalry's code of honor need not stop at women, children, and the aged. Deeds of hard arms and high courage can be done for God. When they are, they save kingdoms and countries, even as they win sainthood.

SS. TERESA, SANCHA, MAFALDA

Portugal's Saintly Princesses:

Sisters in Chivalry and the Spirit

of the Crusades

Three men and three maids

If hagiography has need of history to color it, history has far greater need of hagiography to complete it.

History says the kingdom of Portugal was founded by three men: Henry of Burgundy; his son, Alfonso Henriques; and Alfonso's son, Sancho I. Hagiography grants that these three men founded it; but says it was three women who established it: they were the daughters of Sancho I, which makes them granddaughters of Alfonso Henriques, and great-granddaughters of Burgundy's Duke.

The fact is that, if the three men are needed to lend background and coloring to the lives of the women, the three women are needed much more to complete and color the story of the three men; for Portugal owes as much to Teresa, Sancha, and Mafalda, as she does to Henry, Alfonso, and Sancho — if not more.

Chivalry brought Henry of Burgundy riding into the Iberian Peninsula; for the Moors were pressing the Christians hard. That could not be countenanced by brave hearts and truly Catholic men. So Henry, with others of his mettle, by valorous deeds of real knighthood, drove the Moslem warriors backward. When this had been accomplished, most of the northern knights returned to France, but Henry stayed on the Peninsula. The reason seems obvious when we read that he took as wife the beautiful daughter of Alfonso VI, King of Castile and León. Perhaps it was as dowry, perhaps as reward for his knightly deeds, that Henry came into possession of some land around Oporto, or Porto, which he formed into a tiny feudal principality. This was the nucleus from which came the kingdom of Portugal.

It was Henry's son, Alfonso, who extended his claims and even secured them by conquest, and thus fashioned and actually founded the kingdom. Yet it was the Crusaders and their spirit of chivalry that really completed the work. For the great fleet from the north, on its way to the Second Crusade, stopped long enough to aid Alfonso in wresting Lisbon from the Moors. This not only gave him a capital for his kingdom but one of the finest harbors in Europe.

But the infant kingdom was still too weak to stand by itself. It needed support. Here is where the white monks of Cîteaux entered the picture and gave brilliance to what was at least dull, if not actually dismal. Alfonso, though living a very loose life, was a man of stern, strong faith. Ask no one to reconcile those opposites logically or even psychologically. Accept the bare statement of fact, for it rests on the undeniable testimony of sound history. Somehow or other he entered into correspondence with St. Bernard of Clairvaux. It might have been their mutual tie through Burgundy. At any rate, Alfonso told the Burgundian-born and Burgundian-bred Bernard all he hoped to do with the land his own Burgundian sire had left him on the Iberian Peninsula. Bernard answered his letters. That is why we find Alfonso placing his realm under the protection of the woman Cistercians were calling *"Notre Dame"* — Mary, the Mother of God and of men, the Queen of heaven and all hearts. Not long after this consecration Bernard advised Alfonso to offer his realm to the Pope as papal fief — and advised the Pope to recognize the land as a kingdom. Both men followed Bernard's advice. That is why Citeaux and Cistercians have always been dear to the Portuguese. At least that is the way history tells the story. But hagiography completes that tale as it shows much deeper reasons for this love for Citeaux and all things Cistercian which is in the Portuguese blood and bone. Three of them were the yet-unborn Princesses of the realm: Teresa, Sancha, and Mafalda.

These and others are among the salient reasons for Citeaux's love for Portugal, but earlier than any sanctity, came a donation that was truly princely and which could not but win the return of the love of gratitude. The historical facts not only stir the imagination and emotions; they stir one's faith. In 1147 Santarem, a city and a citadel considered practically impregnable, was assailed by Alfonso and his men. Behind ramparts stouter than any that man could build, the Moors felt safe. But Alfonso had entrusted the daring enterprise to other arms than those of his men. Bernard, and all Clairvaux, Citeaux, and all Cistercians, were praying. Santarem fell. Alfonso, the man of many moral defects, was not wanting in honesty, gratitude, or generosity. He attributed his success at Santarem to the white monks and in appreciation gave them Alcobaça. This famous monastery, founded and endowed by Alfonso, is best described, perhaps, as a small feudal kingdom; for its possessions stretched from eighteen miles above Lisbon uninterruptedly to the sea, embracing no less than thirteen towns, each of which paid tribute to Alcobaça's abbot and dutifully called him "Lord." This abbey one day held over nine hundred monks — while its abbot was feudal lord of over six thousand vassals. But founding and endowing Alcobaça was not enough for Alfonso. He made the abbot of that house Chief Almoner of his kingdom, set him in the Royal Council, and had him in the Cortes as equal to all bishops. On top of all that, Alfonso decreed that an annual tribute be paid to Clairvaux.

This man, as King Alfonso I, reigned from 1142 to 1185. It would be more exact to say he "warred from 1142 to 1185"; for seldom in all his years was he without arms and a busy army. Though guilty of much moral misconduct, he was most sympathetic toward religion and religious. Perhaps it was his way to quiet a very unquiet conscience, or at least a conscience that had reason to be unquiet. Whatever the explanation, the fact is that even before Santarem he had shown his princely prodigality toward religion and religious, when in 1132 he established the Augustinian Canons in Coimbra in a house that rivaled in wealth the Alcobaça-to-be. When he died in 1185, he left his son, Sancho, a well-formed kingdom, and one that had been officially recognized by the Pope.

Sancho I was not to know the years of his father; yet he was to earn for himself the name of "The Peopler"; for it was he who built towns and really settled the Portuguese territory. Perhaps one of his most astute moves was to follow in the footsteps of his father by establishing and endowing religious houses, especially those for members of the military orders. Sancho showed marked preference for the Hospitallers, and by giving them house after house won for himself not only the best disciplined troops in all Europe, with which to fight the Moors, but also garrisoned his frontier towns with the most trustworthy of men.

Yet, in the only history book that tells the whole story, Sancho's claim to immortality will come not from having peopled Portugal, but from having been parent of three Portuguese saints. And if any land needed sanctity at that time, it was the newly founded kingdom on the Iberian Peninsula.

As you have seen, Alfonso, despite his strong faith, was no angel. Sancho proved true son to such a sire. He endowed bishoprics and abbeys with princely liberality; he welcomed new orders to his realm; yet, ever in his company "for consultation" (he said) was a "wise woman." More than that, Sancho was always a thorn in the side to Pope and high ecclesiastics.

But God will not be mocked. He showed that in the history of His Chosen People. He has shown it again and again in the histories of His chosen princes. Yet, He can easily be appeased. Sodom would have been saved for ten just men. Portugal was by three just women.

Their father fought Christ's Church so vigorously that he brought papal interdict on his realm. Their brother, who would succeed their father and become King Alfonso II, would be guilty of such breaches of faith that the Pope would be forced to strike him with excommunication; and he would lead such a scandalous life that God, it would seem, would be forced to strike him with leprosy. Their nephew, who would succeed not only to their father's throne but even to his name, would be such a thoroughgoing scoundrel and utterly indolent administrator that one Pope would be forced to lay him and the realm under interdict, and another would finally depose him and hand the kingdom over to his brother. This latter, bearing the name of Alfonso III, in order to hold his throne would consent to bigamy.

Yet the land was blessed — and still we know that God will not be mocked. In 1178, seven years before he ascended the throne, the heir-apparent, had his first child by his wife, Dulce. They named her Teresa. After two years, another child was born. Again it was a girl. They named her Sancha. Perhaps the Prince was getting a bit anxious and wondering whether he would ever have a boy. During this time the King was busy fighting not only with the infidel Moors, but even with the Christians in the neighboring Spanish states, as he widened and lengthened his own kingdom. Again Dulce gave birth to a child. For the third time it was a girl. After naming her Blanca, Sancho went out to join his father and the wars. But the memory of baby prattle, even though it came from baby girls, soon had him back at Coimbra. Before three full years had passed, his father was dead, he himself was king, and Dulce had given him a boy whom he named after his late father, Alfonso.

A royal marriage

The Infanta Teresa thought herself quite mature, and was treated as such by the servants, by the time her father became King Sancho I and her mother had set the realm rejoicing by bringing forth Alfonso II. Was she not already the Infanta of Portugal — and one day would she not be a queen? She had to act mature.

But that childish maturity changed to something much deeper long before Teresa was out of her adolescence. For before she had left the teen-age, the nobles and knights of León, the proud Spanish state which bordered the young Portuguese kingdom on the west, were bowing before Teresa and pledging her their loyalty and their lives — for she was now their Queen. Rather young to be a queen, yet Teresa need not feel too ill at ease; for her consort, Alfonso IX, was only seventeen.

It was a political marriage. Sancho I had seen what manner of life his father had led. He determined to win for himself allies. He saw that the hand of his eldest daughter could bring him a whole army. It was given, without the least consideration of her heart or head, to the young King of León.

As the wise and witty Dominican, Father McNabb, has said, "It might be questioned whether anything could be less romantic than such marriages as these. In poorer ranks of life, a bridal dowry was usually given with the bride. But in the marriages of kings and queens, a bride was usually given away with the dowry. Politicians, lawyers, and military leaders were always consulted; the last person to be consulted was the bride. The last quality sought in bride or bridegroom was love. Two lives were thus entwined, for better or worse till death parted them, without the one quality that would make their union less than slavery. To such tyranny men and women must submit in order to be kings and queens. The common run of kings and queens escaped from the thraldom of wedlock without love by an open door of sin. Many of these unfortunate women became adulteresses. Some of heroic mould became saints." Of such mold were Teresa and her sisters.

But about this union of Teresa and Alfonso, there was something worse than the mere failure to consult bride or bridegroom. There was an existing relationship that called for an ecclesiastical dispensation. Teresa and Alfonso were second cousins. Portugal's young Infanta knew nothing of such a relationship or of such an impediment. It is possible that the two bishops who sanctioned the match were equally in ignorance. But one wonders how Sancho I could have been. At any rate, Teresa yielded to the wishes of her parent; and "by doing so" — to quote Father McNabb again — "she shows she had learned not only that love is a sacrifice, but that perfect love is a holocaust." For by entering this marriage Teresa would have to give up more than father and fatherland; she would have to forego a way of life that had come to mean more to her than all the kingdoms of the world. For if we are to believe her earliest biographers, she "loved prayer, spiritual reading, frequent Mass, and conversation about the saints, heaven, and God. Above all she took advantage of her position as daughter of the King to give generous alms to the poor. She applied herself with great earnestness to the purifying of her heart and to doing all things out of love for God alone."

Now it is true that practically all the children of kings, especially those who became saints, receive such praise from their early medieval biographers. Yet, in the case of these three princesses, their future lives were such as to all but authenticate the pious platitudes put forth for them in their childhood. Knowing what we do about the Spanish and Portuguese temperament, it is not too difficult for us to accept as true what the Bollandists say about Teresa having to give up her many penitential practices such as vigils, fasts, disciplines, and hair shirts, along with sleeping on the floor, when she took her place beside León's young and spirited king. Then, when we add that Sancho, despite his faults, was a man of firm faith, and that Dulce was a woman of real piety, then insist that the story of Santarem had become legend in the kingdom, and hence, prayer admitted to be more powerful than arms, we have more reason to accept as true those seemingly extravagant statements about Teresa's piety in her early youth.

At any rate, she went to León in 1191. By 1196 she was back in Coimbra, the mother of three children, but no longer a Spanish queen. For the political enemies of Portugal had reached the ear of the Pope and told him of the impediment and lack of dispensation, with the result that the marriage was dissolved.

No records tell Teresa's reactions. But that she had won the lasting admiration and lifelong affection of Alfonso will be attested by later facts — and that is high tribute to the sterling worth of the woman he took as queen when she was not yet out of her teens.

To have been married, become queen and mother; then to have become unmarried and unqueened without ever becoming a widow, before a girl is nineteen, is experience enough to shake a sensitive soul. Yet this strange, sad, and even tragic experience only shaped the soul of the Portuguese Princess, sensitive though it was, for high sanctity.

While in Spain she heard and saw many things; the most stirring, perhaps, being that the history of the land was little more than that of a long Crusade on the part of the Christians against the Saracens and the Moors. The five small states of León, Castile, Navarre, Aragon, and Catalonia were really monuments to fearless men who lived and died fighting for the Faith of Christ against the followers of the Prophet and who, step by step, won the land by dauntless determination and deeds of high valor. The Cid, the man some "debunkers" would have us believe was nothing but a cutthroat barbarian and brutal leader of a robber band, had become the legendary hero of Spain. He was all but worshiped as the "terror of the Mohammedans and the mirror of Christian chivalry." But Teresa's heart went out more to the soldier monks, the Knights of Calatrava. When told that they had been founded by a Cistercian abbot by the name of Raymond, she had to think of her own land, of Santarem, Lisbon, and Alcacer de Sol — and all that Portugal owed to these same Cistercians and their prayers.

When she heard all that was happening in her homeland since her marriage, she had reason to ask more and more prayers from Cistercians, be they soldiers or simple monks. There are those who see in the series of disasters that came upon Portugal a proof that God will not be mocked — even by royalty! Earthquakes shook whole cities and towns and leveled them. Tidal waves rushed in from the sea, then drew back, leaving horror in their wake. Drought was followed by flood. Then came a swarm of locusts to plague the land. And as death-dealing fires burned themselves out, the Moors attacked.

Teresa heard the rumor about her marriage being the cause of this series of disasters. It disturbed her greatly. She became as prayerful as any monk. When Rome finally spoke, while loathe to leave the man whose love she had won, she was happy to offer herself again as victim and return to Coimbra with children men might call illegitimate, but whom Heaven could view only as the progeny of a girl who was ready to obey God when He spoke through her parents and obey Him again when He spoke through His Church. It takes great will power so to obey; yet it requires even greater intelligence. Teresa had both.

When she reached the palace, she found full scope for all her motherliness; for before the thirteenth century began, Dulce had given birth to eleven children.

Studying her sisters and brothers, Teresa saw much to make her happy and some little to make her frown. She was again Portugal's Infanta, but she knew the rule of the realm would fall to the hands of her brother, Alfonso; and she recognized those hands as weak, irascible, greedy, and mean. He had inherited all his father's defects and seemingly few of his virtues. But in Sancha, Blanca, and the beautiful Mafalda, the eldest sister saw all that was best in Portuguese blood. Maybe with these she could establish some sort of balance in the royal family and secure some semblance of the same for the state. She invited her younger sisters to join her in frequent prayer, generous almsgiving, and other projects of a religious nature.

The king hears some strange requests

By 1200 God must have been smiling on the Portuguese Princesses, no matter what Portugal's King and its heir-apparent caused Him to do. For the four eldest daughters of Sancho I were engaged in an enterprise that would win more for Portugal than had ever been won by nobles, knights, or war. In a mountain valley behind Coimbra Teresa had found something which first took her breath away, then set her soul singing.

Riding on a ridge under a bright Portuguese sky one day, talking to God about Portugal and His world, she looked down into a deep rugged valley to where a group of buildings jutted out from the valley wall. Fascinated by the sight, she determined to investigate. A steep path led her to the deserted Benedictine monastery in the valley called Lorvão.

When she returned to the palace, she was alive with questions. Her father satisfied her excited curiosity by telling her that legend claimed the monastery had been in that place since St. Benedict's time; that history recorded how the monks were so sincere that, unbelievable though it appear, they won the respect of the ever marauding Moors. But the late wars, the disasters

that had piled on Portugal since her marriage, and the spirit of
the time had emptied the monastery, so that now the valley was
a possession of the realm.

"Let me have it," said Teresa suddenly.

"Have it?" asked her father. "What for?"

"For the greater good of Portugal. Remember Santarem and
the Cistercians. Give me that valley, and I'll make the old abbey
a fortress."

"But the Moors will never again attack Lorvão."

"No, but Lorvão will attack the Moors if you let me have it."
Then she spoke her conviction that women can be as chivalrous
as men, if not more so; that she could people Lorvão with the
best blood in Portugal by getting many of the ladies of the court
at Coimbra to join her in becoming Cistercian nuns and
dedicating their lives to expiating the crimes of the people and
petitioning God's favor for the land.

Sancho was taken completely off guard. He knew his daughter
was pious. He wanted her that way. But he still considered her
as queen. He would always need the friendship of León and
Castile. She was still young. He told her so.

The Infanta's head shook slowly, and a sad smile played
over her features before she said, "I can be of much greater
service to you as a nun at Lorvão than as queen in any court of
Europe."

The King objected. But his every objection was met with the
quiet but convincing, "Remember Santarem and the Cistercians."

Sancho granted her the entire valley. Soon some of the ladies
in waiting were off for Spain and the Cistercian convents at
Carrizo and Gradefes, where they were to make a special
novitiate, not only learning all the customs of Citeaux, but absorbing the true Cistercian spirit of simplicity and acquiring
that burning sincerity which had men and women living both
for and with God alone. Among the group was Blanca, King
Sancho's third child.

Before that novitiate was over, King Sancho had to admit that things were greatly improved in the realm; and Teresa did not hesitate to insist that the improvement was due to the prayers and the penances of the novices.

His Majesty was thus put in the proper mood to listen to the request of his second eldest daughter, the quiet yet ever intense Sancha. She pointed to the royal property called Alemquer, just outside the small town of Jerabica, and showed how a small group of pious women, living at that modest estate, could do some wonderful work among the poor at Jerabica with very little drain on the coffers at Coimbra.

This child had always puzzled Sancho. Though named after him, she had none of his characteristics except his deep faith. Early in life she surprised him one day by saying she was going to be queen only to the King of kings and the Lord of lords. When asked what this meant, she blushed, then told how she had vowed her virginity to God. The King, puzzled though he was, respected the sacred sincerity of this child and never once tried to use her as pawn in the political chess game being played with Europe as the board.

"If you think you can people it with sincere followers, it is yours, Sancha," said the King. "But beware of parasites."

As Sancha left his presence, the King looked at Mafalda; and he smiled happily. Anyone would have smiled; for the attractive child had blossomed into the court's boast. She had grace and beauty and every feminine charm.

What pleased Sancho more than her physical beauty was the keen intelligence, the quick spirit, and the evident depth of soul in his child. Whoever would have her hand must pay high for it. She was worth a whole kingdom.

And a whole kingdom she brought him when he married her to Prince Henry of Castile.

It was another of those political marriages. Henry was a mere child at the time. Mafalda was little more. Yet she knew what her father wished to overlook. She knew she was as closely related to Henry of Castile as ever Teresa had been to Alfonso of León. Again the marriage was made without dispensation. Fortunately for all concerned, the marriage was never consummated; and neither the boy nor the girl grieved when, a few years later, the Pope declared it no marriage at all. Mafalda lost no time in getting back to Portugal. But when she arrived, she found that, while she had not changed, many things in the royal household had.

Sancha had a small group at Alemquer and was loved by all the poor in Jerabica. They were calling her "the saintly princess."

Teresa was at Lorvão with a much larger group, and these were *bona fide* nuns of the ever growing Cistercian Order. In the community the humblest, most hidden, yet best loved, was her favorite sister, Blanca.

When Mafalda visited the convent, she was baffled by Teresa's appearance. Evidently she had foregone the world; yet she did not appear a full-fledged nun. The younger sister asked her to explain and thus came to know how Portugal's Infanta had given herself to God, yet had to remain linked to royalty and the world.

"I have three children of my own, Mafalda, and twice three of their Majesties — all of whom need care. Our father, the King, is getting old and has been none too well of late. His successor, our brother, Alfonso, needs watching. The properties given us by His Majesty need a wise head and a firm hand to protect and administer them. I am as much of a nun as I dare become at the moment. His Holiness, the Pope, has intimated that both Sancha and I may take vows of religion yet retain our rights over the rich grants father has given us. I hope to take advantage of that dispensation some day. I believe Sancha will do the same; for she is already living the life of a religious at Alemquer — and has been for years."

As she talked, Teresa was studying her younger sister. How

well she knew what a political marriage could do to the heart, the soul, the mind, and body of a princess. But watching and listening to Mafalda she secretly exulted to find that neither the beauty of the body nor the beauty of the mind had been marred by the experience in Spain. No trace of bitterness was found in her words, no shadow of sadness on her soft features.

When Teresa laughingly remarked that they were a strange pair of Spanish queens — each without a king or a kingdom, yet neither of them really widowed, fright appeared for the first time in the eyes of the younger Portuguese Princess; and when she spoke, her voice shook.

She told her elder sister the tense talk that was to be heard in every royal household from León to Catalonia. The infidel followers of the Prophet had become so insolent and strong that the Pope and all Europe feared that the reign of the Christians and very existence of Christianity were doomed in the land south of the Pyrenees.

Teresa had heard something similar from her own Alfonso IX in the years she reigned in León. The Almohades, who had crossed from Africa to help the Moors, had administered a crushing defeat to his father and, as she called him then, her father-in-law in 1185 at Alarcos. Now, in 1211, Portugal's Infanta was inclined to take her sister's alarm and her reports as so much court gossip that was aimed at exciting the nobility to real preparedness. But when Mafalda told her how the Knights of Calatrava, who had been so disastrously defeated at Alarcos, had, only the year before, been driven from Salvatierra, Teresa frowned. She knew this to be the stronghold the Knights had taken as their home in Castile after being driven from Calatrava ten years earlier. She was ready to accept Mafalda's next report; namely, that the fall of this stronghold had stirred Italy and the Pope; and His Holiness deemed it necessary to call all Europe for a Crusade against the Crescent.

Mafalda told Teresa that Germany and France had rallied to

the call of Innocent III, and rumor had it that in the spring of 1212 ten thousand horses and a hundred thousand footmen would come pouring into the Iberian Peninsula. "And Father will have to do his part," concluded Mafalda. "His Knights of Avis, of Santiago, his Templars and Hospitallers will all have to go to battle the Mussulmen. And Citeaux will not only have to bless her fighting men but have all her monks and nuns pray as never before; for they say, no matter how generous the North is with men, the Infidel will outnumber us five to one."

The Infanta thought for a while and then quietly said, "Mafalda, what would you think if I said the most important person in our family is Blanca?"

"What has that to do with what we are talking about?"

"Everything. Most people think that Alfonso, who will surely succeed to the throne, is the important person in our household. He is important, but he is far from the most important. Prayer and penance, if history means anything, is what we need now as much as, if not more than, knights. Prayer and penance appease God. Prayer and penance can rout the Infidel. We can do more for Father and Spain, Mafalda, than any number of knights, be they Cistercian or not. That is why I say Blanca is really the power behind the throne."

"I believe in prayer, Teresa, but only to back up the fighting men."

The Infanta looked deep into her sister's eyes as she said, "What Spain, Portugal, and all Europe need, Mafalda, is love of God. What we have lacked, and what is bringing on all these fears, is the God of love. We believe, Mafalda, but not intensely enough. That is why I say religious are more necessary than knights, and Blanca more important than Alfonso."

"But if all princesses take the veil, what will happen to royalty?"

Teresa sensed the seriousness of the question and rightly suspected that Mafalda was really presenting a personal problem.

She leaned back as she said, "All won't. But if more did, both royalty and the world would be cleaner and much more pleasing to God. We are called nobles. God made us and every human noble. But what have we made of ourselves? You've seen some of the courts of Spain. So have I. We both know some of the facts about our own family. Grandfather was no saint. Father will never be canonized. As for Alfonso, I'm praying that his soul be saved. Royalty is much better off in this ravine of mine with God alone, than in the courts of Europe making mockery of God's great Sacrament of Matrimony by using princesses as political pawns, marrying them to men they may not marry, or to men who do not want to marry them. God will not be mocked, my little sister. If more princesses take the veil, royalty will become more royal; and our Christian lands may be saved."

This had been one of the longest, severest, and most serious talks the two sisters had ever had. When Mafalda accused Teresa of being too hard on nobility, she was told that it was love that prompted such severity — love for God and love for those He had elected to rule. The Infanta spoke earnestly of the value of prayer and penance, not only for the individual soul, but for the realm. Her final words were, "What Portugal, Spain, Europe, and the world need — and what I hope to give unstintingly — is reparation."

Mafalda never forgot that word, nor the ring in Teresa's voice as she spoke it.

The real victors

That same year all Portugal rang with the cry, "The King is dead. Long live the King!" as young Alfonso took the crown to carry on the work of his father. Portugal was not yet a hundred years old. But the difference between the tiny grant of land that lay between the Minho and the Douro which, along with his daughter, Alfonso VI of Castile had given to Henry of

Burgundy in 1095, and the kingdom which Sancho I left to young Alfonso II, was such as to make the monarch gasp. He ruled six large provinces stretching from the Entre Douro-e-Minho in the north, which had been the original grant, to the Alemtejo and the Algarve provinces in the deep south. His seaboard ran a full five hundred miles; his land frontier was even longer. It was a strange land. The northern part, marked mostly by rivers and mountains, held some high plateaus and a few deep, narrow valleys, where life was possible, but rugged. The central portion had broader valleys and larger plains. There life was much easier, but still strenuous. It was only south of the Tagus, in the province of Alemtejo, which was practically all plains, that things were in any way easy. Further south the Algarve grew hilly again, and life became more difficult. It was a land calculated to breed a strong people. The man who ruled it in late 1211 was weak.

His first move was to answer the call to the Spanish Crusade. He did so by sending only a token force of Cistercian soldier-monks. It was the first indication of the smallness that was to characterize so many of his moves. But this handful of Cistercian knights brought glory not only to Portugal and Citeaux, but along with the other knights of France, Germany, and Spain, brought an end to the Mohammedan threat on the Iberian Peninsula.

There can be no doubt as to the identity of the real victors in that astonishing victory at Las Navas de Tolosa. When the armies met that morning of July 16, 1212, the followers of Christ were outnumbered just as Mafalda had predicted the day she talked to Teresa. So confident was the Emir En Nasir that he insolently announced to the King of Aragon that, after completely subjugating Spain, he would go to Rome and purify St. Peter's with the blood of Christians. Counting the knights lined up against him on the plain, no one could blame him for his boast. But Emir En Nasir did not count the myriad hands that were unsheathing the sword of the spirit. He did not number the almost numberless souls that had answered the call of Innocent III for a Crusade of Prayer. He did not know that he was facing the unconquerable force of prayer and the omnipotent strength of penance. Emir En Nasir escaped with his life, but only by fleeing from a field on which he left more than one hundred thousand followers of the Prophet behind him in their blood.

Mafalda, in high excitement, hurried to Lorvão to tell Teresa the almost unbelievable news. She sang the praises of the Knights of Avis, Santiago, Alcántara, and Calatrava. Teresa let her have her moment. She enjoyed the sight of her excited sister. But after Mafalda had told all she knew, Teresa led her to the church where Lorvão's community was singing Office. She let the soft rhythm of the psalmody create its atmosphere of awe and adoration; and not until the choir had sunk back on the tiny seats which allow them to bend over as the chantress sings the oration for the day, did Teresa speak. When Mafalda's eyes were fixed on the bent backs and lowered heads, she quietly said, "You are now gazing at the real victors of Las Navas de Tolosa."

When Mafalda's dark eyes turned questioningly upon Teresa, her older sister smiled and pointed to Blanca standing in the fourth stall on the Epistle side and whispered, "There is one of the greatest knights of Portugal. She was at Las Navas de Tolosa and fought grandly."

Mafalda pulled her sister out of the church, and once the door was closed, flashed around on her with, "What in the world are you talking about? You don't mean to tell me Blanca went to Spain!"

Teresa smiled. "That is exactly what I'm telling you. Not only Blanca, but every veiled head you saw in that choir."

"But, Teresa! — "

Then, taking the younger sister by the hand, Teresa led her

back to the room they were first in, saying, "We really go where our prayers go, Mafalda. These nuns have been in Las Navas de Tolosa. They strengthened the arms of our fighting men in that bitter battle. They really conquered; for you well know that Mohammed was not driven away by the sword. That is why I say Blanca has done more for Portugal than anyone in our family."

Mafalda was frowning as she again exclaimed, "But, Teresa!"

Then the Infanta opened a Bible and read to her sister the story of Moses on the mountaintop and Josue on the plain. With quiet intentness she stressed the line, "And when Moses lifted up his hands, Israel overcame." She paused, looked at Mafalda, then went on with, "but if he let them down a little, Amalec overcame." Again she paused and again she looked meaningly at her sister. Then turning back to the Bible she said, "Listen closely to the conclusion of this story, Mafalda. 'And Moses' hands were heavy; so they took a stone, and put under him, and he sat on it. And Aaron and Hur stayed up his hands on both sides. And it came to pass that his hands were not weary until sunset. And Josue put Amalec and his people to flight by the edge of the sword.' "

She closed the book, bent forward, looked deep into her sister's dark eyes and asked, "Who defeated Amalec: Josue or Moses?"

"I never remember hearing that story before," replied the younger Princess thoughtfully. "I can see what you mean about Blanca and this community . . ."

"Do you begin to see what I mean about Portugal?" interrupted Teresa.

"What?"

"We have enough Cistercian knights. We need more Cistercian nuns. Josue has his men, but where are the hands of Moses — and where the Aarons and the Hurs to stay them up?"

When Mafalda made no reply, the elder sister went on,

"There are more ways than one for saving our country, Mafalda. Love for Portugal can send people to convents as well as to battlefields. Secretly I believe it takes greater love for our land to bring men to Alcobaça and women to Lorvão than it takes to send them across to Spain to combat the Infidel. Love sacrifices, Mafalda; total love becomes a holocaust. Look at Blanca."

That was all that was said that day; but the most beautiful of the daughters of Sancho I and Dulce now had two words to haunt her, "Reparation" and "Holocaust."

The support of sacrifice and the power of prayer

Before the summer of that important year of 1212 had yielded its harvests, Mafalda was back at Lorvão standing beside Sancha, who, with tears, was telling Teresa all that their brother, Alfonso, threatened to do at Alemquer.

"He not only wants the convent and grounds," she cried, "but he says he will wrest from each of us girls every inch of land father granted to us before he died. What are my poor to do? And what of my *Encelladas?*"

"*Encelladas?*" echoed Mafalda. "Who are they?"

"Women who love God enough to wall themselves in from the world. Almost a dozen of them live across the river from Alemquer in tiny cells whose doors have been walled up. I have fed them for years now."

"What a weird way to serve God!" exclaimed the youngest of the sisters.

Teresa looked at her. There was both understanding and reproach in her eyes. When she spoke, the thinnest edge came on her tone. "Not nearly as weird as the way God served us, Mafalda. He did not wall Himself in, it is true; but He did allow others to hammer Him on to a tree. These *Encelladas* are not mad, Mafalda, unless to love God with all your heart is madness. But don't you go worrying about them, Sancha. . . ."

"But I must. His Majesty is most determined."

"His Majesty," repeated Mafalda; and there was high disdain in her tone.

Again Teresa looked at her. And again there was both understanding and reproach in her eyes. "My little sisters," she began, "we must forgive His Majesty, our brother, the King. Our father, Sancho, and his father, Alfonso, both gave extensive grants of land to religious and to quite a few nobles who had served them well. Now all such lands with their revenues are withdrawn from the jurisdiction of His Majesty, the King. I happen to know that at present the royal coffers are almost empty. But to run a government, one must have revenues. Our brother, Alfonso, must run the government. So he will endeavor to recover those lands which will yield the richest revenues. It is all understandable enough. But he is forgetting much. He is forgetting charity such as yours at Alemquer, Sancha. He is forgetting loyalty to our father's name. He is forgetting justice to our father's friends — yes, and even to our father's children." She was smiling confidently as she said, "Don't either of you worry. He will never touch our lands."

"But he says he will send soldiers . . ."

"He does?"

"Yes."

Teresa's smile faded, and her mind became alert. Soon messengers were hurrying to the man whom, for three years, she had called "husband." More messengers hurried to Rome to the one she always called "His Holiness." Still other messengers sped to Coimbra, Lisbon, Alcobaça, and even to Citeaux, telling the truth tersely and asking the support of sacrifice and the power of prayer.

When Alfonso II attempted to reclaim Alemquer, he was met by the threat of excommunication from Rome and the strong, stern-faced soldiery from León. Alfonso IX still loved the woman he had one time called wife. The sympathy of Portugal, from the rugged mountains above Oporto to the southernmost shore of the Algarve, was strongly arrayed on the side of the sisters. The greedy Alfonso II halted before the spiritual arms of the Church, the martial might of León, and the powerful moral force of sympathy. The sisters kept their lands. But that of all their brothers and of many of Portugal's highest nobility was taken by an angry King. Many titles were revoked and the Crown's coffers filled. But the sisters wondered about justice and the wrath of God. So did the Queen-Mother, who knew too well that her son was being more than highhanded.

In 1216, when two Franciscans crossed the mountains from Spain and arrived in Coimbra, Dulce, the Queen-Mother, welcomed them as if from heaven and sent them on to Sancha at Alemquer. With a happy heart the Princess gave the friars a little chapel which stood on her grounds and which had been dedicated to St. Catherine. She told the two men that all the fields surrounding the chapel were theirs too. This was the cradle of the Franciscan Order in Portugal.

The following year the generous Princess did much the same for the Dominicans, establishing them at Monte Junto.

It was from these two centers that the Dominicans and Franciscans went to those possessions Portugal later acquired in Africa, South America, and the Orient. Thus it was that Teresa's successful opposition to her brother's greed had effects in centuries yet unborn and on lands far distant from Alemquer and Lorvão.

But in 1220 she was trembling at one of the effects her opposition had already produced. Sancha had come to Lorvão in great excitement and poured out a story that set the onetime Infanta of Portugal and quondam Queen of León shaking. Sancha said she had been at prayer for Portugal and the world when suddenly there stood before her five young men robed in blinding white with crowns on their heads. The excited Princess thought there was something familiar about their faces, but it was only when they thanked her for having financed their way to martyrdom that she recognized them as the five young Franciscan friars who, only a year before, had stopped at St. Catherine's on their way to the Moors in Mauretania. Sancha had kissed the hem of their brown robes that day, served them a meal, and talked long and enthusiastically with them about God and His kingdom, both on earth and in heaven, then sent them on their way with gifts and promises of prayers.

Now they were back to say that they had been successful, not so much in spreading God's kingdom on earth, but, by shedding their blood, winning their way to His kingdom in heaven. They thanked her for the help she had been to them in gaining this victory, saying that it was not only her presents that enabled them to go to Mauretania, but her prayers that won for them the strength to face death that they might live forever.

Finding Sancha so deeply moved, Teresa thought it opportune time to make a suggestion that had been in her mind for months. "Why don't you bring your *Encelladas* across the river, Sancha," she said, "turn Alemquer into a real convent, and make it strictly Cistercian? Give your charity a permanent form, Sancha. Give God more than all your wealth. Give Him yourself."

Sancha smiled then and confessed that she had already persuaded her *Encelladas* to give up their solitary form of life and live together under the Rule of St. Augustine. "But, after studying Lorvão," she added slowly, "I see certain advantages in the Cistercian way of life. If you will help me —"

"Help you?" broke in Teresa. "Why, I've been pestering Heaven to persuade you for years."

Thus was laid the foundation for what was one day to be the flourishing Cistercian Convent of "The Cells." Sancha chose that name in order to commemorate the *Encelladas* and the walled-up cells in which she first found them. Much against her will, Sancha was made prioress. She would have been happy had they allowed her to sink into anonymity in the depths of the common life and there cultivate the virtue she so admired in her sister, Blanca, and which she called "hiddenness." She also desired more than ever before to practice a mortification of body and soul that would frighten moderns, and offer the same to God as a tribute of thanks for His patience with Portugal and her rulers, even as it would be a petition that He grace the land and all who lived in it. Instead she had to accept the post of prioress and still administer her large estate; for the Pope urged this for the sake of the poor. Thus charity, which had always marked her life, still remained its dominant virtue despite her new and intense attraction to "hiddenness" and mortification, as reparation for the realm.

After her very first visit to "The Cells," the beautiful Mafalda hurried to Lorvão with the excited question, "Is this all necessary?" Mafalda was on fire with feeling as she eloquently drew up her case against Sancha's taking the veil. She spoke of the poor at Jerabica, pointed to St. Catherine's with its Franciscans and to Monte Junto, white with Dominicans; then said that, as Mistress of Alemquer, Sancha had much wider field for real charity and broader scope for effective edification than she would ever have as prioress of "The Cells." Her concluding words were, "She could build the monastery for the *Encelladas* if she liked, but why enter it herself?"

Teresa was amused by this fiery display of logic. She rightly suspected that by this full and clever enumeration of Sancha's works and their marvelous possibilities, Mafalda was but seeking either to quiet her own conscience or seeking reasons that would justify her in imitating her elder sister's latest more. Lorvão's Foundress looked musingly at the mountainside. "I wonder if Christ told that parable of the foolish virgins precisely for the daughters of kings?" she said. "I really do not know. But of two things I am certain. One is that the rich young man who walked away sad was very rich indeed — but not a bit heroic." Teresa paused, turned from the window, and looking straight at Mafalda said, "And the second thing of which I am absolutely sure is this: those *Encelladas* who have turned Cistercian have oil in their lamps, and those lamps will be burning when the Bridegroom comes."

It was not a very direct answer to Mafalda's insistent: "Is it necessary?" but now to "Reparation" and "Holocaust" she added the word "Bridegroom."

State attacks Church

Teresa herself would long since have taken the veil to walk in silence and know the obscurity that shrouded Blanca if she could have settled the affairs of her own three children and felt more sure about the conduct of her brother, the King. In the earliest years of his reign, Alfonso had avoided open conflict with the Church. But Teresa knew that the revenues he had stolen from his brothers and the nobles he had robbed of title were not enough to run the government as he desired. She was not greatly surprised then, though she was greatly grieved, when news came in 1220 that Alfonso had clashed with clerics and taken issue with the Bishop of Lisbon.

The eldest daughter of Sancho I took herself to special prayer; for she well knew that authority in the hands of the cowardly is always used as a bludgeon for injustice, and she knew Alfonso was cowardly. She well remembered how her own father had brought an interdict on the land; and because she knew her brother to be morally weaker than her father had ever been, she knew he would be that much more cruel. This Princess of Portugal knew human nature — at its best and at its worst. She prayed earnestly and did penance with the abandon of the heroic.

But Heaven seemed uninterested. In 1221 news came that Alfonso had seized the property of the Archbishop of Braga.

Teresa wept. Mafalda found her eldest sister in tears and asked what was wrong, what could she do. For reply Teresa made a request. "Please, Mafalda," she sobbed, "let us have another Cistercian convent." When Portugal's youngest Princess asked what she meant, she heard again what she had heard the day she had first come back from Castile. "This realm needs the God of Love, Mafalda, and much more love of God."

Then she explained. Mafalda was the only one of the family for whom Alfonso had shown any affection. She alone, of all the sisters, had not been threatened with the confiscation of her property. Never once had messengers come to her from the King demanding assistance. Yet she held as her own some of the most fertile valleys of the whole realm in those mountains called Serra di Freitas.

Teresa then gave her sister a history that turned out to be a plea for God even more than a story of men. She told how a monastery had been founded at Arouca in the Serra di Freitas years before Portugal had become a kingdom; how God had there been worshiped by men living under the Rule of St. Benedict all the time their grandfather and father were fashioning the realm; how chivalry toward God gradually cooled until finally the few remaining monks left. But it would seem that God had His eyes on that fertile valley and wanted praise to rise from humans who would live there; for nuns soon took over the house and spent their nights and days as St. Benedict had prescribed — in the adoration of God. But history repeated itself, and all too soon God was looking on a fertile valley with an empty house. Now Mafalda could win for Portugal the God of Love, and have some Portuguese women showing some love for God if she would allow that empty house to be filled with Cistercian nuns. Then came the three words that had been haunting Mafalda; for Teresa said, "Let them make *reparation* for the realm, by becoming *holocausts* of love, for the sake of the *Bridegroom.*"

It was done. The Bishop of the place, the Abbot of Alcobaça, and even King Alfonso himself, approved. Mafalda showed herself a real sister to Sancha in her generosity and to Teresa in her maternal interest in the monastery; yet, even after it was built and fully equipped, she stayed in the world. This puzzled Teresa and appalled Sancha.

But then the heavens opened, and a flood poured down. Three Spanish bishops, legates of the Holy See, came to Portugal with a sharp remonstrance from His Holiness, Honorius III, for His Highness, Alfonso II. The King ignored it. Teresa wept. Mafalda grew afraid. The following year the Pope excommunicated the King. Even this had no effect. Yet God wanted both Alfonso and Mafalda for Himself; so He had the Pope threaten Alfonso with deposition, then struck the King's body with leprosy. With the onset of the disease Alfonso read God's handwriting on the wall and capitulated. With his death, Mafalda fled to Arouca determined to show God all the chivalry her brother had failed to show, and by her example to kindle in the souls of all her sisters the spirit of the Crusades for the sake of the Portuguese kingdom.

Off at Lorvão was one who would have rivaled Mafalda in both endeavors, one who was as capable of high chivalry and who was stirred with the spirit of the Crusades; but Teresa did not take the veil yet. She knew something of the spirit in young Sancho II, Alfonso's eldest son and his heir to the throne. He was little more than a boy when crowned in 1223, but before 1230 had shown himself fully mature in crime. Teresa felt sure that the wrath of God was held back only by such things as she had witnessed early that year when she had been called to "The Cells" by a messenger who claimed that Sancha was dying.

It was early March in 1229 that Teresa climbed the narrow, steep path that would bring her up from Lorvão's wild ravine and allow her to hurry to Alemquer so peacefully settled in serenity outside Jerabica. It seemed strange that she should be hurrying toward one so near death — especially one so young. She wondered if the summons were sound. For she recalled that it was Sancha who had cured one who was almost dead from cancer and had calmed another almost distraught from an ulcerated tooth. The nuns had called these works "miracles." Could the "miracle-worker" now be dying? But as soon as Teresa entered the room where Sancha lay, she knew she was just in time. Lifting a crucifix from a nearby table she held it toward her sister saying, "Embrace Him. Embrace Him whom you have loved. Courage, Sancha; He is near. Gather your soul and breathe it forth into the wound in His side."

In one last sigh Sancha gave back to God the soul He had lent to her, that soul which she had poured out in holy chivalry for the sake of Portugal. It was March 13, 1229.

One day a year later Teresa went out to Sancha's grave. News had just come of another clash between prelates and nobles. Standing before the tomb she softly said, "Portugal needs the God of love, Sancha. Her people need the love of God. I'm glad you are here to help me. I'm glad I stole you away."

She was referring to the fact that the day Sancha died, Teresa had begged the nuns of "The Cells" to allow her to wash the body. When they agreed, she suggested that they all go to choir for the hour of Tierce. They all left. When Tierce had been sung, they hurried back to the infirmary but only to find both Teresa and the body had gone. It was the only way Teresa saw of avoiding a dispute. She knew the nuns of "The Cells" would want to enshrine the remains of her sister. She felt she had prior claim.

Down in Arouca, Mafalda was proving that the greatest knights of Portugal were women. As if driven by an insatiable thirst for God, she had plunged into the Cistercian life of prayer and penance. The first few years saw her burning with zeal for choir. Her regularity became the subject of comment by superiors and served as stimulus for her companions. Arouca, fervent before her arrival, became a hotbed for virtue after her entrance. Humility and charity were exceptional. But where Mafalda's Portuguese blood showed most vividly was in her quest for privations and penance. She got permission to empty the straw from her mattress and fill it with bits of broken cork. She asked to be allowed to observe a black fast three times a week the year round. It is said that she disciplined herself to blood, spent whole nights in contemplation, and was finally blessed with the gift of tears. It is all quite violent. But then Mafalda was one who would never do a thing by halves. If she were to give herself to God, God would get all of her.

The first becomes the last

Teresa seems to have expected just such chivalry from the beauty of the family. She smiled contentedly when she heard that Mafalda had lavished a fortune on the embellishment of the shrine of Our Lady of Silva, in the city of Oporto. It appealed to her as eminently fitting that the real Queen of the realm should be venerated in royal fashion at what was the actual cradle of the kingdom, and she claimed it was especially fitting that her shrine should be ennobled by the generosity of the grandchild of the man who had first offered Portugal to our Lady.

When all this good news came to Lorvão, Teresa felt that at last she could give herself entirely to God. Her children were cared for; her immediate family freed from the responsibility of governing; so she knelt at the feet of the Bishop of Sabina and, in the presence of her onetime spouse, Alfonso IX, took the Cistercian habit and became a full-fledged nun at Lorvão.

Of course they wanted to make her abbess right away. But Teresa smilingly pointed to her sister Blanca and asked if it were proper for her, the eldest of the family, to allow one of the youngest to outdo her in chivalry toward God. So she remained a simple nun. For a few years more, however, it seemed as if she were rivaling Mafalda and not Blanca, as she gave away her wealth and properties with a hand that was truly royal.

Mafalda, with her ever practical turn of mind, saw that her bequests showed. She had bridges built across some rivers and established ferry service on others; maintained hospices along mountain passes where weary travelers could escape storms and recuperate their strength. Teresa's bequests recalled her father's generosity. She endowed churches and monasteries and built hospitals. Of course, the rulers of the realm cast covetous eyes toward such wealth and resented such prodigality; but Portugal's people blessed God for the Princesses He had given them.

Lavish as they were with gifts of land and valuables to the people, these same Princesses were still more lavish in the gift of themselves to God. We must remember that these two women were Portuguese; that they knew the sins of the courts of Portugal and Spain; that they were keenly conscious of the conditions of the empire and the entire European world. Then we must recall that they had a love for country surpassed by none, and possessed a chivalry toward God shared only by saints. If we forget any of these facts, we will never understand some of the lines about them recorded by the Bollandists.

Their temperament explains much. Their times explain the rest. Both of these Princesses walked around the cloister with rough hair shirts clinging to the clotted blood they had scourged, or allowed others to scourge, from their veins. Each of them found the fasts of the Rule too meager and obtained permission to deny themselves even the thin meals of the Cistercians. They could have had the posts of prioress or even of abbess. Neither would hear of such. They remained in the ranks as simple nuns and not only engaged in, but it would seem, actually sought out, the hardest, most humbling, meanest, and most menial labors. Their hunger for humility and thirst for humiliations had each burying herself more deeply in the common life and even seeking to be ruled by women of lowliest birth.

Teresa was more successful than her younger sister in sinking into that anonymity which so often singles out the real saint; for the eldest of the children of Sancho I cut herself off as completely as possible from the world she had so long known, courteously, but very definitely discouraging the visits of her noble friends and even of her family. Finally she so disposed things that she no longer needed to handle wealth. This she considered her greatest gain. Mafalda was not so fortunate. She still retained much property and had command over considerable riches.

The Church attacks the State

For almost ten years Teresa knew the joys of solitude and the rapture of that Cistercian silence which allowed her to adore God continuously. But then came the news that Portugal's King, by his brutalities and avariciousness, had so stirred the aged Pontiff, Gregory IX, that the realm was threatened with interdict. Teresa hurried a messenger to Arouca reminding Mafalda of the three words that had come to mean so much in her younger sister's life: Reparation — Holocaust — Bridegroom. It is said that Mafalda wept when the messenger gave her the news and kept on weeping for days after he departed. It is safe to surmise that those tears were not for Portugal and the threat that hung over the realm nearly as much as they were for the God who was being outraged by the rulers of the land.

But neither Teresa's prayers nor Mafalda's tears stayed the interdict. When Sancho brutally slew some priests, the Pope let fall his spiritual weapon. Sancho felt its moral force so keenly that he gave way before its power and, as if to imitate his aunts, threw himself into a veritable crusade against the Moors; meaning this work as reparation and plea for pardon. This King of Portugal has been summed up as "a thoroughly bad man, an indolent ruler, but a brave soldier." That summary, especially its final phrase, was borne out very clearly in this campaign against the Infidel. So successful was he that he was feted by the Spaniards — and to call forth their admiration one must have been a very brave soldier indeed. But this combination of success and admiration proved Sancho's undoing; for at the court of Castile he met a certain Dona Mecia Lopes de Haro. She so completely captured him that he forgot not only his crusade of reparation but even the realm of Portugal.

Mafalda wept even more bitterly when this news was brought her; for Castile's court had once been hers. She wished she could double herself so as to be victim for her nephew who sinned so, and victim also for the court that led him on in his sinning.

These were the events that weighed upon the hearts of these two Princesses and led them to living the Cistercian life of prayer and penance as it has seldom been lived in all its eight hundred years of existence. When they arose shortly after midnight, their souls burned like torches in the dark; and as they sang the psalms of David, that King's lines took on new life and meaning for these two daughters of a king because their kingdom was showing itself as stiff-necked and wayward as ever had the Chosen People.

In 1245, when Pope Innocent IV deposed Sancho and gave the crown of Portugal to his brother, Alfonso, Teresa sighed with relief. But less than three years later she was sighing again, but not from relief. At Oporto's shrine of Our Lady of Silva, Mafalda could be seen weeping; for the court of Castile, to which she would ever feel connected, had outraged not only heaven's honor but even human decency when it forced Sancho's brother, Alfonso, to marry Beatrice, the illegitimate child of Castile's sovereign. Alfonso of Portugal, though already married, yielded; and in order to hold his crown became a bigamist.

This time Mafalda's tears before the shrine of the Spotless One and the aged Teresa's bitter penances at Lorvão won speedy reply; for Alfonso's lawfully wedded wife died before the year was out, and the Pope legitimated the union contracted with Beatrice.

Reparation — Holocaust — Bridegroom now dominated the life of the seventy-year-old Teresa, even as they had always influenced the religious years of Mafalda. But it was really the Bridegroom who was dominating. He was letting the aged nun realize that soon He would be coming. Teresa had a tomb built before the altar of Our Lady of the Rosary and asked that her body be laid there after her death. Now she was seen to enter the tomb more frequently; and those who watched saw her compose her body as she knew others would compose it when it was a corpse — and there, in that position, she would meditate on this thing we call death. Often she took the Cistercian Ritual with her and went through the prayers for those in their agony. She studied her five senses and recalled the words some priest would say as he anointed each in the administration of the Sacrament of Extreme Unction. She even reviewed every step in the Cistercian burial service. And the end result of all such meditating was that, like St. Paul, she "longed to be dissolved and be with Christ."

But even while she lived, the Bridegroom would show His appreciation for her holocaust and reparation: He would give her the power to work miracles.

One day there came to the convent which clung to the cliff at Lorvão a beggar who held out a paralyzed arm as he asked for food. Teresa touched the arm, and it was instantaneously cured. Then the beggar, like so many of his predecessors, though forbidden to say a word about the cure, climbed the steep narrow path and noised the wonder abroad. For days after that, a long line of cripples could be seen creeping and crawling down to the cliff where the convent clung. None left Lorvão in the condition in which they had come.

But perhaps one of her greatest, surely her most characteristic, wonder was worked the day she heard that one of her sisters had died without the Last Sacraments. She hurried to the room where the body lay, knelt in tearful prayer, touched the corpse, saying something like Jesus said the day He took the daughter of Jairus by the hand: *Talitha cumi*. The nun arose.

In 1250, the seventy-two-year-old Teresa, daughter of one king, consort of another, but who for twenty-one years had covered the head that had once been crowned with the simple black and white coif of a Cistercian nun because she loved the King of kings, fell ill. When the end was at hand, she begged to be taken before the high altar in Lorvão's conventual church. The community was summoned; and from the lips of the nun, who was dying but who yet stood on her own two feet, came the command to begin the prayers for the agonizing. Teresa joined in the praying. At the last moment, she slumped to her knees; but valiant woman that she was, she would yet cling to her Christ. Her aged hands clasped the feet of a huge crucifix; and supporting herself on her swaying knees, she asked her sisters to sing the *Magnificat*. With gasping voice she joined them as well as she could. At the verse *Suscepit Israël puerum suum* — "He hath received His child, Israel" — she died.

To her tomb, which was close to that of Sancha, came the crippled and the blind. The few that did not leave cured left mightily consoled. When a heavenly light was seen to glow over the tomb of Sancha, the people of Portugal linked the sisters in a cult called that of the "Holy Queens."

Two years later they had another, who had actually been a queen, to add in their veneration of Teresa and Sancha; for in 1252 Mafalda obtained permission to go from Arouca to the shrine of Our Lady of Silva at Oporto. She would make a penitential pilgrimage on behalf of Portugal. All the way to the shrine, and while at it, she poured herself out in prayer. Her gift of tears, too, was most manifest to the crowds of people who lined the streets and thronged to the shrine to watch "the holy Queen" pray. On her way back she fell ill at a place called Rio Tinto and immediately dispatched a messenger to the Abbess of Arouca, who was not only her spiritual mother, but the executrix of her will. The messenger met the Abbess and several of the nuns of Arouca hurrying toward Rio Tinto; for the good Abbess had been warned in a vision of Mafalda's plight. As spiritual mother to the Princess, she had come to know that Mafalda had a real dread of death; so she was hurrying with extra speed not only to comfort her daughter but to see if she could allay this dread.

When she arrived at the bedside, she found the still beautiful features of the nun alight with joy and heard from her lips words that bespoke not only calmness of mind but surprising serenity of soul. The Abbess could not repress the exclamation, "Mafalda! How is it that you are so filled with joy after all these years of dread of death?"

"God's gift, Mother. He made me prudent enough in life to fear this day, so that, when it actually came, I should be without fear. I go gladly to the Bridegroom to whom I have ever offered myself as holocaust in reparation."

Then turning to the senior nuns, she exhorted them to cling with all their hearts to everything Cistercian and gave example of what she pleaded by now begging the Abbess to allow her to die on the floor once it had been strewn with ashes in the form of a cross. The request was granted, and the loveliest of the Portuguese Princesses died clasping a crucifix to her heart.

She was buried at Arouca. For it was there, she claimed, she had found God; and there she had done her utmost to help Portugal. At her tomb, as at those of her sisters, miracles were wrought.

When the causes of these three were introduced in Rome in the late seventeenth century, no less than ninety-seven miracles were adduced as proof of holiness.

History tells that, shortly after the death of the last of the Princesses, Portugal knew peace as King Denis entered into cordial relations with Rome and even made restitution of all that had been taken from the Church since before Teresa had been betrothed to the King of León. It goes on to tell how Portugal knew a rare prosperity and that the Queen who sat beside Denis was actually a saint. And all doubt about hagiography, with its account of these three Princesses, telling the truer story of the realm than history with its account of the three men, vanishes. "By their fruits . . ."

The Bollandists have but a few fleeting references to Blanca, the first of Sancho's daughters to become a Cistercian. But who would be surprised to learn from God's great book of hagiography that, if Portugal owes much to the sanctity of Teresa, Sancha, and Mafalda, these three owe their sanctity very much to Blanca? It could very well be; for God loves humility — and Blanca was truly humble. That her three sisters are high in heaven there can be no doubt. Yet the suspicion remains, and even grows with reflection, that Blanca may be even higher.

It was in the early eighteenth century that Clement IX canonized these three chivalrous women — and did so because of the spirit of the Crusades they had shown in the thirteenth century. For seven hundred years neither Portugal nor the Cistercian Order has ever forgotten the love these women had shown to a God so often outraged. It was a total love, and total love always means a holocaust.

She is Patroness of Poland — but was never a Pole. She is celebrated as a Cistercian — but never belonged to Citeaux. She was nobly born and linked to royalty — but gloried in her rebirth by Baptism and claimed union with Christ as her only real dignity.

She lived and died in the thirteenth century — yet is as modern as this morning; for she lived the doctrine that is today really coming to life — the doctrine of the Mystical Body of Christ.

We place her here because she was so like and unlike the Princesses who have just engaged our attention. In each case it was a parent who occasioned the sanctification of the children; but in what different ways! The sins of a father stimulated the Princesses of Portugal to give back to God the glory that was denied Him; the sanctity of a mother turned Hedwig to heroic penance and heroic love.

Like Teresa and Mafalda, Hedwig married; unlike them, her marriage was legitimate and in time she became a mother and a widow. Like them she burned with love for her country and would insure its prosperity by penance and prayer; but unlike them she never became a real nun. Like them she had a flaming faith, which was very near vision; like them, too, she built convents and endowed monasteries while her charity ever flowed out prodigally to the poor; but unlike them she was never enriched with the power to work miracles. Could it be because her greatest miracle was herself? Let us look at this woman who never talked to Christ face to face, yet spent her life tenderly touching no other face simply because she took God at His word.

ST. HEDWIG

Patroness of Poland:

The Woman Who Took

God

at His Word

Home-training and family traits

It may strike one as strange that this Patroness of Poland was never a Pole; but the historical facts are that Hedwig was born in what is now Bavaria, lived in what was Silesia, and died at Trebnitz, a town that was not then in Poland.

Yet the Poles have very good reason to venerate this daughter of the Duke of Carinthia, wife of the Duke of Silesia, but widow of the man who one day, at the request of its nobility, acted as Regent for Greater Poland; for she gave to Poland what Patrick, who some say was a Frenchman, gave to Ireland — the example of a love for God which generated a trust that was unshakable.

Born about 1174 into a family of four boys and three other girls, Hedwig should have had a very happy home life; for her father, Berthold, was of the noble family of the Counts of Andecks, rich and powerful, while her mother, Agnes, came from the equally noble family of the Counts of Rotletchs; and at the time of her birth her parents were the rulers of Meran, a town near the castle of Tyrol. Yet she was allowed only infancy and earliest childhood in the bosom of the family; for by the age of seven she was living in the monastery of Lutzingen in Franconia.

Agnes, mother of these four boys and four girls, really shaped their lives before any of them had reached what is called the "age of the use of reason." The eldest boy, Berthold, died as Patriarch of Aquileia; Elebert, the second oldest, became Bishop of Bamberg; the other two sons, Henry and Otho, divided their father's principalities between them and became famed for their valor as soldiers and their virtue as rulers. Of the girls — Agnes married Philip Augustus, King of France; Gertrude married Andrew, King of Hungary, and gave birth to Elizabeth, who would one day become St. Elizabeth of Hungary; the third daughter became abbess of Lutzingen; and Hedwig, the last child, became wife, mother, widow, saint, and Patroness of Poland.

Henry, Duke of Silesia, married Hedwig when she was only twelve years of age. Yet it was not long before this young girl was doing for a baby called Henry all that her mother, Agnes, had done for her. Gradually the castle of Breslau became very like the castle at Tyrol; for in regular succession Hedwig gave birth to three boys and three girls, all of whom she tried to shape as her own mother had shaped her. Henry, the first-born, and Gertrude, the last, were especially dear to Hedwig because of their manifest bent toward genuine piety. With them she could create the atmosphere that surrounded her own childhood and, like her mother, Agnes, talk to these youngsters about God and about being good. Conrad, the second son, was the father's favorite, and would always prove a source of worry to his mother. High-spirited, headstrong, and somewhat selfish, he clouded an atmosphere that otherwise would have been limpid and free.

After the birth of Gertrude, Hedwig approached Henry with

a bold proposal. She suggested that they glorify God by denying themselves. Neither was yet in deep middle age; the warm blood of youth still coursed through their veins; yet Hedwig proposed that they praise God by taking a vow of chastity. Henry did not hesitate, but he wanted to be sure it was the proper thing to do; so he consulted the Bishop of Breslau. This good man stated the facts clearly. If these two members of the land's highest nobility loved God enough to sacrifice their rights to the legitimate expression of their human love, for God's glory and the good of the world, it would be a sacred and sanctifying thing. But he insisted it would have to be an act of love, an act that was fully free, an act that would be an openhanded giving to God. Henry understood him. Shortly thereafter he knelt beside Hedwig and made solemn promise to God of a better thing. It was the turning point in their lives. They had been good before; now they would become great. They had been holy parents; now they would become more than ordinarily holy.

Royalty's generosity and God's strange recompense

Every historian of Poland will call Henry "The Bearded"; for from the hour he knelt before the Bishop of Breslau to take that vow until the hour of his death thirty-two years later, he never wore gold, silver, or royal purple, nor did he ever shave. He would be as simple, as humble, and, as far as in him lay, as holy as his wife. Their holiness began the easy way: that of giving alms and contributing to charitable enterprises. Their first, and perhaps their best, venture was the building of the Cistercian convent at Trebnitz, three miles from Breslau, the capital of Silesia.

Whatever they did, they would do in royal fashion. Thus Trebnitz would not only be founded; it would be endowed; not only would a convent be built, though it took fifteen years of labor, it would have the town of Trebnitz and other estates as sources of income; it would be able to house and feed one thousand individuals every day, and in the beginning one hundred of these would be nuns; the rest would be girls of the dukedom from poor families. These were to be educated as thoroughly as possible and, when of age, would be dowered so that they might marry well; or if they so wished, they could be received as nuns. To the building of this famous monastery Hedwig gave all of her mighty dowry.

And Heaven rewarded such generosity in the way God rewards most of His intimates: by affliction. Hedwig's youngest child, Gertrude, was old enough to be betrothed to Otto of Wittelsbach. This marriage would have meant peace of mind for the mother and happiness for the daughter. But in 1208 Otto murdered King Philip of Swabia, and Gertrude would not think of joining her hand to those of a murderer. Four years later Duke Henry divided his realm between his two eldest sons. Conrad, the younger, was dissatisfied with the division; and the sorrowful mother had to look on while her two children gathered armies and pitted them against one another. Conrad was completely routed and fled the land. A year later a messenger came to the mother and told her her son had been killed in a hunting accident.

Hedwig did not look up as Teresa of Ávila would three centuries later and say, "If this is the way you treat Your friends, Lord, small wonder You have so few." Instead, very like Job, long centuries before, she bent her head and said, "The Lord hath given. The Lord hath taken away. Blessed be the name of the Lord." And then went on about her charities. Into the duchy, with the approval and generous aid of her husband, she brought Augustinian canons, Cistercian monks, Dominican and Franciscan friars. In Breslau, Henry established a hospital of the Holy Ghost. Hedwig matched him with one for female lepers at Neumarkt. But where Henry could not match his wife was in her ever greater withdrawal from the world and her ever closer approach to the Cistercian way of living.

She fixed her principal residence close to the convent at Trebnitz and, whenever possible, went into the community itself, sleeping in the common dormitory, eating in the common refectory, wearing the simple coarse habit, and doing the lowly chores of the choir nuns. God was so deepening the soul of this noble woman that it would become a citadel of faith the strongest enemies would storm in vain, and a wellspring of charity whence love would flow with the prodigality with which energy pours from the sun. The instrument He used most for this deepening was the Cistercian life as lived at Trebnitz.

Hedwig, realist that she was, saw these nuns devoted entirely to prayer and penance. So in her palace she practiced austerities more rigorous than many a nun in her cloister. Beneath her simple gray garb, this Duchess of Silesia wore the stiffest of hair shirts, to which she sewed white serge sleeves, leading many to believe that she was actually fastidious about her dress, when all the while her innermost garment was a torment to her. Over snow and ice she went barefoot to church. Wednesdays and Fridays she fasted on bread and water — and for forty years she never tasted flesh meat.

Of course there were those who remonstrated with her. Even Henry, in the early years of their vow, protested that she was going too far. But Hedwig pointed to the Cistercian nuns and said something like, "They love God enough to give their all. They have faith enough to believe it counts, and hope enough to think it pays. They tell me that penance not only chains the beast that lives within us, but frees the angel so that it may fly. They say it can also tame the beast in others. We have six children. We are rulers of a duchy." Henry let her fast, wear gray, and go barefoot.

But that was not enough for Hedwig, who, judging from the things she did, must have been a very passionate woman.

A new revelation

One day she had asked the Portress at Trebnitz why she was always so kind to her. The surprised nun opened wide her eyes and answered simply: "Because you are Christ." That reply puzzled Hedwig. She pondered it long, but could not fathom its depth. She knew the Portress was sincere, would never think of flattering, let alone deceiving her. Hedwig's admiration for every Cistercian nun was towering. She was often seen to kiss the very ground they walked on, kneel in the places they had occupied in church, and make use of towels and clothing the nuns had already used. Unquestionably her subjective admiration colored the objective reality. But it did not help her understand the meaning of the Portress' statement; so she presented her problem to the Abbess. The answer, of course, was simple. The Reverend Mother just stated what was in St. Benedict's Rule. But such a reply led to further questioning, and this brought out a real revelation for Silesia's holy Duchess.

The secret of Benedictine sanctity, from the hour the boy from Nursia hid himself at Subiaco until the trumpet of Doom is sounded, lies in *Christ-consciousness.* Hedwig learned this as the Abbess explained the legislation drawn up by the Patriarch of the Monks of the West and showed her that it is this that changes men and women into Cistercian monks and nuns and finally transforms both monk and nun into saints. For the Cistercian takes the Rule of St. Benedict literally, which explicity commands that Christ be seen in everyone and everywhere.

Hedwig was too vigorous a realist to accept this seeming lyricism at once. She had seen too much of human society, both at court and among the common people, to be able to understand immediately how Christ is to be seen in every Christian and even dimly discerned in every human being who is not baptized. She protested to the Abbess. That wise woman listened quietly, let the Duchess pour herself out, then opened a Bible that was at hand to the twenty-fifth chapter of St. Matthew's Gospel and read to Hedwig the description of the Last Judgment as given by Christ Himself. The Abbess stressed each pronoun, then paused after each item that was listed. Hedwig heard: "*I* was hungry, and *you* gave *Me* to eat." . . . Then: "*I* was thirsty, and *you* gave *Me* to drink." . . . "*I* was a stranger, and *you* took *Me* in." And so on to: "*I* was in prison, and *you* came to *Me*."

Hedwig had read it many times herself. Yet this day it was coming to her with all the force of an entirely new and utterly unheard of revelation. She listened avidly. This was something new. Something important. When the Abbess concluded with the words: "Amen I say to you, as long as you did it to one of these the least of my brethren, you did it to me," Hedwig felt as if she had heard the very voice of the God-Man.

Her first reaction was sorrow. "I've lived so long, and known so little! I've missed so very much all my life. I wonder if any of my charities have been charity."

The wise Abbess smiled, touched the Duchess lightly on the arm, and affectionately said, "Your Highness has missed nothing so far in life that God did not want you to miss. But now He is opening your eyes to clearer vision. I'm sure you have done all your charities out of love for God. But now He wants you to know how near He is. . . ."

The realist in the Duchess came to the fore. She saw that she did not have to wait for death to sunder the veil before she looked on the Christ — and life on earth took on new zest; and her zeal, a new ardor. Horizons were wider, heaven much nearer.

She could be seen now at the hospital she had erected for

female lepers, and found not only binding up or cleansing their sores, but even bending over and kissing them. Onlookers shuddered; they did not know that the feet the Duchess saw were the same as those to which the Magdalen clung on Calvary's height, and from which she had to be loosed on Easter morn. Hedwig's faith had opened her eyes; no longer did she see only humanity in humans nor did she miss, even in the material world, the sight of "the many-splendored things."

Her house, next to the convent, was often crowded now with beggars, paupers, cripples, and the sick. The Duchess sat with them and ate, or, more often, served them as they sat, after having washed and kissed their feet and replaced their rags with decent raiment. After these poor people had departed, she would show the same reverence for the utensils they had used which she had so often manifested for articles touched by the Cistercian nuns. Her faith was a lively faith; and her charity, a passionate love. Who is there who would not kiss the chalice Christ lifted to His lips in the Cenacle, and cherish the very napkin with which He had wiped His mouth? Hedwig was doing just that.

The doctrine of the Mystical Body is as old as Christianity, and, to a certain extent, just a little older. For it was taught by Christ in the Upper Room the night before He stumbled to the hill; and the Church, which is His Mystical Body, came forth only after His Heart had stopped its beating and His sacred side was pierced. Nor is it only now in the twentieth century that the dynamism of this doctrine is being felt in the Church. Hedwig was driven by it in the thirteenth, and Paul thrilled his hearers with its truth and fashioned their living on its wonder back in the first. This dogma is the heart of all dogma, and this revelation is the center of all Revelation. To live *in Christ Jesus* is the only purpose of human existence; for God the Father is glorified only in His Son. Like all true

Cistercians, Hedwig found God in this truth, and began heaven on earth by *living* her discovery.

Many may think her penances part of the Purgative Way. Perhaps they were at first. But after the Abbess had explained what the Portress had said all life and living had changed.

Her vigils, fasts, abstinence, disciplines, hair shirt, bare feet, poor clothes, and bed of boards had, at first, been for herself and her children. She would bridle all her own and all their passions as far as she could. But once she had learned that she herself was a member of Christ Jesus, then reread what Paul had said about his own sufferings, Hedwig increased her austerities, not to check her own passions, but to "fill up what was wanting to His Passion, for His Body, which is the Church." Her penances became prayers pleading with the Father for the souls of men. This revelation of the doctrine of the Mystical Body had made her not only more Christian, but much more Catholic. Her family was not now just the three boys and girls she had brought into the world, but every human soul God had sent into the world, save those of His Son and that Son's Mother.

The woman wins

Few understood Hedwig. They saw a person who had more power than any other woman in the realm, one who was wife to a man who not only ruled the duchy of Silesia but who was everywhere spoken of as the one who would rule the united duchies which would make up Greater Poland. They knew her to be wealthy beyond their computation, and to enjoy that which wealth could never buy — the love of her subjects. They knew she could have lived in luxury and known all the pleasures that go with power, position, and prestige. Yet they saw her dress more soberly than many a woman of much lower class;

eat more poorly than many of the poor; use her wealth only for the needy; and employ her power and prestige merely to promote the peace of the realm. She greatly puzzled those of lesser faith.

Even her husband, Henry the Bearded, did not fully understand. He is known to have remonstrated with her over what she took at table. Yet he was wise enough to pattern his own life ever more closely on hers; for he divined what others missed; namely, that at the Cistercian convent his wife had grasped a philosophy of life that lit tall candles in her ever earnest eyes, and kept her heart always singing. She told him she had found Christ, and he — though not fully comprehending — was forced to believe; for the happiness which radiated from Hedwig he knew could come from no merely earthly source.

Since 1220 she had lived almost exclusively in the house next to the convent of Trebnitz, and more often than not she wore the habit of the nuns and followed the exercises of the religious day and night. Only her duty to her husband, her children, and the realm kept her from entering all the way and taking the Cistercian vows.

In 1227, however, she had to doff the black and white of the Cistercians and don her somber gray; for word had come from Gonsawa that Henry the Bearded lay there wounded after having been ambushed by Swatopluk, Duke of Pomerania, who had some designs on Silesia and part of Poland. She was still the loving wife, and now more than a gentle nurse. She told Henry how to bear his wounds, and why, even as she tended them. The Cistercian simplicity had not only been mastered by Hedwig, it had mastered her; so now all she could think of, talk about, or teach others was Christ. Henry heard Christianity explained in such a way that he was soon viewing the ambush as part of God's special providence and his wounds as heaven-sent to enable him to "fill up what was wanting to the Passion of Christ." He was being taught not only resignation to God's will, but the favorite Cistercian doctrine of complete abandonment to it.

If Henry had missed any of the consequents of the doctrine while recuperating at Gonsawa, he had plenty of time to ruminate the whole truth a few months later at Plock, where he was lodged as a prisoner. Conrad of Moravia contested Henry's right to the territory left open by the death of Ladislaus, Duke of Sandomir. The Bearded One was eminently successful in battle and established himself as ruler of Cracow. But Conrad had his underground in that city; and one Sunday, when Henry went to Mass, he never returned from it. The next heard of him, he was in chains at Plock.

Hedwig received the news at Trebnitz. Turning to the messenger she simply said, "Thank you. Please God I may see my husband at liberty soon and find him in good health." Perhaps that is all she would have said or done about the matter had not her eldest son, who was now being called "Henry the Pious," gathered an army for the purpose of assaulting the prison at Plock and liberating the prisoner.

The Duchess again donned her somber gray and hastened to Moravia. Conrad had spurned every offer of Henry the Bearded and Henry the Pious. His army was ready, and waiting for whatever force would come from Silesia. But when this lone woman in somber gray walked into his presence, he capitulated. What was it that radiated from this aging Duchess who dressed more simply than many a peasant and spoke as softly as any nun? What was the secret of power of this personality that shone from eyes deep-shadowed from fasts and deep-circled from vigils? What was the source of the silent eloquence that poured from her mere presence; an eloquence that won what mortal might could not wrest from him? Conrad could not answer those questions, but he had to frame them for himself; for never before in all his life had anything like this happened. Henry the Bearded went free. Henry the Pious demobilized his troops. Hedwig went back to Trebnitz, and to her penance and prayer.

When her husband playfully taunted her with want of conformity to God's will and utter lack of resignation to His obvious decrees, made so manifest by her interference with his imprisonment at Plock, he got more than he asked for. Hedwig smiled first to show Henry she knew he was teasing, but then became most serious as she said, "Let no one distort Cistercian doctrine. We live abandoned, completely abandoned to God's will. But while that means we are ever to be humble under the hand of God, it never means that we are not to lift our own hands. If God permits that our house catch fire, He wills that we try everything to put it out. If He permits the river to overflow, He wills that we build dykes to dam it up. If He permits our bodies to sicken, He wills that we take medicine to cure them. If He permits Conrad to imprison the Bearded One, He wills that a mere woman should set him free. When we say God *permits* a certain thing, almost always we mean that He *wills* the opposite. He permits sin; He wills that we be saints. The Cistercians teach abandonment; but there is an activity, an intense activity, to this thing that sounds so passive. It is very like the wild abandon of your troops when they rush into battle, seemingly reckless of their own lives, yet battling wildly all the time to save them. Conformity to God's will usually means opposition to what God has merely permitted. For instance, He permitted you to tease me; He wills that I teach you."

How old the new

The lesson was given with a laugh that night, but it was lived without any laughter almost a decade of years later. In 1237 the nobility of Greater Poland elected as overlord of the realm a mere child, Boleslaus V, and appointed Henry the

Bearded as regent. That made the aging woman at Trebnitz, who so often dressed in somber gray and even more often walked to church over ice and snow with bare feet, the Duchess of Silesia and Leading Lady of Greater Poland.

Hedwig was impressed, deeply impressed; but not as many moderns would expect her to be. She saw the need for more penance and more prayer; need for a deeper contemplative life. For if she and her husband were to be responsible for the welfare of more humans, they must have closer contact with God. Instead of somber gray, she was seen more often now in Cistercian black and white; and spent much more time within the cloister than in the ducal residence. Her bed was left untouched as she slept on the floor, and more than one night was spent entirely in prayers and tears.

Yet in 1238, when news was brought to Trebnitz that Henry the Bearded was dead, the only dry eyes in that huge convent were those of Silesia's Duchess and Greater Poland's Leading Lady. Like a female Job she asked the weeping nuns: "Would you oppose the will of God? Are you forgetting that our lives are His? My dear Sisters, is not our only will that which it pleases God to ordain, be it our own death or the death of our loved ones? Let us not weep for Henry. Let us abandon ourselves to God."

Henry the Pious took over and ruled both Silesia and Greater Poland in his father's stead. This, her first son, along with Gertrude, her last daughter, were all that were left to Hedwig now. Actually these two had been the joy and consolation of her life; for more than any of the others in the family, they had caught her spirit and lived both in and for Christ Jesus. At the moment Gertrude was what her mother had longed to be all the time — a professed nun in the Cistercian convent at Trebnitz. Henry warmed the aged Duchess' heart as he lived up to his title, "The Pious."

Here the Bollandists have a page, describing what took place in the year 1240, but it reads like something taken from our newspapers in 1940. Were one to take a map and trace the happening as it occurred then, all one could say would be: "How history repeats itself!"

Out of Asia poured the Tartars. Their object, all Europe. Running through Russia like a fire, and leaving behind them little more than a fire leaves behind, they swept on through Bulgaria, Ruthenia, and Poland. They turned Cracow into ashes for the winds, then went on to Silesia.

Genghis Khan was dead; but his son, Batu, was carrying on with all the fierceness and fire of his father and enjoying much the same success. These Tartars seemed irresistible. All Europe could be theirs. Their advance was very like that of fierce flame. But when they laid siege to the citadel at Breslau, they were met by another fire — and before it they fell back. A globe of flame dropped from the heavens and hung threateningly over the Tartar camp. The Mongols cowered beneath it. Then withdrew to Liegnitz.

Here Henry the Pious had mustered an army of Silesians, Poles, and Germans. The night before the battle all confessed. The chroniclers say that the next morning all communicated at Mass. Then near Wahlstatt the Christians and Mongols met. It was as bloody a battle as history has ever recorded; and from what the chroniclers say, it would seem that here for the first time some sort of poison gas was used; for they say that "a thick and nauseating smoke, issuing from long copper tubes shaped like serpents, stupefied the Polish forces." Henry the Pious gave wonderful proofs of courage and cleverness in this memorable battle and for a time beat the Tartars back. But then his horse fell under him, and he was cruelly slain.

Hedwig, with Henry's wife, Anne, and the nuns of Trebnitz had retired to the fortress at Chrosne after seeing that Henry's children were safely within the impregnable castle at Liegnitz. Three days before any word of the battle arrived, the aged

Duchess bent toward a certain Dermudis, who was working at her side, and quietly said, "I have lost my son. He has gone from me like a bird in flight, and I shall never look upon his face again in this life."

When the messenger did arrive, it was Hedwig who took Anne in her old arms and with Henry's youngest sister, Gertrude, weeping at her knees, comforted and practically crooned to them the truths that had been her life. "We ought to have no other will than His. God has dealt with my son, who was your husband, and your brother, as it has pleased Him. Praised be God." Then came what should have been a threnody but which actually was a thrilling Ode of Thanks to God, ending in a motherly petition for her son's soul. "O my God," cried this now-wrinkled Duchess, "I thank Thee with all my heart for having given me such a son. Always did he love and honor me. Never once did he cause me pain. To see him alive was my greatest desire; yet I feel a still greater joy in seeing him, by such a death, deserve to be united with Thee forever in the kingdom of Thy glory. O my loving God, with my whole heart I commend to Thee the soul of my darling son."

Three more years were given to Hedwig to "fill up what was wanting to His Passion for His Body, which is the Church." She sheltered Henry's widow with a tenderness her own mother could never have surpassed and at the same time showed to Gertrude, her own daughter, who was now Abbess of Trebnitz, a humility and obedience the most fervent in her community could not equal. Like another St. Paul she preached by word and example only "Christ and Him crucified." And her life was the most eloquent exhortation possible for all to believe as she believed, and live by a faith that was just short of vision.

On October 15, 1243, though those about her did not consider her seriously ill, she insisted on being anointed. She then asked that the Passion of Christ be read to her. As the words of the evangelist, telling of the darkness that closed in on Golgotha, reached her dimming senses and a new darkness closed in on her, Hedwig, like Christ, breathed her spirit into the hands of God.

Less than a quarter of a century later, Pope Clement IV named her "Saint." And from that day in 1267 to this, the Poles have claimed this woman who was not a Pole as their patroness, just as the Cistercians the world over have honored and yet do honor her who was not a real Cistercian. And she, who never talked to Christ face to face in this life, learned in the other that she had done nothing else all her days.

These three women, each named Ida, reflect the thirteenth century so fully and sum up Cistercian spirituality so completely that they merit treatment as a unit.

Ida of Nivelles was born in 1199.

Ida of Louvain died in 1300.

Ida of Léau lived and died in the middle of the century.

Chronologically, then, they form a unit: giving us the entire century. Socially the unit is just as complete; for one was from the wealthy upper classes; another a daughter of a middle-class, well-to-do farmer; the third, a poor orphan. Their lives, seen against such a backdrop, show us the economic strata of the century. Finally, the very different educations given to each enable us to see the heights and depths that existed in this age which gave to the world the quintessence of art, literature, painting, sculpture, and thought.

But what especially cries for their unification in one essay is their spirituality. These three Idas, as different as morning, noon, and night, in every other respect, were as like as three peas in a pod when it came to seeking, finding, walking with, and loving God. They were three women with but a single love. They merit special attention.

IDA OF { NIVELLES / LÉAU / LOUVAIN }

Three Women

With but a

Single Love

Shocking!

Some modern psychologists and a few present-day psychiatrists may nod knowingly when they learn that both Ida of Louvain and Ida of Nivelles had a very unhappy childhood. Ida of Nivelles ran away from home when she was nine, then begged for herself and seven women who posed as pious, before entering the convent. Scoffers at the religious life may sneer when they hear that Ida of Louvain became a silent nun because the fame of her sanctity brought such crowds to her home that life was rendered intolerable. When they are told that Ida of Léau entered the Cistercian life just after reaching her teens; then, after meeting Christ in her postulancy, wished to die immediately so that she might live with Him forever, they may nod to the psychologists and psychiatrists indicating that she is their case.

But the sanity of these three Idas makes many another human being look insane. These three women never forgot what many of our modern psychologists and psychiatrists seem never to have known; namely, that the human soul is a capacity for God and nothing else. With an insight clearer than most of these professionals, they recognized the keenest hunger of the human heart and the most burning thirst of the human soul to be a hunger and a thirst for God. With a wisdom that seems to have been lost to our day, they realized that all the unrest in the human mind, all the uneasiness in the emotions, all the gnawing dissatisfaction and galling sense of frustration are really nothing but our soul-deep instinct for joy and our innate drive for Him who is the source of, as well as the culmination of, all true joy.

Unquestionably in each human soul there is a deep-seated unrest, an unrest that tells poignantly of our need for God. A recognition of the existence of this need would lead to the solution of most of the unrest that is sending more and more people to psychiatrists and mental institutions. No one of these three Idas ever reasoned her way either to the existence of the need or to the solution for the unrest. Yet when only nine years of age Ida of Nivelles knew its existence and found a way to satisfy it. It was to let herself out a window in the dark of night while her relatives wrangled in a room below, arguing how best to marry the girl off so as to be rid of a cumbersome orphan. Ida had with her only the clothes on her back and a psalter.

It was the year 1208. The young girl had just lost her father and found herself not only orphaned but unwanted. In her anguish and loneliness one thing stood out in the memories of the bright years before her father fell ill; it was of the occasions he had allowed her to cross some of Flanders' most marshy fields in order to visit Christ in the village church of Nivelles. She remembered, too, a tiny house beside the church; but, as she hurried across the muddy fields in escaping from her relatives, her thoughts were of Him who was in the church and not of the house that was shadowed and sheltered by the church's wall. Yet, when morning came, the hungry, homesick, lonely, and lovesick child went to that tiny house gladly when its pious inmates sympathetically invited her.

For the next six years that tiny house was her home. Better, perhaps, to say she ate and slept there, brightening the lives of seven aged women with the sparkle of her youth, while she made the church her real home. The Christ in the tabernacle became her real Friend, and it was to Him she paid her thanks for the kindness of the women who had taken her in. In no time it was evident to the old ladies that they were receiving much more than they had given; for Ida not only brightened their lives with her ready laughter and the warmth of her generous affection, but by her begging obtained more fuel and food for them than they had ever known before.

That was the childhood of Ida of Nivelles — orphaned — a runaway — a beggar.

But for modern scoffers more positive "evidence" is offered by the childhood of the Ida who died at the end of the century. If these men will say that they know exactly why the Ida who was born at the beginning of the century entered the Cistercian convent at Kerkem, which was later moved to La Ramège, how much more absolutely they will speak of the reason Ida of Louvain left home and became a nun at Roosendael!

This Ida was born into a well-to-do middle-class family, which seems to have been ridden by that ambition we of the twentieth century know so well. They wanted more than economic security and social standing; they were materialistic enough to crave real wealth and long for luxury. They never understood their spiritual-minded child, but they did know how to persecute her.

Ida liked to go to church often. That was bad enough. But when she began to stay up late at night or rise in the small hours of the morning in order to pray, the family became more than unsympathetic. When they found out that she slept on a mattress of vine branches, wore a hair shirt, and took a discipline; when they heard her singing hymns up in her room or reciting psalms and canticles as she worked about the house, their attitude turned to antagonism. When she wanted to go to church, she was locked in her room. If she took this quietly and began to sing the hymns and canticles that have been written to praise God, they mocked her by off-key chanting or by taunting cries. If she grew quiet, so as not to provoke them to what she took to be real irreverence, but turned herself to silent prayers they would make all sorts of unmannerly noise so as to disturb and distract the locked-in girl. One time when she asked if she could fast in preparation for an approaching feast, they said, "Certainly" — then let her go without any other food save the flowers of a linden tree for eleven full days.

Can you not hear our omniscient psychologists and psychiatrists saying "masochism" as they read of Ida's practices?

Claire Boothe Luce, in her introduction to her book, *Saints for Now*, has offered an explanation that does not explain away, but enlightens what it allows to remain. She writes: "When we encounter the grim asceticism of some saint of the Middle Ages, we consider his conduct morbid, if not insane. That is because we live in an Age when a scratch sends us rushing off to the medicine chest for iodine and a band-aid. We would be less scandalized by this manifestation of asceticism if we were to recall that the saint lived in an Age when the most excruciating torture was publicly administered to malefactors and criminals. We might then see that his particular mode of holiness was to take upon himself a measure of the pain society was currently inflicting on its sinners and, in effect, he was saying, 'If torture is to be the lot of the sinner, then torture is my lot; for all are guilty in the eyes of God.'"

All the love in this mad world of ours is not self-love; so it is worth while to distinguish between masochism and asceticism. There are some few of our fellow rational beings, in the present and the past who love and have loved God as He commanded that He be loved: "with all thy heart, all thy strength, all thy mind, thy whole being." This is and has been especially true of

women. And never was it more true than of the three women
before us: Ida of Nivelles, Ida of Louvain, and Ida of Léau.
And right here, as well as everywhere else, the point might as
well be made: when one loves God with the all-out love He
demands, then that one will find himself or herself loving all of
God's creatures, especially those who are rational creatures, with
a very similar love — one that is all-out. Then he or she will
long to make reparation to God for the sins of man — her own
and her fellows. Now reparation for the sins of men is most
assuredly anything but masochism. In its perfect form it is not
even asceticism. It is merely love's ardor forcing one to love as
did He who took the sins of the world upon Himself to die on
a criminal's cross.

But, perhaps, some of our contemporaries may still think that
they can explain the entrances of Ida of Nivelles and Ida of
Louvain into Cistercian convents by pointing to the unhappy
childhoods of these two women. But what will they offer as explanation for the entrance of the other Ida whose childhood
was as different from these two as day is from night?

Ida of Léau was born just about the time the little beggar girl
and orphan was leaving Nivelles to enter Kerkem. This Ida's
father was a farmer who won his livelihood from those fields of
Flanders that lay outside the little town of Leeuwen, or Léau.
Unlike the parents of Ida of Louvain, he wanted his daughter
to be happy and knew there is an intimate relation between
health, holiness, and happiness. He fed and clothed her well.
He sent her to the best school in the neighborhood, one con-
ducted by some Beguines. These able women not only taught the
child the rudiments but quickened in her such a love for learning that young Ida was up in the earliest light of dawn devouring her books.

Ida's father, like all good farmers, was up with the sun. When
he found his child up before him and poring over her lessons
by this silver light, he was highly pleased but just as highly

puzzled. For he had another daughter, just a few years older than Ida, who was just the opposite. She seemed allergic to all forms of study. When this energetic father found his younger child as avid for prayer and piety as she was for book-learning, he knew a joy he had never expected to know, and encouraged her in every way he could. He gave her as much of his company as his farm work would allow. He taught her all he knew of wild life and of domestic animals. He showed her flowers that only nature lovers can find, and made her days not only pleasurable but very profitable. For every bit of progress she made at school or at home he had a reward that not only pleased but stimulated the child. As time went on, he urged her to study the art of manuscript copying, and thus laid the foundation, all unwittingly, for something at which Ida would excel in her later years in the convent.

Yes, Ida of Léau had a charming childhood. Yet at the age of thirteen, two years younger than that at which poor Ida of Nivelles took the step, she entered the same Cistercian convent that now housed the former beggar — that at La Ramée, or La Ramège.

The Solution

If the psychologists and psychiatrists would look in the first book of the Old Testament and the first book of the New Testament; or more pointedly, if they would consult St. Paul in his first letter to the Corinthians, they would find an explanation that does explain, and a truth not to be found in their manuals. Genesis 2:24 says: "Wherefore a man shall leave father and mother and cleave to his wife; and they shall be two in one flesh." Matthew 19:5 puts these same words on the lips of the Word, Incarnate Truth. And Paul renders perfection perfect when in 1 Corinthians 6:17 he says, "But he who is joined to the Lord is one spirit." All three are talking of love.

Love sent these three girls to the convent. A passionate love; one that wanted both to possess and be possessed. A fearless, unfaltering, flaming love; one that counted no cost and admitted no compromise. These girls had found the "pearl of great price." They had come upon the "treasure in the field" — that field would be theirs, cost what it may! They had met their Man. He was the God-Man. They would be Godlike.

Not because their childhood had been unhappy, or because they were sad; not because they were warped of soul, or twisted in nature; but because they were straight and true and thorough-going women, they showed their passionate pride in the possession of a heart that could be given away and a body that could be denied that their deep souls might be filled with a love this world knows too little of.

Why is it that so few moderns ever make a fuss when some girl wants to sacrifice herself to a career on stage or screen, or devote her every energy to some profession? Why is it that they accept as normal the wholesale forfeiture of social standing, economic security, proud name, and powerful position for what they recognize as human love; yet will look askance at any young lady who wants to "throw herself away" on Jesus Christ — the most beautiful of the Sons of Men, Incarnate Wisdom, the Splendor of the Father and Omnipotence Itself?

These three Idas became Cistercians because they wanted to follow the only career open to all humans, in which no mortal need ever fail — the career of loving God.

The tiny beggar girl of Nivelles is one of the most charming female characters one will meet in literature or in life. She was all heart, a being who radiated a warm affection to all her fellow humans. This little orphan was French. Kerkem, which moved to La Ramège, was Flemish. Ida did not know the Flemish tongue; but there is a language of the heart which needs no lexicon, no grammar or rules of rhetoric. When she entered the cloister at La Ramège a Flemish nun was sitting disconsolate, enveloped in an aura of sadness. When this tiny French girl came over and sat by her, and smiled into her sad eyes, the sad eyes and the entire countenance lit up with joy. Ida had said nothing with her tongue; but her presence, her personality, her whole being was eloquent.

So universal was the effect of this charm — which is but the overflow of truest charity — that when shortly after her profession, Ida fell suddenly and mysteriously ill and it was announced that there was little hope for her recovery, the entire convent of La Ramège got down on its knees and stormed heaven with prayers, begging God to allow them to keep this radiant spiritual personality in their midst a few more years. The result speaks well, not only for Ida and the Heart of God, but for the nuns of La Ramège; for Jesus appeared to one of them to assure her that Ida would be allowed to remain with them for over a decade of years.

Clare Boothe Luce writes that the saints bring afflictions on themselves because of their love for others. An incident in Ida's life illustrates this truth. The father of one of the nuns had just died. The grieving Sister made a sign to Ida asking her to pray for her father's soul. Ida agreed, and immediately began to beg with an ardor that makes such prayer irresistible. The following day the nuns were out in the fields harvesting. During the rest period Ida sat down by a shock of wheat sheaves and again lifted her mind and heart in pleas for the soul of the nun's father. Of a sudden there opened before her a view of purgatory; and there she saw the soul of him for whom she was praying. The anguish of the soul so moved Ida that she cried out to God, asking Him to afflict her instead and to take the man's soul to heaven.

God answered that cry. Ida was struck there at work with a fever that kept her in almost intolerable pain for the next six weeks. At the end of that time she was told that the soul for whom she had cried had been freed the day she called from beside the sheaves of wheat — and that her six weeks of agony had taken the place of his punishment.

How true it is that when the feminine heart has been set aglow with the tiniest spark of divine love, grace finds it as docile to its slightest touch as is the lightest feather to wind; and the woman's will shows itself capable of a generosity and perseverance we seldom find in man.

That is not said to flatter, nor in any spirit of chivalry. It is simply being somewhat scriptural and very true to fact. Women have often been called "the weaker sex"; we read in St. John (19:25): "There stood by the cross of Jesus His mother, and His mother's sister, Mary of Cleophas, and Mary Magdalen." St. Matthew adds: "and many women were there" (27:53). Where were the men?

It was a woman who anointed His body at Bethany. It was a woman who wiped His face on the road to Calvary. It was women who wept as He stumbled beneath the cross and staggered toward Golgotha. And it was the Woman of all women, the one who bore Him, who stood by Him until He died.

Be it said to their credit it was no woman who betrayed Him; no woman who denied Him; no woman who condemned Him; no women who fled when He was captured; no woman who nailed Him to the cross or dug His side with a spear.

He is the One who drew these three Idas to Cistercian cloisters. Once they were within those walls, they found a liberty that allowed them to love as all great women love — utterly and to the end.

The tiny beggar of Nivelles found herself in the cenobitic life — which means that she was surrounded by souls that knew the same hunger and thirst, had the same desires and determination, were being urged on by the same tremendous love.

We have seen enough of the Cistercian life by this time to know that it holds certain difficulties for women that it does not hold for men, and even more peculiar hardships, naturally speaking, than would be found in other cloisters with different rules. The Cistercian interprets Benedict literally; and Benedict, with all his temperance, is a strict taskmaster. There is a steely discipline to his organized regime which grates on the very nature of woman, who is guided by feelings, impressions, emotions, in a more marked manner than is man. In her, reason is less dominant; yet the prime requisite for a balanced, integrated, and properly orientated life in religion is reason. If the religious life is not based on, directed by, and fully controlled by principles, it is not religious, nor is it really life. But to live by principle requires reason, and even demands a strong and inflexible will. Now it is no disparagement of the women to say that just as reason is not ordinarily dominant in their intellectual life, neither is inflexibility of will markedly their volitional characteristic. They can be willful, it is true; but that no more means the same as strong-willed than does "strongheaded" mean the same as "powerful mind." So women, by their very nature, are faced with hazards, difficulties, and real obstacles in the cloister which men do not have to face.

Yet, by that same nature, they have advantages men can never hope to have. Woman has a sense and an intuition for the supernatural that is denied man by his nature. By an instinct of her very being, woman needs to believe that behind the material world there is a deeper, more mysterious, and infinite one. By disposition she will joyfully accept sacrifices when they are idealized; for she has an innate tendency toward sacrifice. So the cloister, especially the strict Cistercian cloister, can awaken all that is best in the feminine make-up and channel its every energy to their highest ends. Since by temperament she is highly sensitive to all that is good and beautiful, the cloister is an ideal setting for her, because, there, horizons widen and ever widen to a world that is all Goodness and Beauty, since it is God.

That analysis of woman is necessary if we are to understand the actions and the reactions of these three Idas. In our day it has been said. "It takes courage rather than strength to be a Trappistine." And the Trappistine of today is the Cistercian of the thirteenth century. But who has ever associated courage habitually with the "weaker sex"? Yet for eight hundred years there have been "Trappistines."

Will you believe it?

Ida of Nivelles was tiny — one of those delicately formed, small women who, even up to old age, remain doll-like. Yet she went into a cloister where courage is in high demand. She had been the joy of her father, the joy of the seven pious women for whom she begged, and became the joy of La Ramège from 1214 to 1231. Her woman's nature is as sound an explanation as any. This tiny orphan was true to her nature. She loved. Hence, she found joys, at times bitter ones it is true, but joys nevertheless. Everything she did in the cloister was done out of love for Love. Consequently, she radiated joy. Ever mindful of Christ, she was ever thinking of Christians; most especially those near her — her sisters. Small wonder she became the joy of La Ramège. Utter unselfishness always wins hearts, creates an atmosphere that is alive with peace and joy. But how account for Ida's unselfishness?

She came, a French girl, into a Flemish convent. A difficult situation in itself; one that seems calculated to drive a girl in on herself and to produce selfishness. More, she came from a most strange environment and after a truly soul-searing experience with life and people. She came, an uneducated beggar, into precincts that are sacred and silent, where the mind and heart must reach heights where God and angels dwell, or starve and shrivel. Difficulty seems to be piled on difficulty when one analyzes the situation in which this tiny girl found herself at Kerkem. Yet she became its joy. For before her father had died, she had come to know Christ. That knowledge fills all voids, educates the unschooled, gives meaning to what looks meaningless, and puts romance into life and living. In the six years of beggary, the church was really her home, and the tabernacle the heart of that home. When she entered Kerkem, St. Benedict said to her in his Rule, "See Christ everywhere." That is as good a summation of the Rule as can be made; and this young, uneducated orphan, by instinct, if not by intuition, saw into that Rule's central core.

With her as with Ida of Léau, it was not a transformation that was effected by asceticism so much as a full flowering that was brought about by mysticism. The charm and simplicity of this tiny nun, whether one looks at her manner of prayer or studies her visions, engenders the conviction that she was specially taught by God just how to walk with Him.

You have already seen her cross the cloister, sit by a disconsolate nun, and by a simple look and affectionate smile brighten the world for that Sister. Her prayer life was as natural, as simple, and as charming as that. She merely looked around and saw God everywhere. She heard God speaking those silent, peaceful, loving words which have in them an infinite depth of tenderness. From such looking and listening, her heart was filled to overflowing; joy poured out.

Theologians can call it the gift of Knowledge and analyze its function if they will; but for our purpose it is enough to say that this tiny creature, whose person sparkled and whose presence diffused joy, had learned somehow or other that the Holy Ghost is the Sculptor in the Trinity, who shapes souls artfully if they but yield themselves, and His one model is the Christ. Her devotion to this Sculptor won for her what was given the Apostles in the Cenacle. One feast of Pentecost, as Ida sat in the refectory thinking of the uncreated, eternal, substantial Love of the Father and the Son, her face became a blaze of light. Conscious of the happening, she lifted the very ample sleeves of her cowl to hide what God was doing; but the splendor spread all about her. Then suddenly He who had been formed in the immaculate womb of Mary by the power of the Holy Ghost stood before her cloaked in a blazing light. Ida ate nothing that Pentecost Day, yet dined sumptuously. After this Pentecostal Banquet Ida was like St. Paul; she knew no one save Jesus Christ — and Him crucified.

Her devotion to the Mass and the Victim of that Sacrifice, to the Prisoner of the tabernacle, the God veiled beneath the appearances of bread and wine, won for her the rending of the veil before the darkness of death approached, and allowed her to see Him whom it will be heaven to gaze upon for all eternity. One Christmas Eve she lay in her cell in the infirmary sick, but not so sick as not to be absorbed in thoughts of the little One whose Mother wrapped Him in swaddling clothes and laid Him in a manger. Suddenly she felt herself transported in spirit to the convent's church — and there, at the Consecration of the Host in the Midnight Mass she saw in the priest's hands what Mary laid in Bethlehem's straw. She was down for the Mass of the Aurora; for this was a Christmas Day without parallel in her whole life. At the Consecration in this Mass, she saw the same thing happen. Transported now with joy, she stayed in the church awaiting the major Mass of the day. When the Consecration took place, she almost hesitated to look up. Yet, she knew this was the moment for which she had been waiting all morning. When she did lift her eyes, they fell on the form of Jesus, but now no longer an Infant but a Boy of about twelve or thirteen. Her Christmas gift this year was to have that Boy come running to her as she knelt in choir, throw His arms about her neck, and kiss her.

"A sick woman's fevered imagination," the scoffers will say. But can they deny it was a delightful bit of imagining? And what if it all be fact?

Evelyn Underhill has said, "We meet mystics in the East and the West; in the ancient, medieval, and modern worlds. Their one passion appears to be the prosecution of a certain spiritual and intangible quest; the finding of a 'way out' or a 'way back' to some desirable state in which alone they can satisfy this craving for absolute truth. This quest, for them, has constituted the whole meaning of life. They have made for it, without effort, sacrifices which have appeared enormous to other men; and it is an indirect testimony to its objective actuality, that whatever the place or period in which they have arisen, their aims, doctrines, and methods have been substantially the same. Their experience, therefore, forms a body of evidence, curiously self-consistent and often mutually explanatory, which must be taken into account before we can add up the sum of the energies and potentialities of the human spirit, or reasonably speculate on its relations to the unknown world which lies outside the boundaries of sense."

That sounds like anything but a page from the Bollandists. Could it be because they who wrote what these Jesuits have gathered were wiser than our wisest scientists, and more intellectual than our greatest intellectuals? Could it possibly be that they believed that the Christ who appeared to a Magdalen weeping outside the empty tomb, the Christ who caught fish for frustrated fishermen, the Christ who allowed a Thomas to dig His side and hands with unbelieving fist and fingers was, as St. Paul proclaimed, "the same yesterday, today, and forever"? What is to prevent Jesus from appearing to a cloistered contemplative that did not prevent Him from appearing to a doubting Thomas and to the disappointed pair heading toward Emmaus?

In his essay on *Mystics as Adventurers,* Father Gillis writes: "I apologize. Argument is really out of place. Let us close, not with argument, but with affirmation. There have been on this earth, and there are today, men and women who by crucifixion of the flesh and discipline of the soul have fitted themselves for strange and wonderful spiritual experiences, raptures, ecstasies, visions, not merely after the fashion of poets, artists, composers, and other men of genius, but supernatural experiences quite transcending the native powers of man. The heavy sod to which our leaden feet are fastened, is to the mystics comparatively unreal. Reality for them is elsewhere. They have plunged into that Reality. . . . They have gone in quest of God, and they have found Him. They have snatched a few minutes of Eternal Life, even before bodily death. A wise man will not deny their experience, still less ridicule it, but contemplate with awe the holy daring of those who have gone forth, in the flesh or out of the flesh, into a region that we know only by hearsay and by faith, a region that we shall have to die to conquer."

Did Ida of Nivelles have to pay for her entrance into that region? For thirteen years she was nagged — that is about the only word for it — by devils. Now it would be in the form of an ugly dog suddenly springing up in front of her, now as a chattering monkey, or some such annoying animal. One night the door of the dormitory filled with flames, and in the midst of the burning stood three devils of horrible aspect glaring at the tiny nun. Suddenly out of that flaming fury a soul leaped, ran to Ida's place, and hid under the covers of her couch. The young nun knelt, called on the Holy Ghost, made a slow reverent sign of the cross, and was relieved to see the flames and the devils vanish. She remained kneeling, praying on hour after hour for the soul she had seen run under her covers. Late that night God came to her, assured her the soul was saved and that now she could take her rest.

This little beggar girl really knew how to bargain with God. She could get what she wanted because she bargained the way God loves to be bargained with. She offered herself as victim for those whom sin had victimized.

But victimhood was only one aspect of the life of Ida of Nivelle — and not the dominant one. To picture her as a suffering victim would be inaccurate. The true picture is that of a simple little woman who was all charm and warm generosity.

Some of her experiences, supernatural ones at that, lead one to believe that life for her was what it is for very happy children. When we read that our Lady came to her with Jesus as a Child, allowed the little nun to take Him in her arms, press Him to her heart, and kiss Him, we suspect that our Lady saw Ida as we do.

Her last Pentecost on earth was that of the year 1231. On that day she fell into an ecstasy which seems to have lasted until Trinity Sunday and to have been God's way of preparing her for her last earthly task: that of suffering bravely until the following December. Then she went to Him whom she had always loved.

On the day of her burial, a boy was cured, by her intercession, of an angry toothache. A little later, a Dominican friar, who was undergoing the same torment, called on the tiny beggar girl and received instant relief. That is how Ida of Nivelles became the patroness for all those who suffer from aching teeth. But what endears her to all sensitive souls is that charm which Cistercian cloisters will give to all feminine hearts and personalities if they open themselves as did this little orphan — a charm like that of the most winsome child.

God-intoxication

In the same convent of La Ramège, twenty-nine years later, another Ida died in circumstances that must have awakened echoes in the memories of those few who were there when Ida of Nivelles died. On a Sunday in late October of 1260, Ida of Léau was given Holy Viaticum. She had been in the infirmary for three long years, during which she suffered not only the dissolution of the body that disease slowly brings on, but that desiccation of the spirit which spiritual dryness brings to the soul. But this woman had a will, and that will sparked her mind to believe. She knew that these three years, so painful to her, could be much more pleasing to God than those of decades before when she enjoyed ecstasies and visions and had such mystical lights and intuitions that she astounded learned theologians by her discourses on the Trinity and the Hypostatic Union. Now that they were giving her Viaticum, she felt that the end of darkness and even of the half-light she had enjoyed in ecstasy was at hand — for the best of visions when compared to the Beatific Vision is dull indeed. Ida knew this well and felt that the blindness of all her days was soon to be over. After receiving the Host, she asked the attending nun to place a veil over her face as she made her thanksgiving. It was done. But soon, from beneath that veil, came a heavenly light, which grew until it filled the room. In the midst of this splendor Ida of Léau left La Ramège for the unveiled splendor of God.

But there were many other things in the life of Ida of Léau that remind us of those in the life of Ida of Nivelles. In fact, as one reads the biography of Ida of Léau, scenes seem to reappear — yet always with a color and a fragrance that make them different and give definite stamp to the character of this nun who was the convent's most gifted calligrapher and copyist. For instance, Ida was in choir for one of the night Offices of a great feast. She was following St. Benedict's injunction that as she sing she be conscious of the fact that she is "in the presence of angels who ever look upon the face of God." Suddenly the Madonna appeared to Ida, held out the Infant for her to take. The nun embraced the Child and was truly "in heaven." But then, in the midst of her delight, she awoke to the fact that it was her turn to intone a psalm, something she had to do with arms hanging by her side, or "in ceremony," as the Cistercians name the posture. The excited Sister did not have time to hand the Child back to our Lady; so naïvely she said, "Watch out for Yourself, Jesus; I have to sing in ceremony." She dropped her arms to her sides, intoned the psalm faultlessly, with the divine Child clinging to her neck.

That has been called "one of the most delightful visions to be met with in the annals of Cistercian mysticism." It contains countless lessons, but the greatest of these is love.

Ida had loved God from childhood. She entered La Ramège at the age of thirteen. While still in her postulancy she had an experience so deep, so transforming, that it can only be called mystical. She heard Christ speaking in the very substance of her soul and found herself so filled with love for Him who spoke that she asked then and there that she be allowed to suffer everything on earth so that at death she could fly straight to that Voice.

Whether she realized it or not, she was asking for a purification that is veritably a "trial by fire." Her experiences tell us how pure is the all-pure God and how immaculate a soul must be before she can enter His presence.

Ida could not sleep at night. It was not insomnia. No bodily ailment or nervous affliction kept this healthy daughter of a Flemish farmer awake. It was God searing her senses by allowing onslaughts to be made on her will, and searching her soul by permitting fierce attacks on her faith. She was being tempted, tried — purified.

It can be a terrifying experience, in which one grows convinced that he or she is not only displeasing to God, but has been abandoned by Him — and deservedly so, because of unworthiness. Then it is that the will must bend the understanding to a steady and steadfast affirmation of belief even when the whole being feels that it is not believing — belief in God and in His love for the lowest and least of His creatures, and very especially of His undying love for this soul which already seems dead without having been loved.

It makes the world dark, pitch dark. Ida's remedy for this blackness was to go to Him who is called the "Light of the World" — but she saw no light. In her dryness and semidespair she went to Him who called Himself a "Fountain of living water, gushing up into hope everlasting" — but found no water and knew little hope. She received Holy Communion as often as superiors would allow her to — yet came away with only her will bending her intellect to go on saying, "I believe. I believe."

But once God was satisfied that Ida was sincere and had been sufficiently purified, He granted her peace. Then she knew a form of prayer that was hardly praying, as we conceive it, yet was highest prayer; for it was not just lifting mind and heart to God; it was being absorbed in Him. Especially after Holy Communion did she experience this wonder and joy. On Sundays, when allowed to receive, the whole day would pass in such absorption. On other days she would sit in a favorite nook of hers, whence she could look into the church and see the dove-shaped container which held the consecrated Hosts. It was the same kind of looking and loving that is revealed in the story of the peasant and the Curé d'Ars. "What do you do all day as you sit here in church?" the peasant was asked by the Curé. "Oh, I just look at Him, and He looks at me." It was as simple as that — and just as sublime.

With this Ida, as with the one who would follow her, the Blessed Sacrament was the passion of her life.

In those far-off days Cistercians still received Holy Communion under both Species. After receiving the Host from the hands of a priest, it was customary for the nuns to descend from the predella of the altar, bow, walk behind the altar, and on the Gospel side receive the Precious Blood through a tube administered in a chalice by a deacon. Often Ida would receive God in the Host, then become so absorbed in Him that she would wander out of line and be unable to find her way around the altar. So absorbed was she that she did not complete her Communion, and finally had to be led back to her place in choir unconscious of everyone and everything except the Host in her heart.

Magnificent as such consciousness of the reality of God's

presence is, the Superioress of La Ramège did not find the consequences of this consciousness so magnificent, especially when two or three others imitated Ida or actually experienced this marvelous awareness and absorption in God. So the good Abbess made the rule that anyone who could not conform to the custom of the house, should refrain from receiving the Sacrament.

Hard lines for one in love. Yet they taught Ida and the Cistercian world — and can teach the rest of the world — the value of Spiritual Communion. The nun obeyed her Abbess, but she had also to obey her heart. That desired God; that craved for union with Him; that yearned for Communion. And Jesus answered that yearning by producing the same effects in her soul because of this Spiritual Communion as she had experienced after receiving the Sacrament. In fact, He went further, as if to reward her obedience, and granted an increase of intimacy and a deeper, faster union. So Ida wrote an epigram in Flemish to the effect that the chalice administered by Jesus through His ministers is indeed filled with delights, but that which He administers Himself is not only filled, but overflowing.

Love can be agony

The third Ida, she of Louvain, had a very similar experience, and given, no doubt, for the identical purpose: to teach us that we are to become attached to God, and only to God. Ida of Louvain came to the convent much later in life than her two namesakes and after a much fuller and varied spiritual experience and mystical formation.

As we have already seen, she had an unhappy childhood and an adolescence that was simply a protracted persecution from her father and family in a vain effort to put an end to her efforts to praise God and show Him appreciation for life by love, and detestation of sin by penance. The opposition had the effect that such opposition always will have in persons of character: it screwed Ida's determination to the sticking point. This will to love God and to manifest that love became the passion of her life. She well knew her obligations to her parents and family, but was even more conscious of her obligation to God. The First Commandment was first with Ida. She grew ever more keenly aware of the truth that the only acts befitting a human being are those of prayer and martyrdom. She would spill out her life before God in adoration, or she would spill it out before men in attestation to her belief that God is God, and to her conviction that what she loved lived. She was praying all she could. She was also enduring a veritable martyrdom.

Parents and family might prevent her singing canticles to Christ, interrupt her private prayer, and utterly disrupt her meditations; they might keep her from going to Christ in the Sacrament; but they could not keep her from thinking and loving. While doing all in her power to promote peace in the home, she became ever more in love with the Prince of Peace and imperceptibly with His Passion. Any deep thought of Christ leads to Calvary. All real love for Christ finds itself crucified. Ida of Louvain soon came to know that love can be agony. She anguished to find His body red with wounds and wet with blood, while her own flesh was entire. Love, to be real love, must be an exchange. We seem to have forgotten that. We tend to take it to be an exaltation of one's ego, a triumph of selfishness. But Christ is Love who would share man's misery — and any man who would love Christ must share His Calvary. Ida knew this. She told her Love that she would share everything with Him, know what He had endured not only in her mind and affectionate soul, but even in her flesh.

And now what happened to St. Francis of Assisi on Mount Alverno in 1224 happened to Ida of Louvain. Her hands, feet, side, and head came to hold the marks of His Passion, the imprint of nails, spear, and thorns. In Ida's case the lightest touch of these wounds from softest garment caused her agony. Yet she would not be without this testament to the truth of her love for Him who became Man out of love for her. No, not for an instant would she be without the pain; but the marks were another matter.

Here is where Ida of Louvain shows herself the real lover. The stigmatization caused a sensation in Louvain. Imagine the reaction of her parents and family when both the curious and the reverent came to the home even as they throng to Konnersreuth now. And imagine Ida's embarrassment. To save her family and yet keep God's nearness she did what few of us would think of doing. She begged God to allow her the pain of the stigmata without the external signs of His great manifestation of love. God could not resist such a plea. So people were disappointed when they arrived at Ida's home and saw white hands and clear brow, and feet without trace of blood or sign of nail print. But Heaven was not disappointed as it looked and saw a lover giving that unquestionable proof of love — suffering.

Our scientific age has taken apart this occurrence, too. Just as the learned will tell you that ectasy, psychologically speaking, is a purely natural state of emotion; namely, sympathetic love; and illustrate the phenomenon for you by using the familiar example of the human eye and the sun, telling you that just as the eye is blinded when it stares at the sun, so is the individual taken out of himself when in mystical contemplation he stares at God. Therefore ecstasy is clearly seen to be a weakness of human nature just as in the case of the eye with the sun. But these scientists go further and tell you that stigmatization is nothing but a psychosomatic phenomenon as natural as a cold sweat from great fright, or a flush from surprise and pleasure. They claim that experience shows that these wounds and even their bleeding is the effect of deep emotion and nothing else. They prove their claim by producing the same in hysterical persons under hypnotism.

Medicine, physiology, psychology, parapsychology, and psychiatry should have interest in stigmata and stigmatists. So should theology and theologians. Over three hundred proved cases of genuine stigmatization are known in the Catholic Church. Ninety-five per cent of these were on women. Granted that women are more emotional than men, can it be granted that they are 95 per cent more? Granted that hysterical subjects bleed when under hypnosis; need it be even thought that all stigmatists were hysterical or any of them hypnotized? Suppose for a moment that it is a psychosomatic phenomenon due to deep emotion; is it not sad that more of us do not have emotions that are deep enough to make us so like Christ? But what will these learned men say about this girl who wanted the share in the Passion that was so painful without the signs of the Passion that produced the pain? Will they be wise enough to see that beyond the psyche is the soul, and deeper than all emotions is love? On this point Father Gillis writes: "A wise man will not deny their experience, still less ridicule it, but contemplate with awe the holy daring of those who have gone forth. . . ."

We, at least, can say with him, "Argument is out of place. Let us close not with argument, but with affirmation. . . ." Ida of Louvain loved Christ to such an extent that she became like Him even in His wounds.

Love transforms

Our paganized world, so skeptical of virtue, cynical about love, contemptuous of genuine devotedness, has been shaken out of its supercilious attitude and awakened to the fact that passion for a cause and devotion to an ideal can transform a man, even the most brutal, into some semblance of a lover. The Russian Revolution has made many a revelation to moderns, but none more timely and true than that love for, devotion to, absorption in a cause can make a man ready, not only to suffer for it, but even ready to die. That fact should make all keenly sympathetic with those who are in love with Him whom Communists hate, and move all to the highest admiration for those who are possessed of this "passionless passion" to prove their love by becoming like Him of whom St. Paul has said, "He loved me, and gave Himself up for me." These women loved God and gave themselves up to Him.

The persecution continued at home — so did Ida's prayer. The combination of both somehow or other developed in her a spirituality that was predominantly Eucharistic — possibly because nowhere, not even on the cross, has Christ shown such abasement and love. Pilate was able to say, "*Ecce Homo*," even though the humanity was frayed and made a folly; but when the priest says, "*Ecce Agnus Dei*," while holding up a Host, not even the semblance of a man is seen. Ida would adore continuously the God-Man so fully present under those humble Species. Christ rewarded her devotedness by giving her a supernatural sense of His presence in the Blessed Sacrament, so that she was aware of the nearness of her Beloved even when there was no outward sign to tell her He was there. For instance, on one occasion, she visited a holy recluse who had obtained permission to have the Blessed Sacrament reserved on the altar of her oratory. But this fact was kept secret. No outward sign was given to indicate that God was there. Yet Ida was not with the recluse two minutes before she somewhat ecstatically exclaimed, "My Father is here!" and bent low in adoration before the altar.

The expression is uncommon. It strikes one as strange until we recall the line of Jesus, "I and the Father are one." Then we have to marvel at the depth of this girl's theology.

It is said that after her adoration and her visit, Ida went to town and bought the recluse a sanctuary lamp.

So intense was her devotedness to Christ in the Sacrament of His Love that it spurred her to the magnificent daring of petitioning Rome to grant her permission to receive Holy Communion every day. Rome made its usual discreet and exhaustive inquiry; then satisfied with the sincerity and the sanctity of the petitioner, granted the extraordinary favor.

When she used it to her heart's delight, she caused more and more comment in Louvain. People in those days were not accustomed to the sight of a girl receiving Communion daily. But they could not deny the evidence that is always eloquent — that of the fruits of this Sacrament revealed in Ida's everyday conduct. She seemed to grow visibly more pure, more joy-filled, more kind, and ever more gentle and generous with her fellow humans. Her reputation for sanctity, so justly deserved and dearly won through prayer and persecution, brought crowds to her home. This disturbed not only her parents and family, but upset Ida herself. She prayed ever more earnestly for light. She wanted to know where she could love God without drawing all this attention to herself. And her gaze was turned to the Cistercian convent at Roosendael.

Cloistered there, Ida saw she would escape notice. But she wondered if she could love with the liberty love demands in a convent where seemingly no liberty is allowed. She had yet to learn that the Cistercian nun devoted the entire activity of her being to God — and such a total devotedness is the acme of love and loving. She entered and found that this seemingly loveless place, with its life that was so rough, harsh, and forbidding in its external appearance, was the one place in all the world that a woman, made for love, was perfectly at home. She immediately saw why. She found these women living for and with God alone. They had foregone all other intercourse that they might devote all their energies to One, and only One. Ida soon found the source of the joy that filled the convent and understood why these poor walked their ways conscious of their wealth. Detached from everything on earth, they were attached to the earth's Creator. Now her prayer became one long act of gratitude.

But she was not in the novitiate three days when she was

facing the greatest disappointment of her life, and being asked her biggest sacrifice. She was told that it was customary for novices to receive Holy Communion but thrice a year. She bowed her head, but her heart was breaking. She cried to God, and God heard her. The very next day, when the professed of the community approached the altar for Holy Communion, Ida, by some strange phenomenon, bilocation or something similar, found herself in that line and received the Sacred Host and the Precious Blood. Yet no novice or professed noticed the happening! This continued until the end of her novitiate. Small wonder that her life was one of joy and gratitude not unmingled with awe at God's strange ways.

But Christ Himself was to teach her that there is more to the Eucharist than thanksgiving. He would impress upon her that it is the Sacrament of unity as well as of union; that it unites us to the Whole Christ, not simply to the Head; that the Love here manifested is universal; that when we receive Holy Communion, we should be conscious that we are united to Christ not only as He is in Himself, but as He is in all His members. This is how Christ taught the lesson: He appeared to Ida offering her a very pretty coronet of intertwined crosses and jeweled flowers. He then told her not to fear the austere Cistercian mode of life; for He would always be with her. Then He explained to her the ineffable mystery that is Divine Charity, showing her how He gave Himself whole and entire to her, and whole and entire to each of her sisters, whenever Holy Communion was administered.

It was an impressive lesson — and undoubtedly an important one. To this moment of her life, Ida had been something of an individualist. Now she was entering the cenobitic form of life. It would demand much more charity. It would call for the very generosity of God. She should give herself whole and entire to each of her sisters. It was also a lesson in humility. Ida had been specially graced by God and exceptionally gifted all these years.

She was far advanced in what is called the mystical way. Christ would show her that, so long as He is in a Host, no soul ever has reason to pride itself on special favors; for He offers Himself whole and entire, Body and Blood, Soul and Divinity, to each who will approach worthily. He was very subtly telling this young nun that there is no grace greater, no grace comparable to Holy Communion; so she need not be puffed up with her visions or rapts. God is all to all.

That truth sends us back to Ida of Léau. . . . One Christmas Eve she was in the infirmary unable to go to church for the night Office or the Midnight Mass. Her spirit, of course, was in the Bosom of the Trinity and at Bethlehem; the eternal decree of the Incarnation and its fulfillment absorbed her attention. Suddenly into that little room came a flood of light and in its midst the Blessed Virgin with her Child. Holding the Infant out to Ida she said, "Here is my beloved Son. He is just now born. I have no dearer gift. I give Him to you and to *all your sisters.*"

What Christ taught Ida of Louvain, Mary had taught Ida of Léau. They were to be gifted, greatly gifted; but they were not to think that their sisters were denied the greatest of gifts — the Christ.

The medieval monk who was the biographer of Ida of Louvain has a remark here that is as instructive as it is amusing. He says that after this vision Ida was so radiant with supernatural light that, "if she had been suspended from the ceiling, she would have made a fine lamp, illuminating the whole house." Appreciating his hyperbole, we need also appreciate Ida's charity. She was alight with joy not only over her own good fortune, but over that of her sisters. And that is living the doctrine of the Mystical Body as St. Paul has preached it. "If one member glory . . . all rejoice with it" (1 Cor. 12:26).

These three Idas loved Christ with the all-out love of the all-sacrificing heart of real women. That is typically Cistercian.

They loved Him very especially in the Eucharist. That, too, is specifically Cistercian and contemplative. They were formed by the liturgy; and because they lived the liturgical cycle, they walked with Christ throughout the entire year. And that is as Cistercian as the white cowl of the choir religious or the brown of those indispensable helpers called lay Brethren or lay Sisters; it is as Cistercian as Citeaux. Liturgy is life with and in Christ Jesus. That is why Citeaux was founded; that is why it yet flourishes.

Ida of Louvain lived this liturgical life or this life in Christ Jesus until the dawn of the fourteenth century. It is said, somewhat abruptly, that she died "peacefully and uneventfully after a long illness." The first adjective is acceptable; but no death after such a life and no death after a long illness can ever be called uneventful. The grand larceny committed by Him who said, "I shall come like a thief in the night," is always the greatest event of such a life — and after such an illness. What must it have been for Ida of Louvain after all her glimpses of glory and moments of heavenly intimacy? What must it have been for her to see Him face to face after so many fleeting visions?

And that last long illness . . . what that must have meant to Ida, to Christ, to the entire world! Final purification for her, of course; but completion of His Passion for Him; and salvation for uncounted souls.

These three women had a single love — Christ. But because of that single love they gave their hearts and their lives to humanity and its countless billions. Christ died for all mankind. Every true Cistercian lives for Christ and dies for Christ and therefore lives and dies for every human.

In 1702 the Holy See confirmed the cult of Ida of Louvain. Even now she is venerated as one of the Patronesses of Belgium. And April 13 is one of the big days on the calendar at Louvain; for on that date they honor the woman who bore Christ's wounds and ever walked with God.

Three sisters who were saints have been united in one essay. Three saints who were not sisters have been similarly joined. We can close fittingly, then, by uniting two who were joined as closely as mother and daughter; for Mechtilde mothered Gertrude to the spiritual life and to marvelous intimacy with God.

Furthermore, since we opened this book with a woman who showed us Christ's Sacred Heart, there is appositeness in closing it with two women who will show us the Immaculate Heart of Mary as well as the Sacred Heart of Jesus. Moreover, these women not only walked with God; they lived ever at home with Him.

ST. MECHTILDE

Songstress of Special Grace

ST. GERTRUDE THE GREAT

Herald of Divine Love

* * *

Two Flames of Love

Ever Surging

God's nightingale

Mechtilde of Hackeborn was born the year of St. Hedwig's great grief — 1241 — in the ancestral home of the powerful Thuringian family of the Barons of Hackeborn and Lords of Wippra, situated in the little town of Eisleben in Upper Saxony. It is said that she was cousin to Frederick II — but it would seem that the relationship affected neither! How true the story is we do not know, but it is told that Mechtilde was such a weak wisp of a thing that it was feared she might not survive the bright light of day and the first winds of our weary world; so they rushed her to the church for baptism the very day of her birth. A young priest who was just vesting for Mass, the story goes, yielded to the pleas of the godparents; and once he had changed Mechtilde from a sin-stained pagan to a child of God, he very calmly reassured all that the child would not only live, but live long enough to become a great figure in the Church.

At the age of seven Mechtilde was taken by her mother to the convent at Rodersdorf in order to visit her elder sister, Gertrude, who had entered among the Cistercian nuns a few years previously. It is said that the child so fell in love with the life that she put on quite an act, crying bitterly and begging to be allowed to stay and join Gertrude. To some this might appear like a childish whim and the crying something of a temper tantrum. But Mechtilde's parents were wiser. They knew there is no such thing as "accident" in the world that is governed by the wisdom and the will of God. But they were far from being convinced that this attraction was without its human element. Mechtilde had always loved her older sister with a very special warmth and depth. The solution speaks well for the hearts and the heads of Mechtilde's parents. They allowed her to stay at Rodersdorf — but only as a boarder in the convent school.

Three years later Gertrude, though only nineteen years of age, was elected abbess of the monastery. Unquestionably that had much to do with young Mechtilde donning the white wool and the black scapular of the Cistercian choir nun a few years after — in 1255 or 1256. Young, of course, to begin such an austere existence; but not too young to begin loving God with all her heart.

Two years later Abbess Gertrude sent for her two brothers, Albert and Louis. She would have a very serious conference with them. When they arrived, they were told something of the history of the house. They learned that the community had come to Rodersdorf from Mansfield, where it had settled in 1229, after having been sent out from the mother house of St. James in Halberstadt. Gertrude told her brothers that, while Rodersdorf was much better than Mansfield had ever been, it was still far from what was needed for a Cistercian community, because it lacked sufficient water. The brothers accompanied their sister on a tour of inspection about the monastery grounds, then went home to think and talk the matter over. Not long after that meeting, word came to Gertrude that Albert and Louis had found just what she wanted at a place called Helfta. It had water aplenty — and she could have the place as a gift from them. Gertrude accepted their gift; for while she knew that Helfta was very near their ancestral home, and that ordinarily it is not good for cloistered nuns to be so close to home, she also knew that the now seventeen-year-old Mechtilde was spiritually much more mature than her biological age; hence Helfta would not be bad for her, and would be very good for the rest of the community. So to Helfta they went.

Those dates and names are very important. For they show that the Helfta community was really the continuation of the colony that had been sent out from the Cistercian convent of St. James in 1229. It stayed at Mansfield for only five years. It was at Rodersdorf for twenty-four. The date 1229 is most important. For only the year before, in 1228, the General Chapter of the Cistercian Order had decreed that they would accept no more convents under its jurisdiction; though they had no objection to religious women wearing the Cistercian habit and adopting the Cistercian manner of life. It was a measure demanded by practicality. It was not that the men lacked generosity; but only that the women had more than the men could cope with. Already there were nine hundred convents in Europe for whose spiritual welfare abbots were responsible, to which they had to send worthy chaplains, and at which they had to make an annual canonical visitation. It was just too much for the men. So Mansfield, Rodersdorf, and Helfta, though Cistercian in name, habit, and manner of life, were not Cistercian officially or canonically, since they were never under the jurisdiction of the General Chapter. Could this be one explanation why some historians have called the convents Benedictine (which was true history) and led a few hagiographers into giving the impression that Gertrude of Hackeborn, her sister Mechtilde, along with Gertrude the Great were Black Benedictines (which is not true hagiography!)?

If the monastery at Gethsemani made a foundation today which followed all the customs of Gethsemani, wore the same garb, and lived the identical life, but which, owing to a ruling of the General Chapter, was not under that Chapter's jurisdiction, would you call it a Trappist-Cistercian monastery, and its men Trappist-Cistercian monks, or would you name it and them Benedictines? That is the story of Helfta; for the foundation charter of St. James at Halberstadt calls it a *Cistercian* establishment, and Count Burkhard, in giving that community a site for a foundation at Mansfield, calls the sisters "nuns of the Cistercian Order"; a document dated February 12, 1262, bearing the signature of Ruprecht, Archbishop of Magdeburg, describes the nuns at Helfta as "religious of the Cistercian Order." Finally, Abbess Gertrude, Mechtilde's elder sister, in every extant letter describes herself as "Gertrude, by the grace of God, Abbess of Helfta, a convent of the Cistercian Order" — and in one of these letters tells us how a foundation made from Helfta in 1253 followed the "observances of Citeaux." So, despite lack of official connection with the General Chapter, it seems that one is quite safe and far from inexact if he calls Mechtilde, Gertrude, and all at Helfta Cistercian nuns; even while he admits that those who name them Benedictines, while not entirely wrong, certainly give a very wrong impression.

So we have it clearly now that Mechtilde of Hackeborn entered Rodersdorf in 1248, as a child of seven, to be educated by the Cistercian nuns there, among whom was her much loved elder sister, Gertrude. It is worth while noting that in such convent schools the *Trivium* (grammar, rhetoric, and logic) was always taught, and in some of the more select the *Quadrivium* (arithmetic, geometry, astronomy, and music) was also added.

From what we know of Mechtilde it seems safe to say that Rodersdorf was among the select class; for to think of Mechtilde is to think of music.

She was a gifted child, and before Gertrude was elected abbess, had already attracted the attention of the more competent teachers and was being very specially coached particularly in music; for nature had endowed the girl with an unusually sweet voice. In fact, Christ Himself, in later years, called Mechtilde "His nightingale." Unquestionably this youngster could have become a very spoiled child. For she had looks, talent, intelligence, nobility of blood, powerful relations, and everything else that attracts attention and wins affection. In no time she could have become "Little Mistress" of that Alumniate and had the enamored nuns, wittingly or unwittingly, doing her will. The opposite happened. This favorite of Fortune became one of the most docile pupils in the Alumniate and acquired something that would later flower into beautiful humility, patience, self-control, and true charity. The credit should go, undoubtedly, to the elder sister, Gertrude.

In fact, no one can be wrong in giving this elder sister credit for most of the sanctity that blossomed into the marvelous mysticism of the two Mechtildes: her own sister and the one known as Mechtilde of Magdeburg, along with the even more marvelous mysticism of Gertrude the Great. For, from what we know of the Benedictine Rule and the Cistercian manner of observing it, we know that the spirit of any one house depends, under God, almost entirely on the spirit of the First Superior. In the history of sanctity and mysticism Helfta towers over the others, and her surpassing height was attained in the last half of the thirteenth century, in the very years she had as abbess, Gertrude of Hackeborn.

Gertrude was only nineteen when elected to the office, and not quite sixty when God called her home. Yet in those forty years she mothered Mechtilde to sanctity and saw to it that she,

in turn, mothered Gertrude the Great. Thus, due to her, the
Church won two mystics whose writings greatly influenced
saints and scholars, rulers and writers, century after century,
down to our own day. Teresa of Ávila, the great Suárez, St.
Francis de Sales, M. Olier, the saintly Father Faber, and Dom
Guéranger all confess they owe the Helfta mystics a great debt.
But no one of them would be wrong in making their checks
payable to Gertrude of Hackeborn; for she was the abbess under
whom Helfta became the most famous convent in all Germany,
and practically in all Europe, for its asceticism and mysticism.

Although she has never been called "Blessed," has never enjoyed the slightest religious cult or veneration, it still remains
true that, if we are grateful to God for Mechtilde and Gertrude
the Great, we must be grateful under God to Gertrude of
Hackeborn. From the writings of her two spiritual children, it
is not too difficult to discern how thoroughly Cistercian Helfta
was, and what was the secret of Abbess Gertrude's astounding
success.

"Find God in song"

It was in 1251, just three years after young Mechtilde arrived
at Rodersdorf, that Gertrude became Lady Abbess. With a
prudence more than natural, she insisted that her choir nuns be
educated thoroughly, not only in the sciences pertaining to the
monastic life, but even in what we can call the liberal arts. The
Latin found in *The Herald of Divine Love* and *The Book of
Special Grace* — which contains most of the revelations made
to our two mystics — is no ordinary "schoolboy Latin"; it flows
from the pen of one who had studied under a master and who
had been thoroughly schooled in the use of that tongue, which
besides being melodious, can be made wonderfully rhythmical.
The light, sound, color, splendor found in the visions tell that

every talent, from mind, memory, and imagination to eye, ear, and touch had been carefully trained.

But Gertrude knew she had immortal souls to shape for eternity even more than minds and wills to mold and mature for time; so she wisely insisted that Sacred Scripture, that work of God, should be the book of books for all in the convent and the convent school at Rodersdorf.

By the time her two brothers gave her Helfta as site for her convent, Gertrude had clothed her younger sister in the black and white of the Cistercian choir nun and because of her exceptional voice named her Chantress of the convent. It was a big assignment for one so young. Perhaps only those who have held this office can appreciate all that was entailed in that appointment. Mechtilde was responsible for the tone and tempo of the entire choir throughout those seven or eight hours each day that were spent singing the praises of God. She had to set the pace for all processions and know every note in each Mass — and there is a separate Mass each day in Lent, every Sunday of the year, and the individual feasts of the liturgical cycle. At a very conservative estimate Mechtilde had to know the proper of at least a hundred Masses, the common of perhaps ten, the antiphons, versicles, responsories of some hundred and fifty Offices, besides the psalms, hymns, and canticles. And to master that amount of matter is by far the simplest part of her task. The more difficult lies in the fact that she has to train young and old, those blessed with voices and ears, and those who are tone-deaf if not stone-deaf. It can be a nerve-racking task. Mechtilde held it all her religious life — and it sanctified her.

One can easily imagine the seventeen- or eighteen-year-old girl coming to her sister and saying, "But, Gertrude, I came here to seek God, not to be a songstress. I came to make melody in my heart, as St. Paul puts it; not to teach music. How can I seek perfection or make any spiritual progress while running a choir?" It is a natural, normal, and quite common objection. If Mechtilde was as human in all things as she shows herself in so many, we can be quite sure she made this protest; for every beginner in the contemplative way of life is jealous of anything that will take him or her from full and direct attention to God. But Gertrude could have been short and sharp. "Find God in your song," she could have said. "Let the choir sanctify you." And if we take one example as typical, we can see how Mechtilde was wise enough to outwit the wily one and make what could have been a distraction a means of more intimate union. A responsory in one of the Offices of the Blessed Virgin had the words, *Ostende te, Maria* — "Show thyself, O Mary" — and on the second syllable of the word *ostende* was a neum or jubilus of exceptional length. Mechtilde noted that it was divided into nine parts; so, wise virgin that she was, while singing each separate part, called each separate choir of angels to join her in the petition and practically compel Mary, who was their Queen, to listen to the plea. In *The Book of Special Grace* we read that Mechtilde and the angels were often so successful in their pleading that Mary came down to the church literally on clouds of angel wings.

Of course, St. Benedict has prescribed that all have their minds concur with the words their voices are uttering; but not every cantor or chantress, far less every member of the choir, is as happy in fulfilling that prescription as Mechtilde seems to have been. Music really lifted this girl to mysticism. But it was only because of the purity of her intention and the intensity of her attention.

Love and loneliness

In 1261 a child of five was brought to the convent at Helfta. Her name we know. But everything about her origin — her parents, her place of birth, the social standing of her family, her ancestry and relatives — has escaped recording. Some would have her an orphan who had been committed to the care of the nuns by some charitable soul who took pity on the homeless one. Others would have her related to the reigning family. But that, undoubtedly, is confusing Abbess Gertrude with this child Gertrude, who would one day be known as "Gertrude the Great." From her writings it would seem that she was born in Germany, but not at Eisleben. Too bad; for that town, which will ever have to bear the stigma of having been the birthplace of Luther, could bear to have one like Gertrude call it her natal place. From these same writings two other facts are evident: the first is that her parents, whoever they were, never had any contact with the girl once she had entered Helfta; and the second is typical of sanctity — Gertrude never ceased to pray for them.

Of course she was placed in the Alumnate, over which the Chantress of the convent was now Mistress. Thus did God bring together two who would give Him what He has craved from every human from that occasion in the timelessness of eternity when the Trinity took counsel and said, "Let Us make man to Our image and likeness" (Gen. 1:26).

To Abbess Gertrude it seemed that history was repeating itself as she watched the child Gertrude manifest the same quick intelligence, the same winsome ways, the same surprising talents her own sister had shown thirteen years earlier. Teachers were doting on this youngster, too. But, though the Mistress of the Alumnate was only twenty years of age, the Abbess knew her sound sense and substantial piety; so she did not worry. She knew Mechtilde would neither spoil the child nor be spoiled by her. When the Mistress and others told the Abbess how much they felt attracted to the little one whom everyone was now calling "Trutta," the rock of common sense replied, "Who isn't? But let us remember, she belongs to God — and so do we." Her advice to Mechtilde will be recognized as pre-eminently wise by modern psychologists and hailed as solid and sound by alert modern educators. It boiled down to: "Keep that child busy. Channel those energies. Develop that mind and heart. Love her — for we are at home only in the neighborhood of love — but do not love her too much. Above all, do not allow her to fall in love with herself."

If we accept young Gertrude's own testimony, without sober criticism, we would conclude that she fooled her Mistress and fell in love with learning. For in the first chapter of the second book of that priceless volume of revelations which is called *The Herald of Divine Love* — which is, incidentally, the only book Gertrude composed herself — she claims that within her was a "fortress of vainglory and curiosity which her pride had raised up," and adds: "I have the name and habit of a religious to no purpose." But one must read the self-accusations of saints not only carefully but very critically. She entered the cloister before she reached the age of use of reason. She was under the care of Mechtilde, who was already far along the road that leads to mystical union, and under Abbess Gertrude, who was ruling a house that would soon be famed for its holiness. She was kept at her *Trivium* and *Quadrivium* by a wise Mistress and able teachers. How great a sinner could the girl have been?

It is true, as St. Bernard has pointed out, that the pursuit of learning merely for learning's sake, will dry up a soul that is supposed to be seeking God; and undoubtedly young Gertrude experienced something of a drought the month before she had the vision which changed her life. The dry spell began before Christmas — and that is important.

Anyone sensitive to the meaning of words and the wealth of meaning in melody who has once heard the *Rorate Coeli* of Advent rendered by another soul sensitive to the same two meanings can never forget the verse, *Consolamini, consolamini, popule meus; cito veniet salus tua* — "Be comforted, be comforted, my people. Speedily will thy salvation come." It would seem as if Jesus could no longer stand the pleadings of His people who for all the weeks have been crying to the "clouds to rain down the Just One." He will not wait for Christmas; He calls already from His Mother's womb, as He called to the Baptist in his mother's womb the day Mary went "with haste into the hill country" and sang the first *Magnificat.* The *Quare moerore consumeris?* — "Why is it that you are eaten up with sadness?" — is almost a divine complaint — and the melody heightens the poignancy of the question.

As one walks the cloister in loneliness — and loneliness comes some time or other to every human soul, even those in the cloister — the haunting lilt of these lines may drift into his or her consciousness and like some cloud that is being carried across a darkening sky only to be suddenly goldened by a burst from the setting sun, the sudden, strong *Salvabo te, noli timere* — "I shall save thee. Never fear!" — burnishes the query and querulousness in the *Quare moerore* — and not only all fear but all loneliness is banished. It is a beautiful and haunting melody and seems to have been written just to lift some sorrow. One who knows a little of the cloistered contemplative life along with something of the human soul, may well suspect that Gertrude was haunted by this song in late December of 1281 and early January of 1282. At any rate here is her own description. . . .

"I was in the twenty-sixth year of my age when, on the Monday before the Feast of the Purification of Thy most chaste mother, in a happy hour before Compline . . . being in the middle of our dormitory and having inclined to a senior religious as our Rule prescribes, on raising my head I beheld Thee, my most loving Love, and my Redeemer, surpassing the beauty of the children of men, under the form of a youth about sixteen years old, beautiful and amiable; attracting my heart and my eyes. . . . Thou didst utter these words: 'Thy salvation is at hand. Why art thou consumed with grief?' . . .

"When Thou had spoken thus, although I knew corporally I stood in the place I have mentioned, it seemed to me, nevertheless, that I was in choir . . . and that I saw Thee place Thy right hand in mine, as if to ratify Thy promise. Then I heard Thee speak thus: 'You have licked the dust with My enemies, endeavoring to suck some drops of honey from among thorns. Come back to Me, and I will inebriate thee with the torrent of My divine pleasures.'

"When Thou hadst said these words, my soul melted within me; and, as I desired to approach Thee, I saw a great hedge between Thee and me, so long that I could not see an end either way, and the top of it appeared to be set with thorns, so that I could find no way to return to Thee. . . .

"As I wept over my faults and crimes, which no doubt were represented by the hedge which divided us . . . Thou didst take me by the hand and place me near Thee instantly, effortlessly. . . . Casting my eyes on the hand that had helped me, I recognized, O sweet Jesus, Thy radiant wounds. . . ."

There, in embryo, we have all of Gertrude the Great's mysticism; for there we see the call to renounce all things that are not Christ for the sake of possessing Christ; that burning desire for His love; the poignant sense of one's own powerlessness coupled with an utter and absolute confidence in the omnipotence of the wounded Christ — and especially of the wounded Sacred Heart. But the point we stress here is that it came, somehow or other, out of the liturgy; and this, you know, can be traced back to Mechtilde, her mistress of novices and mistress of chant, thence to Gertrude the abbess, who had so wisely ordered things at Helfta that every earnest soul saw that the twin sacrifices were the wings that would lift them to God. The *Sacrificium Laudis* (the Divine Office) and the *Sacrificium Missae* (the Mass) raise every loving Cistercian monk and nun to Him who is the object of the first and the subject or victim in the second. St. Benedict has reduced it to unity in his Rule, speaking only of the *Opus Dei*; but the Canonical Office in the

Middle Ages and today is for the choir monk and choir nun the setting for the Mass.

Mechtilde was forced by her very offices of chantress and mistress of novices to center her soul in the *Officium* and the *Sacrificium*. Gertrude, her spiritual child, made of the Breviary and Missal two fountains whence living water would be found ever rising up in rich profusion.

Song of flame

It is always amusing to find out just how old is the new. In our twentieth century the entire religious world has been stirred with doctrines that seemed and sounded new. Thérèse of Lisieux gave us "spiritual childhood," and Elizabeth of the Trinity the *"laudem gloriae"* or "praise of glory." Benigna Consolata has astounded us with "divine intimacy," and Dom Lehodey has comforted and consoled with the doctrine of "holy abandonment." All these seemingly new doctrines are found not in seed only, mind you, nor in tender bud, but in full-blown flower in the thirteenth-century Cistercians, Mechtilde and Gertrude the Great. And these growths are seen to be typically Benedictine blooms, for they stem from the liturgical life and are deeply rooted in the twin Sacrifices of the Office and the Mass.

Elizabeth of the Trinity found the phrase *in laudem gloriae* in St. Paul's Epistle to the Ephesians, where he tells how "the Father of our Lord, Jesus Christ, hath predestined us . . . according to the decree of His will to *the praise of the glory* of His grace. . . ." Elizabeth conceived her vocation to be just that; so thereafter she regarded every act, every suffering of her life as an act of praise — praise of His glory who had bestowed upon her His grace. This simplification and unification of life has won much attention in our complex and very confused day; but far from being new, it is as old as creation itself. To be a praiser of God's glory is not only the vocation of every Christian; it is the very purpose of every single creature that has answered the divine *Fiat* and come into being. Habacuc sang of it six hundred years before the coming of Christ when he said, "His glory covereth the heavens, and the earth is full of His praise" (3:3). And Mechtilde of Hackeborn and Helfta had made it her life six hundred years before Elizabeth of the Trinity was born. Mechtilde's position as chantress would have forced this upon her if the Rule of St. Benedict had not already opened her eyes to the profound depth and the heaven-piercing height of her vocation by the phrase, *nihil praeponatur Operi Dei* — "Let nothing be preferred to the *Opus Dei*." And what is the *Opus Dei* but the praise of His glory?

Because she saw this so clearly, Mechtilde loved every neum and every note in the Divine Office and inspired all under her with the same love and the same purpose. That is why Gertrude could write in the twenty-second chapter of the second book of her *Herald of Divine Love*: "Once when reciting the Divine Office with extraordinary fervor, each word uttered appeared to dart like an arrow from my heart into the Heart of Jesus, penetrating It deeply and filling It with ineffable satisfaction. From one end of these arrows, rays of light shot forth like stars, falling on all the Saints, but especially on the one whose festival was being celebrated; from the lower end of these arrows drops of dew flowered forth and fell on the souls of the living and refreshed also the souls in Purgatory."

Who would not love every neum and every note when each can be such a praise of glory?

But it was not every day that Gertrude and Mechtilde saw each note "fly like an arrow" to fill the Heart of God with gladness, heaven with starry splendor, and purgatory and earth with refreshing dew. And it is in the same twenty-second chapter of her book that Gertrude tells us about it. One day while trying to attach a special intention and thus give special attention to every word, she awoke to the fact that her mind was wandering and her will was asleep. In sadness she cried, "Alas! What fruit can I hope to obtain from this exercise when I am so unstable?" She got an immediate answer to what she may have meant as a rhetorical question; for our Lord appeared, held out His Sacred Heart to her as a burning lamp, and said, "Have confidence. My Heart is always ready to repair your defects and make up for your negligences."

Gertrude wondered — and feared. Our Lord comforted her with this explanation: "If you have a beautiful and melodious voice, and take pleasure in chanting, will you not feel displeased if another person whose voice is harsh and unpleasant and who can scarcely utter a correct sound wishes to sing instead of you and even insists upon doing so? — Thus my Divine Heart, understanding human inconstancy and frailty, desires with incredible ardor continually to be invited, either by word or sign, to operate and accomplish in you what you are not able to accomplish yourself. Its omnipotence enables it to act without trouble; its impenetrable wisdom allows it to act in the most perfect manner; and its joyous and loving charity sets it afire with desire to do just that."

Two other happenings may be given here as characteristic of Gertrude's and Mechtilde's life in the cloister. One day Gertrude heard a most melodious sound, like that coming from a harp; then these words were sung to her: *Veni mea ad me. Intra meum in me. Mane meus Mecum.* — "Come, O Mine own, unto Me. Enter, Mine own, into Me. Abide, Mine own, within Me." She waited wondering what this love-song meant — and from such a Lover. Our Lord appeared and explained, "Come to Me, because I love you and desire that you should always be present before Me; therefore I call thee *Veni mea ad me.* — Because My delights are in you, I desire that you should enter into Me. *Intra meum in me.* — Finally, because I am the God of love, I desire that you remain indissolubly united to Me, even as the body is united to the soul, without which it cannot live for a moment. *Mane meus mecum.*"

Once when Mechtilde was chanting the Office (and worried no doubt about young Gertrude, who seemed too active for a contemplative and so busy about many things as to be too busy for the one necessary thing), she saw our Lord seated on a high throne around which her much loved Trutta walked and walked and walked. Mechtilde watched and noted that Gertrude never once took her eyes from the face of the Master; yet while walking and looking she seemed, at the same time, to be fulfilling many different duties with meticulous care and exactness. Mechtilde mused on that vision long. She did not want to miss a single intimation or lose the slightest connotation. One day while musing, the whole thing was explained to her thus: "This is the image of the life My beloved Gertrude lives: thus does she ever walk in My presence, never relaxing in her ardent desire to know and to do what is most pleasing to My Heart. As soon as she has ascertained what it is that I wish, she executes it with care and fidelity, then promptly passes to some other duty. Thus her whole life is a continuous chain of praise consecrated to My honor and glory."

Small wonder Abbess Gertrude found the eyes of her younger sister and those of her charge, Trutta, sparkling with excitement and splendor. They had looked on things souls long to vision, and heard sounds from another world. All came as reward, as it were, for doing their duty and seeking the will of God. Sanctity is simple — just as simple as all that; union with God easy of attainment. And human eyes can look upon "the many splendored things" if human wills only open them aright.

Teachers from another world

Mechtilde learned this lesson from the wisest woman who

ever lived, one who is called Seat of Wisdom; for Mechtilde had taken as Spiritual Directress none other than Mary, the Mother of God. In a certain sense the center of Mechtilde's life was the *Ave Maria* and the votive Mass of our Lady beginning with *Salve, Sancta Parens;* for the Chantress of Helfta believed utterly that she who was Mother of God was also her mother. To the Virgin Mary she went with everything: joys, sorrows, triumphs, failures, problems, puzzles, perplexities. And she went as a child — as one who had all the unquestioning love and unclouded confidence a child has in a parent she considers not only infallible but omnipotent. The charm and simplicity and deep dogma in it all makes one almost weep. For instance, this woman, who was mistress of the Alumnate, mistress of novices, and a chantress who really enchanted with her song, went to Mary Immaculate to beg forgiveness for a slip she had made. She went as a child and was received as a child! Like many another loving mother, Mary Immaculate took Mechtilde's chin in her hand and, looking deep into the nun's eyes, made her promise never to do it again.

Was it from her elder sister, the Abbess, that Mechtilde had learned this wisdom? That would be hard to establish from either *The Book of Special Grace* or *The Herald of Divine Love.* Yet it is a very logical supposition. For Abbess Gertrude knew that it was Mary who had mothered the Physical Christ, giving Him flesh of her flesh. Who else could mother the Mystical Christ? Who else could mold members into the likeness of her Son? Who, but Mary?

No one but God can tell all that Mary means to the life of the soul. He, and He alone, who said to us through St. John, "Behold thy mother," can properly exegete those words. But it is not difficult to tell what it was Mary heard and what she understood when He said, "Behold thy son." She knew she was commissioned to form Christ in all who would allow her to mother them.

So devoted to the Mother, it is not surprising to find Mechtilde in love with Him whose Sacred Heart was formed under her Immaculate Heart, and longing to be lost in it as completely as possible. At Mass one day she looks up at the time of the little elevation (in those days they did not have the major Elevation of the Host as we have it today immediately after Consecration), and she sees not the priest but the Christ, and He is holding in His hands not the Chalice and Host but His Heart. It shines like a lamp of dazzling brilliance, filled to overflowing with liquid light which falls in drops of fire all about it. Desiring to have her own heart poured out into His, she prays earnestly for this favor and suddenly finds herself, as she puts it, "swimming in the Sacred Heart just like a little fish in the ocean."

One vision of the Sacred Heart that filled her with intoxicating joy was that in which she saw rays of burning light streaming from the Sacred Heart and lancing their way straight to the hearts of the individual members of the Cistercian Order. Inebriating this assuredly was, but Mechtilde was not so taken out of herself as not to pray, *Fiat! Fiat!* to that vision.

And where did all this intimacy with Christ and His lovely Mother lead these nuns? To a confidence and a trust that culminated in a complete, uncompromising abandonment to the will of God. This, in its turn, gave them a peace that was absolutely imperturbable. This trait in the saints and the saintly often sets lesser souls marveling. But the logic of it all has been set forth lucidly by the saintly Cardinal Newman when, after reflecting on the fact that God had created him for some definite service, had committed to him some work which He had entrusted to no other, a mission which was his and his alone, and one which he might never know in this life, but which would be told to him infallibly in the next, he says, "I am a link in a chain, a bond of connection between persons. He has not created me for naught. I shall do good. I shall do His work. I shall be an Angel of Peace, a preacher of truth in my own place while not intending it, if I but keep His Commandments. Therefore, I will trust Him. Whatever, wherever I am, I can never be thrown away. If I am in sickness, my sickness may serve Him; in perplexity, my perplexity may serve Him; if I am in sorrow, my sorrow may serve Him. He does nothing in vain. He knows what He is about. He may take away my friends. He may throw me among strangers. He may make me feel desolate, make my spirits sink, hide my future from me — still He knows what He is about. Still will I trust Him!"

Who could fail to trust Him after such reasoning — and that reasoning is correct. Job taught it to us long centuries before Newman learned it from suffering. But Gertrude the Great learned such logic not from the Scripture of God but from the very Word of God, Truth Itself. Jesus one day showed her a bride walking with her spouse in a garden filled with roses. The groom plucks beautiful blooms as they stroll, and hands them to his beloved. She, entirely lost in her spouse, pays next to no attention to the flowers he hands her, but merely adds each to the bulging bouquet simply because it comes from his hands. "It is the same with a soul that has faith," said Jesus. "She walks, as it were, in a garden and takes every rose from My hand with delight. If I give her sickness or health, or even take her out of life, it is all the same to her, since it comes from My hand. Being full of confidence in Me, she relies implicitly on My goodness."

Give your heart away

From a study of Lutgarde, Mechtilde, Gertrude, and St. Bernard, it would seem that the traditional Cistercian system was, first, childlike devotion to Mary as our Mother, who then leads us to the Sacred Heart of Jesus, and His Humanity floods us with such love that we arrive at a headlong, holy abandonment — and this produces in us peace, courage, confidence, and unshakable joy. It is as simple and as natural as all that — and just as sublime and supernatural. But the apex is never reached without suffering. How could it be when she is the Sorrowful Mother and He the suffering Jesus?

It is no matter for wonder, then, that Gertrude tells us how she, in the first year of her intimacy with Christ, prayed thus: "O most merciful Jesus, engrave Thy wounds upon my heart with Thy most Precious Blood, that I may read in them Thy grief and Thy love; and that the memory of Thy Wounds may ever remain in my inmost heart to excite my compassion for Thy suffering and increase my love for Thyself."

Again and again she repeated that prayer. Then one night, as she sat in the refectory . . . "I perceived," she says, "in spirit that Thou hadst imprinted in the depth of my heart Thy Sacred Wounds, even as they are on Thy Body; that Thou hadst cured my soul by thus imprinting Thy Wounds on it; and that to satisfy its thirst, Thou hadst given it the precious beverage of Thy love."

But this was not enough for either the mystic or the Master. We read, "To so many favors Thou hast added an inestimable mark of Thy friendship and familiarity, by giving me in various ways Thine Own Most Sacred Heart . . . to be for me an overflowing fountain of delight; now giving It as an entirely gratuitous gift; and now exchanging It for mine as a clearer sign of our mutual familiarity."

That is the way Jesus loves. He gives His Heart away — but takes yours in Its place. Passionate love is always prodigal in its giving, yet demanding in its possessing. At the beginning of this thirteenth century we saw Jesus with a woman who was in love with Him and with whom He was in love. He exchanged hearts with Lutgarde. Now at the century's end we find Him once more with a woman who loves Him and whom He loves. Once again there is an exchange of hearts.

What is this woman who walked so constantly with God

saying by this symbol? What is the Sacred Heart Himself saying? If it were not clear from the wound in that Heart, then
Gertrude's life, as that of Lutgarde and Mechtilde both before
and with her, make it unmistakably evident. Jesus would exchange hearts with everyone baptized if they would be as generous as these women and be willing to suffer so as to complete
His Passion.

It is the great Tauler who says, "When our Heavenly Father
has decreed to adorn a soul with exalted gifts and to transform
it completely, it is not His custom to cleanse it gently, but to
plunge it in a sea of bitterness, to drown it therein, as He did
the Prophet Jonas." That is realism and truth. Hence we are not
surprised to learn that from the time she received the stigmata
in her heart until her death, Gertrude's life was one of continuous sufferings. One attack of illness kept her from choir for
an entire year. She was not only calm in this suffering but
actually joyous; for Mechtilde had taught her that suffering
brings the soul closer and closer to Him who saved all souls by
suffering. Mechtilde could tell her protégé this; for she knew
every feature in the face of suffering.

Intimates tell secrets to the world

In 1290 Abbess Gertrude fell ill. For almost forty years she
had been leading souls to God. As abbess she knew she had to
administer the convent, but she also knew her greater concern
was to govern the community, and to do so as St. Benedict
would have all his superiors govern — as the father of a family,
not as president of a corporation or the head of some large institution. His monasteries and convents were to be homes; and
every individual dwelling therein, a member of the family. So
Gertrude of Hackeborn mothered all under her, and made the
shaping of their souls her prime concern. Now, reduced to help-
lessness by her sickness, she would hand this all-important task

over to another. She had had the consolation of seeing her family grow holy and her convent become a seedbed for high sanctity. But she well knew what constant care such blooms demand, and she felt that she could not answer that demand from a sickbed. So she wished to resign. But young Gertrude told her that it was God's will that she remain in office until the end. It was a reversal of roles — the Abbess receiving the will of God from a subject. But Gertrude of Hackeborn was wise with the wisdom of the holy. She accepted the statement as true, and did her bravest and best to rule the convent from her cot. The end came in 1291, and for a time our two mystics felt like orphans.

From the year of her sister's death until that of her own seven years later, Mechtilde lived on Golgotha. Constant illness had Christ's nightingale singing in her heart and telling her intimates, Trutta and an unnamed nun, that she was "swimming in the joys of God" — surrounded by them, she said, as a fish by water or a bird by air.

These were the intimates who gave the world that precious volume, *Liber Specialis Gratiae;* for, unknown to Mechtilde, they committed to writing all the visions she told them about. When Mechtilde heard of it, she sang a mournful note; for she feared to reveal "the secrets of the King." But Jesus Himself calmed those fears by telling her He had helped the conspirators in the compilation; for it was His will that these special graces should be known to the world.

His will was accomplished — and is still being accomplished. Boccaccio tells us that the book was brought to Florence shortly after Mechtilde's death in 1298 and popularized under the title, *La Laude di Donna Matelda.* The Florentines took "Matelda" to their hearts as only Florentines can, memorized her prayers, and even had them written on their walls.

After God had taken her Abbess and her Mistress from her, Gertrude longed with ever growing intensity for the other world.

For decades now it could be said that she had lived in three worlds simultaneously; for besides being alive to this world and living ever in the presence of Him who is the Lamp of the other world, she was ever conscious of what lies between — that Limbo where joy is just short of the joy of heaven, and pain almost as intense as the pain of hell: purgatory.

Like Lutgarde and Mechtilde, because of her entire love for God, Gertrude the Great was enamored of every soul in purgatory. And it was the Sacred Heart Himself who kindled ever greater sympathy and love as He spurred her on to more intense activity on their behalf when He revealed to her that He was as grateful to anyone who delivered any of these souls as He would be had they delivered Him from captivity. Gertrude, of course, made the "heroic act" — offering all she did for the souls who were suffering. Imagine her joy when Christ told her first, that for each verse of a psalm *many* souls were released from purgatory, then added, "As for yourself, each movement of your tongue in psalmody liberates a soul from flame and sends it to the glory of Paradise." That meant with each syllable Gertrude pronounced, God gained the glory of another soul in His eternal kingdom. It is not hard to see why Gertrude the Great and every great Cistercian is enamored of the *Opus Dei.*

But now Gertrude came to know an incurable sickness, a languor no earthly physician can cure, and an illness, which undoubtedly aggravates whatever physical disease the saintly may be suffering; she was fevered with a longing for home.

Some say she was a chronic invalid for the last twelve years of her life. Others simply state that she suffered seven severe illnesses. But the important part of any sickness is not its length or its depth, not its height or its width, but only the way it is accepted. When Gertrude the Great lay in what was to be her final illness, our Lord appeared to her and said, "Tell Me, My beloved, that you languish with love for Me."

Trutta looked up piteously and replied, "O Lord, how can I, a poor sinner, say with any truth that I languish with love of Thee?"

Our Lord's answer should stimulate all. "Whoever offers himself willingly to suffer anything in order to please Me," He said, "tells me that he languishes with love of Me, provided that he continues patient and never turns his eyes from Me."

The thought of death was constant with Gertrude in her last years. Every Friday she would retire into solitude and there recite the litanies and prayers that are said for those in their last agony; pondering on their marvelous meaning; drawing courage and consolation from the power she saw them to possess.

In the last book of *The Herald of Divine Love* we read that on one of these Friday afternoons "Gertrude beheld herself reposing in the arms of our Lord, under the form of a fair young maiden, in her last agony. At the same time there appeared an immense number of angels and saints surrounding her. In their hands they held censers, by which they offered to the King of Glory the prayers of the Church. As the litany for the dying was said, Gertrude saw each of those whose names were invoked, beginning with Our Lady and her Guardian Angel, approach both to assist and to congratulate her. Finally the Son of God inclined toward Gertrude and lovingly embraced her, absorbing her into Himself, as the sun in its meridian splendor absorbs a drop of dew. Then did her soul appear to be received into the Heart of her Spouse, and she was surrounded and penetrated by Him as iron is inflamed in a fire."

In 1301, when some liver complaint was pronounced incurable, Gertrude set about her immediate preparation for death by using "The Exercises" she had drawn up for others some years before. They consist of setting apart five or seven days for a real retreat; one in which the individual reviews life from the hour of Baptism up to the moment of Judgment and sees both how much there is to be ashamed of and how much more to make her grateful. Gertrude opened her retreat by receiving Holy Communion, then spent the next five days in union with God, reflecting on His goodness shown in the Sacraments and their graces; then trying to realize just what it means to die.

As the end approached, her desire to be with God and her physical sufferings increased, both being almost beyond endurance. Yet she bravely turned to the Sacred Heart and told Him that, despite her longing to be home with Him, she would willingly stay in exile until the Day of Doom if such were His good pleasure. As reward for such generosity our Lord assured her that He took her will for the deed and that her generosity so pleased Him that at her death many souls would be converted on earth and many more delivered from purgatory. Then He added that she would soon be home.

The date of the fulfillment of that promise is uncertain, but most now accept that given in the Cistercian Menology — November 17, 1302. She had her name inserted in the Roman Martyrology in 1678, and this is looked upon as equivalent to canonization. Her feast is kept on November 16. The King of Spain asked, and obtained, permission that she be named Patroness of the West Indies.

Now Gertrude the Great is in the Heart of God; and those words of Jesus are actualized, "You will find Me in the heart of Gertrude."

For more than two hundred years *The Herald of Divine Love* was practically unknown. Then, in 1536, Lanspergius, a Carthusian monk, made it known to the world by a new edition, which proved to be the forerunner to innumerable others down to our own day. As Ailbe Luddy has put it, these writings show Gertrude to be "of all Christian seers since Apostolic times, the most consoling."

That is a large statement. Yet, when one reads her writings and finds in them nothing but confidence and trust in the Sacred Heart; visions that are alive with a rich, radiant optimism;

and a teaching that stresses the mercy of God, telling sinners again and again, that the infinite tenderness of Jesus will swallow up all their mistakes if they will but abandon themselves to His love, one sees that the large statement is something of an understatement.

Even more than Lutgarde, who was the first we saw walking with God, Mechtilde and Gertrude, who shall be the last in this book we shall see doing the same thing, teach us how easy it is to understand God, and how utterly free from difficulty is life with Him, if we will be simple enough to do our assigned duties with the intention of pleasing Him.

"If anyone will read this book," said Jesus to Gertrude, concerning *The Herald of Divine Love*, "for his own spiritual progress, I will draw him to Me in such a way that it will be the same as if I were holding the book in My own hands, and associating Myself with him in his action. . . . I wish your writings to be an irrefutable testimonial of My divine Love in those later days, in which I plan to do good to many souls."

That is why Lanspergius, Blosius, Suárez, Teresa of Ávila, Olier, Faber, and Guéranger think so highly of Gertrude. That is why we say she is another of those wonderful women who walked with God.

Lanspergius, anticipating the objections that may arise to the visions just set forth, writes: "But some will perhaps object that these revelations were made to a woman and, either despising or suspecting the whole female species, will think that, no matter how holy a virgin or woman may be, she must of necessity be frail, unstable, and having nothing manly about her. As if holy women have not often been more constant in virtue, more ready for martyrdom, more chary of their chastity, more full of mercy, more intent on averting God's anger, than many men; and have given us examples of virtue which are very often far superior to those of men. We men, therefore, should rather be confounded when we reflect on them, and look up to the whole sex with veneration."

This monk will be chivalrous, but he will not be chauvinistic. After that last remark he goes on to say that women are weak and can easily be deluded; but, so long as they are humble, they will neither deceive nor be deceived. Then he says something strikingly true: "God speaks to whom, and through whom He pleases, and makes no distinction of sex unless it be to give more abundantly to the weaker when they are humble and devoted."

After going through Scripture and showing the various women whom God used either to prophesy or even to rule His people, beginning with Debbora and ending with Elizabeth and Ann, he goes on: "I say nothing of *the* Female, the Virgin Mary, the most worthy, not only of all women, but of all created beings; for it is not seemly to compare her with anyone, since she excels them all as the sun outshines the stars."

But the good Carthusian will not quarrel with us if we say *she* walked with God — and is the model for every woman; yes, and for every man.